Food for Tho
The Free Food Cookbook

Gluten Free
Casein Free
Allergen Free
Toxin Free

Cook Yourself Clear of Allergies,
Autism, Auto-Immunity, Cancer
& Nutritional Impurities

Kotsanis Institute
Constantine A. Kotsanis MD,
MD(H),CCN
Beverly D. Kotsanis, BS
With
Greater Tots Organization
Founder, Kendra Jean Finestead, M.O.M.

Food For Thought
The Free Food Cookbook: Gluten Free, Casein Free, Allergen Free, Toxin Free
All marketing and publishing rights

Copyright 2012, Constantine A. Kotsanis MD, MD(H), CCN,
Beverly D. Kotsanis, BS, and Kendra Jean Finestead, M.O.M

Printed in the United States of America.

ISBN: 1468053116
ISBN 13: 9781468053111

Food for Thought
The Free Food Cookbook

Gluten Free * Casein Free * Allergen Free * Toxin Free

Cook Yourself Clear of Allergies, Autism, Auto-Immunity, Cancer & Nutritional Impurities

Constantine A. Kotsanis MD, MD(H),CCN

Beverly D. Kotsanis, BS

With

GREATER TOTS.org

Founder: Kendra Jean Finestead, M.O.M.,

Mom On A Mission

Disclaimer

The information in this book is not intended to diagnose, treat, cure, or prevent any disease. Only your personal medical professional may do so after a complete history, physical examination, and testing. You should consult a healthcare professional when introducing any dietary changes or if you notice any adverse effects from the consumption of any particular ingredient. The information and recipes included in this book are a guide only. In no way should this book be used as a substitute for your own physician's advice. Kotsanis Institute, Greater Tots Organization, and/or their affiliates bear no legal liability for what you choose to feed your child or yourself.

The information included in this book is based upon Dr. Kotsanis's personal clinical experience treating patients for more than twenty-eight years, as well as review of published scientific literature and medical studies. Dr. Kotsanis integrates both mainstream and complementary medicine. This practice, known as functional or integrative medicine, embraces principles and treatment methods that may or may not be accepted or embraced by conventional medicine providers, individual physicians, or other health care institutions.

Because of the possibility of human error or changes in medical sciences, neither the authors, publisher, editors, nor any other party who has been involved in the preparation or publication of this work warrants that the information contained herein is in every respect accurate or complete. They are not responsible for any errors or omissions or for the results obtained from the use of such information. This is especially true when a person makes changes to dietary intake and lifestyle based on any of the information described in this book and a bad result occurs.

Kotsanis Institute and Greater Tots Organization are in no way affiliated with any of the brands mentioned in our recipes other than being a consumer. The brands listed are simply our personal favorite selections for each particular recipe. Substitutions can be made, but be sure to consult the ingredient lists when doing so as other products may have different ingredients.

The recipes provided are the intellectual property of Kotsanis institute and Kendra Jean Finestead. All rights reserved to Kotsanis Institute and Kendra Jean Finestead, founder of Greater Tots Organization, unless written consent is given for reproduction.

The people in this book are real. Their stories are true. Some of their names, identifying characteristics, and facts have been altered to protect their privacy.

Dedication

I dedicate this book to the parents who have children with autistic spectrum disorders. These parents and their children have been my greatest teachers. I also dedicate this book to my wife and children for their encouragement and deep understanding of the healing science of nutrition. This book is a labor of love. The recipes contributed from the moms of ASD children and my office staff were the most inspiring. I am wishing everyone who follows the recommendations of this book to have a healthy and vibrant life.

Constantine A. Kotsanis, MD, MD(H), CCN

I dedicate this book to my mother, who is an amazing Greek cook and who always made the foods that kept me healthy and gave me an appreciation of the vast variety of flavors on the planet. And to my children, whose understanding of our long work hours and lots of traveling has allowed us the freedom to learn and innovate. Thank you for your patience.

Beverly D. Kotsanis, BS

To my diplomatically patient, brutally honest, and perfectly understanding husband, I thank you beyond words for believing in my passion. To my sweet little bear, my neuro-typical "tot" who is always so kind and concerned for his older sister, I love you beyond words. To my Molly, I dedicate this work to you, for you inspire me each and every day... beyond words! Together, you and I are going to help some kiddos, just as promised.

Kendra Jean Finestead, M.O.M.

A Special Note From
One Parent To Another

I am many things, but I am a mother first and foremost. As mothers or fathers, our heads are piled high with the many hats we must wear, and adding a chef's cap to the pile may have never been of interest to you in the past. Now you find yourself thrown chef's-hat-first into not only a world of cooking, but one in which every meal you make plays an important role in the health and well-being of your most precious possession, your child.

Our own special-diet success story inspired me to pay forward what I learned through my efforts and struggles. Our lives changed when we changed our daughter's diet; moreover, I have been ultimately blessed to be able to help other families start their own success stories. From what I have learned so far, here is the wisdom that I would like to impart:

First, do not fear.

Second, let go. It is very easy to be overwhelmed by the barrage of new information on changes you will need to make to help your child recover. Things you will need to know that are in this book include nutritional information that is specific to your child's condition and how to buy healthy groceries. This sounds like a lot to have on your plate at a time when you are in an emotional upheaval over the health of your child. But in the end, you will be glad you made these changes.

Do yourself and your family the biggest favor of all and let go of the burden. Take one big cleansing breath, hold it in tight, and slowly exhale. As you blow that air out, blow away the doubt (trust yourself as a mother or a father). Blow away the pity (as parents we take on a lot of our child's suffering, when the reality is that they don't feel the same as we do about their situation). Blow away the rulebook. Throw it out the window and rewrite the pages to your own story. Each child on the spectrum has a completely different set of rules—you are the best author for your child's book! And blow away the guilt, because no matter what age your child or what has been or could have been done in the past, the fact that you are here now speaks beyond measure for you. Your child is so deeply blessed to have you and to be given the opportunity to reach his or her fullest potential. Pat yourself on the back!

Finally, smile. Smile big and smile often. Embrace the journey and find yourself moving at your own pace toward your goal. There will be good days and there will be bad days; the road of autism is guaranteed to provide a colorful terrain. It is so important to "eighty-six" the stress surrounding your special diet by planning ahead, getting creative, and truly making happy food for your special little eater. Your joy will be infectious, so consider it the most important ingredient in all of your dishes!

I wish you the best of luck in learning the ins and outs of your special diet and I am thrilled that you have taken on the challenge. Amazing results can come out of the smallest changes, so I am excited for the possibilities that lie ahead for you and your family. You have been given a fantastic gift. You have been given the opportunity to achieve a miracle twice with one life!

Eat FREEly

Kendra Jean Finestead

Contents

Foreword By Doris Rapp, MD

What you are holding in your hands right now can be summarized in one line: what a fantastic great cookbook! This is not a book with turnip and quail recipes but practical, down-to-earth, everyday eating. The clear message throughout this book is that the answers you need are here in detail.

As you turn page by page, you will find that this cookbook is much more than simply a compilation of unique gluten, casein, and allergen–free recipes. If these are your major dietary challenges, this book will prove to be a special gift from Kendra and the entire Kotsanis team.

If you have other food problems, this book will also prove to be surprisingly helpful, because it is absolutely overflowing with food tips of all kinds. There are special sections about water, toxins, nutrition, shopping, label reading, storing foods, etc. Many answers of this type are needed, especially by those families with children who have cancer, autism, and/or food allergies.

Food for Thought, The Free Food Cookbook is a genuine labor of shared love created by the union of one special mother and a special doctor and his team. Kendra combined her personal input with that of many mothers of children with autism, allergies, cancer or auto-immunity. These mothers were all faced with similar familial dietary challenges. Some of the recipes have been adapted specifically from their own children's tried-and-true favorites. Their practical knowledge, combined and blended with the vast expertise and enormous skills of Dr. Kotsanis, his wife, Beverly, and their team have been united to create this extraordinarily helpful and complete Food for Thought book.

The authors of Food for Thought have totally different backgrounds, so their shared expertise contains an enormous amount of medical and non-medical knowledge, of the type not included in ordinary cookbooks. Not everyone needs to know everything that is explained so well in this book, but if they do, you can be assured that the information is here.

Dr. Kotsanis must have had a dream team who repeatedly kept saying, to each other, "Now, what else might mothers of special children possibly need or want to know?" You will have great difficulty finding some aspect of foods, cooking, or nutrition that has been left out.

If you are looking for answers, be assured that they are in this book. Everything you need, want, or should know is included. It might prove to be the best and certainly, the most complete, detailed, and comprehensive gift you ever discovered to help those who are food challenged in some way.

It is not only for those who have gluten, casein, or food allergies. It is for anyone who wants or needs to know more about their diets and maintaining optimum health. Any homemaker, any student in nutrition or medicine, and particularly any mother of a child with autism, allergies, cancer, or auto-immune health issues, will find this book to be a veritable treasure of practical information. Be assured, this book will not only contain what you are looking for, but it definitely will contain the type of practical details you need, such as special food sources, Internet addresses, and phone numbers.

The recipes are located in the middle two hundred pages of the book, and these are enhanced with valuable "power boxes," with "tips and tricks" on each recipe page that include additional nutritional information or suggestions. These can include, for example, tips concerning how to better prepare or substitute some ingredient in each recipe.

The beginning and ending sections of this book contain pearl after pearl. Which foods are most nutritious and why? What food myths exist? What determines your level of energy and what you can do about it? There are parts of the book that contain essential information you might need.

Dr. Kotsanis summarizes how we should eat and introduces the simple eating guide, Nature's Food Pyramid, as the foundation to achieve optimal health. There are back-to-back tables of all sorts regarding certain types of foods, nutrients, and minerals. There is also special information about how to cope with the challenges of school lunches and eating out. Special information about microwaves and the dangers of electromagnetic energy is included. There's even a section explaining which pots and pans are best and why. Every health aspect of what most people might want to know in relation to what is good or bad about water is discussed.

Food for Thought explains why the label "organic" is so important to our health and why the label can be deceptive. There is a chapter that discusses how to do organic container gardening, how and where to shop, and how to store and freeze food. Also included is information on where to buy special hard-to-find ingredients or foods. Nothing is left out.

In the latter part of the book, you'll find measurements, equivalents, food substitutions, and a wide variety of resource tables with lists of other diet books and food sources. Special additional information, mainly to help mothers of children with autism or cancer, is also included. Many resources, addresses, tables, and back-to-back pearls discuss other pertinent aspects of allergies and wellness.

The major aim of Food for Thought: The Free Food Cookbook is to help children with gluten, casein, or other food allergies and anyone else who wants or needs to know more about these topics. This book truly has something for everyone who is concerned about what they eat and how they feel.

So read on and enjoy. Keep this book handy in a prominent spot in your kitchen. It will, in time, become a bit tattered and torn, because the answers you need and want to keep your family happy and healthy are here. This book represents a true labor of love from Kendra Finestead, Dr. and Mrs. Kotsanis, and many others at the Kotsanis Institute. Relax, enjoy, and eat. Begin with anticipation and optimism. You are about to be pleasantly surprised.

Doris J. Rapp, MD

*Board Certified in Pediatrics, Allergy,
and Environmental Medicine,
Clinical Assistant Professor of Pediatrics at SUNYAB,*

Author of *Our Toxic World: A Wake Up Call and 32 Tips That Could Save Your Life,*
dorisrappmd.com or drrapp.com

Acknowledgments

During the course of any project there always must be someone steering and helping everyone stay on course. Our executive director and project manager, Marge Woodard, has been the captain of this ship. Marge knows quite a bit about navigating, both figuratively and literally, as she has captained boats on many seas and rivers all over the world in her "spare time." She has managed to take many people with very busy schedules and has accomplished a feat as unbelievable as herding cats. (She is also a cat lover.) Marge, we all thank you and are extremely grateful for your diligence and patience. This project could not have been completed without you.

We would be remiss if we did not acknowledge the many patients and parents of patients who shared their tips and tricks for food substitutions or hiding of mystery ingredients. We have learned as much from our patients over the years as we hope they have learned from us.

And last but certainly not least, many thanks to the clinical staff in our office, who have also contributed their recipes and tips, not to mention the thousands of hours spent on the phone coaching patients through the lifestyle and dietary changes that would ultimately help them get healthier. A hearty thanks to staff members and care managers Jana Miller, Pam Rust, Lindsay Kirkwood, Allison Saltar, and Nicole Wallace for your contributions, compassion, and conscientiousness.

Introduction

BY BEVERLY D. KOTSANIS

I'm a foodie. I love to cook, and I love to eat. So when my husband and our two children developed health issues and had to modify their eating habits, I was challenged to create meals that eliminated their allergic foods. This was more than twenty years ago. During this time we have met thousands of parents with children on the autism spectrum, and their greatest challenges have been in the feeding of their children. The Kotsanis Institute and the Greater Tots Organization have joined forces to create this compendium of information to help the special-needs population attain optimal health through the diet and lifestyle changes outlined here.

Constantine A. Kotsanis, MD, my husband, began practice in 1983 as a board-certified otolaryngologist. The medical practice that we built together since then has evolved from a traditional mainstream practice into what is now the Kotsanis Institute, which is a functional medicine practice.

Functional medicine, also called integrative or complementary medicine, is a patient-centered, individualized approach to health that combines many different disciplines and focuses on restoring the functions of the various bodily systems to a dynamic balance by using a combination of nutrients, medicines, botanicals, homeopathics, and various other forms of energy medicine. It does not use medications to turn off symptoms.

The Greater Tots Organization was founded by Kendra Jean Finestead. After her daughter was diagnosed with autism, Kendra threw herself into the nutritional and lifestyle changes that would help her daughter recover. But that was not enough. She decided that there were thousands of moms trying to navigate the same course. So she set out to become a resource for parents who were overwhelmed by facing the autism spectrum.

Writing this book has been a labor of love. It's a roadmap to hypoallergenic eating and is a result of many years of collecting recipes that help alleviate the symptoms of autism and other behavior disorders such as attention deficit and hyperactivity.

This book is unique in that it is a collaborative effort between a medical doctor, his staff, and the mother of an autistic child. But beyond being just a collection of recipes, it tries to explain why eating this way is beneficial and explains how other parts of our contemporary lifestyle may also adversely affect your health.

Most medical doctors have no training in matters of nutrition. This is because their training is focused only on using medicines and surgery to correct health issues. When there is a shift in the health of the population that is as great as we have seen in the past 30 years, thoughtful leaders in the medical community ask, "Why? What has changed and how do we deal with these new epidemics?" These are questions we began to ask in the late 1980s.

When I was a child in the '60s, I attended a private elementary school in Chicago with 800 students from kindergarten through eighth grade. We did not have a school nurse, nor did we need one. No one in any of my classes was on psychotropic drugs, had asthma, or ever got really sick. My only memory of classmates being sick is when they got chickenpox or other childhood diseases. Today, school nurses are kept very busy as their role has expanded to providing continuity of care for some very sick children. (http://www.medscape.com/viewarticle/442679_5)

Many children today have been exposed to a myriad of chemicals, toxins, genetically modified foods, life stresses, and electromagnetic fields, the likes of which did not exist in the '60s. These conditions are profoundly changing our DNA. Epigenetics is the study of how environmental factors impact an individual's gene expression; that is, how they affect the way in which a given gene's instructions are carried out. Many of the treatments for today's maladies manipulate these epigenetic expressions using nutrients and lifestyle changes.

Since the late 1980s, we have seen each succeeding generation become sicker. There is no question that we are observing a serious weakening of the gene pool. But if we begin to understand the importance of food and the environment, we can begin to turn the tide around.

It is our hope that this book will raise awareness of these issues and help you navigate a clear path to health.

How To Use This Cookbook

Let food be thy medicine and medicine be thy food.

Hippocrates

The recipes in this book are preceded by reader-friendly, easy to understand discussions of how food sets the direction for health, nutrition basics, food myths, and logical solutions. Doctor Kotsanis addresses "Nature's Food Pyramid," which establishes a foundation to achieve optimal health and healthful living. Kendra Jean Finestead discusses shopping, recipes, tips, and tricks for parents like herself. Beverly D. Kotsanis discusses preparing the home for healthy cooking and living and shares the recipes our patients have requested.

At the Kotsanis Institute Medical Clinic and Greater Tots Organization, our patients, moms, dads, and families always come first! We are passionate about helping them. This book is their book.

They tell us they face overwhelming challenges and need help and guidance. Questions most often asked of us include:

- How do I make my home a healthy environment to live in?
- What about the water we drink?
- What is EMF (electromagnetic frequencies)?
- How do I shop and where can I shop for the "right" foods?
- What do I stock my pantry with?
- What should I look for on food labels?
- What do those additional ingredients that sound like "Greek" mean?
- How do I deal with school lunches for my child?
- What are some guidelines for dining out?
- What are the food allergies?
- We need healthy recipes!

Consult Your Physician

It is important to consult your physician first and ensure that thorough testing is completed. This will provide the fact-based foundation to address specific health issues and to recommend further changes specific to your individual biochemical profile. When testing is complete, customization and individualization to each person is crucial to successfully change the diet and accelerate healthy improvements.

A Quick Start With Healthy Shopping

We help you find the "Right Foods." Look for the sample shopping list in chapter 4. You can find a digital copy of the list on our cookbook website, www.foodforthoughtbook. com. Customize your own list and just check off the ingredients you need for this new adventure in cooking and eating.

Shop at your local health food store if you have one. If not, chapter 4 has a list of healthy food sources with names of stores that may be in your area. Also, find lists of specialty food manufacturers and companies that will ship to you. Visit local farmers markets for weekly shopping trips and fresh organic fruits and vegetables.

Shop organic. While some people think it may cost more to shop organic, the truth is you will be paying far less than if you eat out, and you will also save money in the long term on health costs.

A Quick Plan

The best way to assure that you follow your doctor's recommendations is to set time aside once or twice per week for cooking that week's meals. Cooking early and freezing helps you better measure portions, which will keep you from wasting. Many recipes in the book can be used left over or frozen for later meals.

Food Substitution Charts, Measurements, And Equivalents

Look for these charts in chapters 4 and 5, where you will find specific substitutions. Also find this information consolidated in chapter 16.

Applications (Apps) And Websites

Consult the addendum section for favorite applications to download for shopping, recipes, nutrition calculators, tools, and techniques. Find current social media websites. Let us know if you recommend other apps, websites, and social media sources. We encourage you to contact us! Go to our website at www.foodforthoughtbook.com. Recommendations will be updated there frequently.

The Great 8 Food Allergies

Did you know that there were eight primary allergens? We focus on these common allergens in chapter 5, since they impact most people who have allergies or food sensitivities.

Make This A Family Adventure

You will find that it is easier to make these changes if your entire family switches to this healthier nutritional intake, emotionally as well as health wise. You will see additional health benefits to other members of your family. These benefits may include better heart health, lower risk of cancer, weight control, generally less illness and infection, and improved mental health. Our autistic, learning-challenged, allergy, and cancer patients will find it easier to concentrate. Digestive difficulties will come under control. Adhering to these dietary guidelines will help control allergies and reduce inflammation.

Cut Yourself Some Slack

Changes do not have to happen overnight. For some families it is best to make changes as you shop and replace existing foods already in the kitchen. If the offending foods are not in the house, it is much easier to accept the changes (and harder to "cheat"). Remember, if you try to implement change too quickly, the stress can outweigh the benefit. So please, cut yourself some slack!

Words of Encouragement

For people beginning to learn how to cook with new and alternative ingredients, the challenge may seem overwhelming. It does not have to be difficult! For our moms with difficult-to-feed children, rest assured that we have gathered helpful hints from other moms just like you. This information appears interspersed throughout the pages of this book as well as in all of our patient education materials.

Patients in our clinic benefit not only from our knowledge of nutrition, immunology, and medicine in general, but also gain the benefit of helpful information on meal planning, shopping, and cooking. Our care managers help patients shop and are available for the myriad of questions that come up. We "hold our patients' hands" along their journey, and our hope is that this book will help launch you on your way.

Remember that the change you make in your eating lifestyle is the single most important change you will ever make for your family's health. Your efforts will be well rewarded.

A Final Word

We are passionate about continuous improvement, learning, and sharing with our patients, families, and customers. We encourage you to visit our website, foodforthoughtbook. com. Find answers to your questions, a customizable shopping list, recipes and links to helpful websites for even more resources to support you on your journey.

Food For Thought

HOW TO READ THE RECIPES

Our recipes are uniquely formatted to make it easy to decide which recipe is right for you and your family. Ingredients are presented in order of use. They are gluten-free, casein-free, toxin-free, and, when not noted, allergen-free.

Each recipe highlights key foods, nutrition facts, and ingredients in a "Power Box" so that you understand the health benefits and to help you get to know and appreciate your food a little better. Individual nutrients, vitamins, and minerals are a small part of a large landscape that is our bodies. Power Box points are merely a reiteration of the power that lies in our food choices. As always, it is important to work with your health-care professional for a complete health plan.

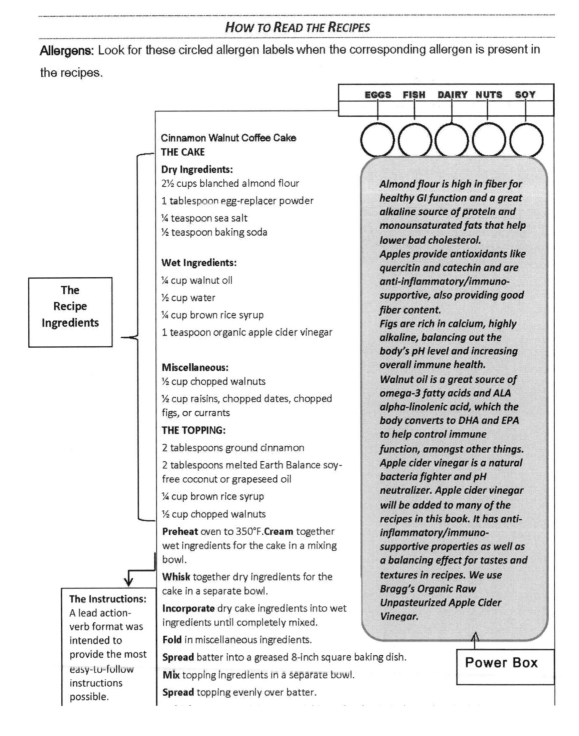

HOW TO READ THE RECIPES

Allergens: Look for these circled allergen labels when the corresponding allergen is present in the recipes.

EGGS FISH DAIRY NUTS SOY

The Recipe Ingredients

Cinnamon Walnut Coffee Cake
THE CAKE
Dry Ingredients:
2½ cups blanched almond flour
1 tablespoon egg-replacer powder
¼ teaspoon sea salt
½ teaspoon baking soda

Wet Ingredients:
¼ cup walnut oil
½ cup water
¼ cup brown rice syrup
1 teaspoon organic apple cider vinegar

Miscellaneous:
½ cup chopped walnuts
½ cup raisins, chopped dates, chopped figs, or currants
THE TOPPING:
2 tablespoons ground cinnamon
2 tablespoons melted Earth Balance soy-free coconut or grapeseed oil
¼ cup brown rice syrup
½ cup chopped walnuts

Preheat oven to 350°F. **Cream** together wet ingredients for the cake in a mixing bowl.

Whisk together dry ingredients for the cake in a separate bowl.

Incorporate dry cake ingredients into wet ingredients until completely mixed.

Fold in miscellaneous ingredients.

Spread batter into a greased 8-inch square baking dish.

Mix topping ingredients in a separate bowl.

Spread topping evenly over batter.

Almond flour is high in fiber for healthy GI function and a great alkaline source of protein and monounsaturated fats that help lower bad cholesterol.
Apples provide antioxidants like quercitin and catechin and are anti-inflammatory/immuno-supportive, also providing good fiber content.
Figs are rich in calcium, highly alkaline, balancing out the body's pH level and increasing overall immune health.
Walnut oil is a great source of omega-3 fatty acids and ALA alpha-linolenic acid, which the body converts to DHA and EPA to help control immune function, amongst other things.
Apple cider vinegar is a natural bacteria fighter and pH neutralizer. Apple cider vinegar will be added to many of the recipes in this book. It has anti-inflammatory/immuno-supportive properties as well as a balancing effect for tastes and textures in recipes. We use Bragg's Organic Raw Unpasteurized Apple Cider Vinegar.

Power Box

The Instructions: A lead action-verb format was intended to provide the most easy-to-follow instructions possible.

CHAPTER 1

Food: The Compass for Your Health

HOW FOOD SETS THE DIRECTION FOR YOUR HEALTH

The goal of a good diet is to supply your body with all the proper water, amino acids, fatty acids, carbohydrates, and minerals it needs to create good clean energy, and the building blocks with which to build the cells and structures of your body. Food is broken down by our bodies and used in the production of energy. Some food becomes the material that will make our bones, muscles, blood, and other tissues. Thus the phrase you are what you eat. If you eat food that contains synthetic ingredients, the body will not recognize those molecules as food but rather as an invading substance. This will begin a cascade of immune responses that can cause many types of health and behavior problems.

However, what do we mean by clean energy? The body has two ways of breaking food down to produce the energy molecule known as adenosine triphosphate (ATP). The first and preferred method is when the body has the time to thoroughly process the food in the digestive tract, then carefully absorb it and take what it needs. This should be an efficient process that reduces undesirable by-products and undigested food. This method gives you the most energy to support your activity, to support the beneficial flora living in your gut, to keep the immune system running smoothly, and to get the best cell integrity for the tissues of your body. It is like a car: use the right fuel, keep it well in tune, keep all the fluid levels checked, make sure the tires are aired up, and keep it free of rust, and it will last you quite a long time.

However, this method of getting energy is too inefficient for stressful fight or flight circumstances, times when you absolutely must have the energy now—if you are late to class, fighting off some thief, or running from a lion. For that, the body makes ATP more quickly but far less efficiently. There are more by-products and undigested food left to accumulate in the intestines, which in turn will invite an overgrowth of undesirable bacteria and fungus, setting up an inflammatory environment. In our car analogy, this is like realizing that you are late for work and have no time to check your car for fluids, gas, or if you are backing over your kid's tricycle. You need to get something done immediately, and you will worry about cleaning up after yourself later. This quick energy is for times of distress; later the body will mop up its mess.

But what if the body feels it is constantly in distress and operating in this dirty-energy mode twenty-four hours a day, seven days a week? Environmental toxins and food-borne allergies can put one into this constant mode of distress, making one sick. Then the toxins and by-products from this dirty-energy mode will continue to build up with no time to repair or clean anything up and will cause the body to sicken, lower the immune system response, and make the body a ready target for pathogens. The unprocessed food will continue to accumulate in your intestine, acting as fertilizer for some new harmful flora while killing off the beneficial ones. Pretty soon, your car is rusted and old, flies swarming around it, and a couple of scruffy-looking cats calling your back seat their home.

There are toxins enough in the air, water, and environment that we cannot control. However, what we eat, we can control. When we maintain optimal health through a proper diet, our bodies will be a lot more ready to fend off the attacks coming from the environment. It is a war, and the enemy in front of us is our environment; we do not need poor nutrition compounding the stress on the body.

When an unrecognized food or an environmental toxin stresses the body, the immune system is triggered. Antibodies are sent, special proteins are released, and inflammation occurs, like when you get a bruise and it swells up. The body does not care if it is a bacteria or a particle of food invading it, all incoming foreign matter is checked. Therefore, if you eat the wrong foods or foods that you may be allergic to, then that reaction can elicit an immune response as well, which can generate sickness and inflammation all over your body.

Besides allergic reactions, many foods are processed with chemical ingredients that can be toxic, such as aspartame, Equal, Sweet-N-Low, NutraSweet, Canderel, AminoSweet, Sugar Twin, cyclamates, saccharine, and many more. Then there are the additives, such as MSG, nitrates, and highly processed foods like HFC, preservatives, and things that leach into the food from their containers, such as BPA from plastic bottles, mercury, and lead. Artificial colorings are found not only in food, but also drugs, toothpastes, mouthwashes, and cosmetics. The disinfectants you use to clean your kitchen and bath should be nontoxic natural alternatives.

Even that plastic bottle you use to hold your otherwise toxin-free water is made with dangerous BPAs, which can leach out just from sitting there. Imagine what even BPA-free plastics will do inside a microwave; your food will be coated with something more than butter. Then there are nonstick chemical coatings. Better to stick with stainless steel, cast-iron, and glass.

It all adds up. The body takes in all these toxins in a constant assault. You can minimize exposure as much as possible, but you still need to make sure that your cannons are loaded with the right ammunition. This proper ammunition can be supplied by the intake of proper nutrients as described in Nature's Food Pyramid (chapter 2) and for food sensitives by following the gluten-free/casein-free (GFCF) diet.

NUTRITION BASICS FOR NON-DOCTORS

Two things control what you are and will become: genetics and the environment. Genetics determine your makeup; they tell your body how to form and grow and what to do. It was once thought that genes were written in stone, but epigenetics is the study of how the environment can affect your gene expression and rewrite what your genes do. Your environment not only includes the air around you, radiation, poisons in your environment, and the like, but everything you ingest as well. All it takes is for one toxin or allergen to affect the way your strands of DNA unfold and refold, altering the way your genes express themselves, for you to develop a new disease or ailment. Likewise, if you have a negative genetic predisposition that is not expressed, proper attention to diet and environment can keep the disease state from expressing.

Poor nutrition and environmental assaults can affect the pH balance of your gut, killing off the beneficial flora that thrive there, altering the way food is absorbed, or causing excessive permeability in your gut, creating a "leaky gut." A leaky gut can mean food does not get digested or absorbed properly and creates sites ripe for infection. However, how can one's gut become damaged? Poor diet, excessive use of some medications (such as antibiotics), parasitic and bacterial infections, and toxins can all set the stage for leaky gut. This is a state of excessive inflammation. Inflammation is a protective attempt by your body to remove the harmful stimuli and initiate the healing process.

The results will be felt in your gut first, commonly in the form of constipation or diarrhea. However, you must realize that whatever goes into your gut ends up in your other organs and brain as well. So if your gut is inflamed, other parts of your body will also become inflamed, including the brain.

To see how eating properly can actually help with certain conditions, such as autism spectrum disorders (ASD); let us start at the very beginning.

If we have clean water, clean air, and healthy plants that are full of nutrients, when we consume that food, the digestive system processes it more easily through digestion, absorption, and elimination. In addition, there are about 100 probiotic species in the gut, and most of them are beneficial, aiding in digestion and encouraging the immune system to do its work properly. If the normal flora is plentiful in the gut, it discourages inflammation and permeability and boosts digestive efficiency and absorption. When food is digested and absorbed correctly, you create optimal clean energy and are supporting all the body's systems to keep them in balance.

The energy and nutrients are then delivered in a very efficient process that supplies the cells and supports the DNA, the metabolism, and the process of restructuring the body itself. Every cell in your body has a lifespan, after which it gets recycled and replaced by a brand new cell. These new cells are built from the components derived from what you eat, so it is important that you eat correctly to supply the best building materials for this construction process to continue smoothly. Would you build a skyscraper from balsa wood? Then why build your body from the dietary equivalent? The nutrients you take in keep you running, thinking, and rebuilding your cells to support the constant restructuring of your body.

ASD is an example of what happens when the body is supplied with sub-par building materials and cheap fuel. However, since the body is constantly renewing itself, there is a high likelihood that a nutrient-dense diet along with a clean and chemical-free environment will help new cells renew in better condition. You just have to give the body a chance.

GLUTEN AND CASEIN

Why The Gluten-Free Casein-Free (GFCF) Diet?

There are two types of immune responses. The first is referred to as IgE, an innate immune response. The second is referred to as IgG and is considered immune sensitivity or food allergy. Wheat and milk are highly common causes of immune response and immune sensitivity in our population. So what is the difference between avoiding "wheat and milk" and avoiding "gluten and casein"?

Wheat is wheat. It is a grain that is highly consumed, especially in the standard American diet. Grains are inflammatory foods and are therefore not supportive to our immune systems. Gluten is the protein (actually a combination of the proteins gliadin and glutelin) found in wheat, as well as rye, barley, and many cross-contaminated oats. Casein is also a protein. It is the sister-protein to the more well-known whey protein and is found in animal milks. Milk as we buy it from our grocery store is a very inflammatory food. All animal milk is inflammatory. Human milk is the only milk that humans need the first two years of life. Additionally, human milk is the only milk that is alkaline. All other animal milks have an acidic pH. Nut milks are OK.

Metabolic Malfunction

The problem with gluten and casein beyond the immune reactions is a malfunction in actually metabolizing the proteins. It was discovered that the large peptides gliadomorphin and caseomorphin were showing up in urine samples of patients diagnosed with autism. The proteins in this form should typically not show up; they should have been metabolized. Gliadomorphin and caseomorphin are neurotoxic when absorbed and may affect immune and brain function. There is much research being done on this theory, but the results speak for themselves. Many thousands of families have seen results as we have seen with our own children and patients.

This led to the conclusion that many people diagnosed with autism spectrum disorders and AD(H)D may benefit from removing these elements from their diet. Although there are many variations of elimination diets for ASDs, in most cases removing gluten and casein proves a vital component on the path to recovery.

The peptides from gluten and casein are important because they can react with opiate receptors in the brain, thus mimicking the effects of opiate drugs like heroin and morphine. These compounds, called neuropeptides, have been shown to react with areas of the brain such as the temporal lobes, which are involved in speech and auditory integration. Neuropeptides also decrease the ability to feel pain and affect cognitive function.

However, some people may not show a food allergy to milk or wheat but may have the peptide problem, and vice versa. So a permeable gut (which is very common with children with ASD) plus insufficiently broken-down proteins results in neurotoxic peptides left to wander in the bloodstream.

Gliadomorphin, or gliadorphin, and caseomorphin are opiates that derive from gluten and casein. These opiates can cause various symptoms and behavioral differences, which is why we see such noticeable changes when removing them from these children's diets. They are hallucinogenic and addicting, and they can cause inattentive behavior, silliness, spacey behavior, poor eye contact, high pain tolerance, mood changes, and picky eating habits.

Enzyme Deficiencies

DPP-IV (dipeptidal-peptidase 4) is an enzyme that is responsible for the breakdown of gluten and casein. A lack of or an interference with DPP-IV breakdown is highly common in children with ASD. More research is needed to confirm the reasoning behind this enzyme deficiency. It is our opinion that it is a trickle-down effect of the past few generations of environmental toxin exposure and chemical alterations made to our life source (our food and water). The truth is that DPP-IV deficiency is a common issue. It makes sense, then, to avoid gluten and casein.

Because of this important dietary intervention, all of the recipes in this cookbook are gluten-free and casein-free. The presence of allergens dairy, eggs, fish, nuts, and soy are listed in the top corners of each recipe if necessary.

Let's talk about autoimmunity briefly. One study conducted on animal proteins in relation to disease found evidence that milk can actually lead to autoimmunity and can certainly exacerbate the disorder.

Allergies, autism, autoimmunity, and cancer are all conditions of an inflamed bodily response. Therefore, it makes great sense to remove those foods, which would promote an inflammatory response.

Life is one big, bold, and sometimes bewildering game of balance. Fitting a special diet into the mix is sure to provide ups, downs, and in-betweens. In this first cookbook, we seek to share with you the perfect balance of practicality, nutrition, epicure, and whimsy. We hope that you will find inspiration in this group of recipes and will get in touch with your inner chef.

FOOD MYTHS AND LOGICAL SOLUTIONS

Food Myth: If I take gluten and casein out of my child's diet, he or she will be missing key nutrients from the whole-grain breads and the milk that are so healthy for children.

The truth is simply this: the grains your child most likely eats are not as whole as you think. Most "whole wheat" breads you purchase at the local grocery store are filled with yeast, sugars, and highly processed starches and are by no means healthy for you; especially in the quantities in which they are consumed in the standard western diet.

The milk that you can purchase from the grocery store has had all of the key nutrients burned out of it in the pasteurization process. Because of this, the vitamins that milk is so famous for must be added back in or "fortified."

There are some great articles on the truths behind milk at the website www.mercola. com. Dr. Mercola states in an article titled Who Knew This Cocktail of up to 20 Chemicals Was in your Glass of Milk, "A single glass of milk can contain a mixture of as many as 20 painkillers, antibiotics, and growth hormones." He goes on to state, "Pasteurization transforms the physical structure of the proteins in milk, such as casein, and alters the shape of the amino acid to one that your body is not equipped to handle. The process also destroys the beneficial bacteria typically found naturally in milk and drastically reduces the micronutrient and vitamin content."

There are plenty of sources of calcium that are true food sources, like sesame seeds; orange, yellow, or red peppers; and oranges. As for your vitamin D, the best recipe is spending ample time outside!

Food Myth: I tried the Gluten-Free Casein-Free Diet and it didn't work for us.

One of the biggest reasons why people find that a gluten-free casein-free (GFCF) diet fails to work for them is sugar. The problem with sugar is starch and not carbohydrates. Carbohydrates (carbs) are found in healthy food choices too, so do not avoid carbs. Instead, as a general rule, you should avoid or at least limit starches. Why? Because all starches turn to sugar in the body and, if not used, get turned into fat.

So merely replacing cakes, cookies, and other baked goods with the gluten-free versions of these treats is not the correct path to take when setting out to accomplish true results from the GFCF diet. "Gluten-free" does not by itself equate to a healthy diet, and similarly "organic" by itself does not equate to a healthy diet. It's just not that simple, which is why a number of diets fail. It's like saying that if you just keep the car gassed up and tires filled that everything will always be okay; sometimes you have to check the engine as well.

In addition to keeping sugars in check, it is important to note that simply reducing the gluten or casein is not going to get you to the results we are presenting. Dr. Syd Baker has a well-circulated metaphor that seems to explain this precisely: "If you are sitting on a tack, no amount of aspirin will make it feel better. If you are sitting on two tacks, the removal of one does not result in 50 percent improvement from the symptoms."

As solutions to the above problem, a number of alternative diets have popped up that go beyond the standard GFCF dietary model. If you are still not seeing results with the standard gluten-free casein-free diet, here are a few alternatives and variations to consider. Many times, families find that a combination of GFCF and one or more of these diets get them the best results.

Lod (Low Oxalate Diet)

Oxalates are present in a lot of plants and fruit that we eat and in virtually all seeds and nuts. Ordinarily, the gut will not absorb much of the oxalate from the diet, and the oxalate will be metabolized by the flora or just leave the body with the stool. Under other conditions, a lot of the dietary oxalate is absorbed. Some children notice major improvement in gastro-intestinal discomfort when they avoid food high in oxalates.

Scd (Specific Carbohydrate Diet)

This variation eliminates all starches and feeds the body only food that will be easily and quickly digested. The idea is that yeast and other baneful flora will not be given an environment in which to thrive or even live in. Thereby, the gut flora is rebalanced.

Rotation Diet

On a rotation diet, you rotate the foods you eat, eating foods from the same food family on a three – or four-day spread to "trick" the immune system into not developing immune responses to new foods.

Bed (Body Ecology Diet/Candida Diet)

This diet is an anti-yeast diet, with no sugars, fermented foods, or fungus permitted. It includes very few grains and a proper balance of acid to alkalinity intake.

Gaps (Gut And Psychology Syndrome) Diet

Visit www.gapsdiet.com for more information. This diet is very closely related to the specific carbohydrate diet. Dr. Natasha Campbell-McBride implements principals of proper food combining, like separating your fruits from your carbohydrate/protein meals. This can be very effective when battling yeast overgrowth.

Feingold Diet

The Feingold diet program is all-encompassing, addressing both food and environmental products. You can find information on this diet at www.feingold.org. They also have a newsletter with great research on chemicals in our foods and environment. The Feingold protocol eliminates all artificial phenolic additives and high salicylates. Some symptoms of phenol intolerance include dark circles under the eyes, red face or ears, hyperactivity, impulsivity, aggression, self-injury, sleep disturbances, inappropriate laughing, bedwetting, dyslexia, tics, and seizures.

Weston A. Price/Nourishing Traditions

Weston A. Price's studies and subsequent recommendations for nutrition are based on his worldwide studies of endogenous cultures and how their diets affected their health. His principles were made popular in author Sally Fallon's book Nourishing Traditions. These principles include pure animal protein sources (grass-fed beef, pastured chickens, and eggs) and saturated fats from sources like avocado, coconut oil, and raw butter. The Weston Price/Nourishing Traditions belief is that cholesterol and saturated fat are in truth good for overall health. These diets also include sprouting grains, seeds, and beans for ease of digestion. They also suggest raw dairy and fermented foods. For more information, see any of the published works by Dr. Weston A. Price and Sally Fallon. (There are also interesting findings in the works of Frances M. Pottenger, whose studies are a collaborative of the Price-Pottenger Foundation.)

CHAPTER 2

Nature's Food Pyramid

HOW THE BODY GETS ITS ENERGY

The best dietary recommendation or advice is to simply observe what the human body is made of and "eat what you are!" The human body requires energy to survive, repair, reproduce, and communicate. But where should this source of energy come from? Surprisingly, the best source is *not* carbohydrates.

So Where Is My Energy Really Coming From?

All functions of life are powered by ATP, which is the "supreme fuel molecule." What super unleaded gasoline is for the car, ATP is for the body. ATP energy fuel can derive from a variety of proteins, fats, and carbohydrates. However, carbohydrates are not essential nutrients. Essential nutrients for humans are essential amino acids (proteins), essential fatty acids (fats), vitamins, minerals, oxygen, and water.

Nutrients are categorized as essential and nonessential. Essential nutrients are unable to be synthesized by the human body (either at all or in sufficient quantities) and thus must be consumed by the body from its environment. Nonessential nutrients are those nutrients that can be made by the body; they may also be absorbed from consumed food.

The body's physical structure is comprised of a combination of proteins and fats, but no part of the body is actually composed of carbohydrates. It would make sense, then, that a more rational approach would be to use proteins, at four calories per gram, and fats, at nine calories per gram. Next to water, fats and proteins are the two most prevalent macronutrients in the human body.

Are Fats and Proteins Better Energy Sources than Carbohydrates?

Stryers's textbook, *Biochemistry,* specifically states in chapter 17, on fatty acid metabolism, that "triacylglycerols are highly concentrated stores of metabolic energy." In chapter 18, on amino acid degradation and the urea cycle, Stryers adds, "Amino acids in excess of those needed for the synthesis of proteins and other biomolecules cannot be stored, in contrast with fatty acid and glucose, nor are they excreted. Rather surplus amino acids are used as metabolic fuel."

Here again, the logic is repeated. Protein and fats can be used as an efficient source of metabolic fuel.

But Eating Fats and Proteins Will Increase My Cholesterol and Triglycerides!

The mainstream population has been erroneously led to believe that eating carbohydrates is a healthier and more intelligent choice than fats and proteins. Medical science appears to differ, however. It is stated in the medical texts that eating excess carbohydrates forces the liver to convert them into triglycerides and cholesterol.

A Woeful Tale of Triglycerides and Cholesterol

"When glucose is not immediately required for energy, the extra glucose that continually enters the cells either is stored as glycogen or is converted into fat. When the cells approach saturation with glycogen, the additional glucose is then converted into fat in the liver and in fat cells and then is stored in the fat cells." (Arthur C. Guyton, MD, *Textbook of Medical Physiology,* 7th ed. (Philadelphia: W.B Saunders, 1986), 816.)

Fats and Lipids: The Great Communicators

Much has been written about fats and lipids. Obviously, a diet sufficient in proteins will also provide many of these much-needed nutrients. World-renowned nutrition expert Nora T. Gedgaudas, CNS, CNT, adds:

Most organs and tissues in the body, including the brain, actually prefer, if we let them, to use ketones, the energy-producing by-products from the metabolism of fats. There is abundant evidence that many modern disease processes, including those resulting in cardiovascular disease, elevated triglyceride levels, obesity, hypertension, diabetes, hypoglycemia, and cancer, to name a few, are the product not of excess natural fat in the diet, but of excess carbohydrates.

Once again, it is not the fats that elevate, it is the carbohydrates! Multiple studies ranging from Framingham, the Minnesota State Hospital Trial, the Veterans Clinical Trial, the Puerto Rico Heart Health Study, and the Honolulu Heart Program have all shown a consistent and distinct lack of correlation between dietary fat, dietary or serum cholesterol, and heart disease.(Colbert, MD, *Dr. Colbert's "I Can Do This" Diet*, (Lake Mary, Florida: Siloam, 2010), 12.)

It's Not the Fats—It Is the Carbohydrates

Thus, eating external sourced dietary fats (exogenous) really does not increase the internal fat levels (endogenous). In other words, eating carbohydrates raises the cholesterol level more than eating the fats. The fats actually have a dampening effect on the liver's own internal production.

This, again, is clearly illustrated in Arthur C. Guyton, MD, *Textbook of Medical Physiology*, 7th ed. (Philadelphia: W.B Saunders, 1986), 816.)

An increase in the amount of cholesterol ingested each day increases the plasma concentration slightly. However, when cholesterol is ingested, the rising concentration of cholesterol inhibits one of the essential enzymes for endogenous synthesis of cholesterol, thus providing an intrinsic feedback control system to regulate plasma cholesterol concentration. As a result, plasma cholesterol concentration usually is not changed upward or downward more than ±15 percent by altering the amount of cholesterol in the diet.

Guyton continues by adding, "Ingestion of fat containing highly unsaturated fatty acids usually depresses the blood cholesterol concentration a slight to moderate amount." Finally, "The blood cholesterol also rises greatly in diabetes mellitus."

In a Nutshell

Increased ingestion of carbohydrates (both simple or complex) does more to increase the blood levels of cholesterol than eating proteins and fats, both of which are major constituents of the human body. Regarding proteins and fats, the body takes what it needs from outside sources while compensating for its deficiencies and excesses with internal controls.

The Energetics of Life

Steve Gagne, in his monumental work, *Food Energetics: The Spiritual, Emotional, and Nutritional Power of What We Eat,* explains the entire realm of energetics as it pertains to the food choices and methods of preparation of these foods. He states, "Ancient peoples, through their relationships with the plants and animals providing their food, understood that their food conveyed the unique energetic qualities of its source, such as swiftness from wild deer and groundedness from root vegetables." Food is not only composed of macro- and micronutrients, but it also conveys the subtle rhythms, harmony, and energies that are so important to the expression of optimal health. This concept is absolutely the most astounding evidence to support the health-building qualities of eating properly.

Gedgaudas sums it up best when stating, "So many taboos…have likely risen from the perception of 'you are what you eat.' Consider instead, that you are what your metabolism does with what you eat." So if you eat vegetables, you are a veggie, if you eat fruit, you are a fruit, if you eat meat, well, you are meat. Therefore…

Eat What You Are!™

Credit and appreciation to Robin C. Hyman, DC, for the model concept and article content.

Nature's Food Pyramid and content contribution by Constantine A. Kotsanis, MD, MD(H), CCN.

NATURE'S FOOD PYRAMID

The Logical Approach to Health

The first question should be why, with the standard food pyramid previously promoted by the USDA, do we need a new one? As was said before, a more logical approach would be to examine what the body is composed of and derive out the food pyramid hierarchy that sustains the body from there. Such a common sense approach has a few benefits. Namely, it does the following:

- Helps prevent and reduce inflammation, infection, and disease in the body
- Delays aging
- Improves overall health
- Supplies a nutritionally sound dietary foundation for optimal health
- Provides the optimum anti-inflammatory natural approach to "eating for life"

Thus, besides promoting overall health simply by feeding the body just what it needs, these dietary guidelines may also help counteract ongoing chronic inflammation, which is most often the root cause of serious diseases, including heart disease, cancer, Parkinson's and Alzheimer's, age-related disorders, and autoimmune diseases such as rheumatoid arthritis and lupus.

Nature's Food Pyramid is a proportional guideline upon which to base daily food choices. It is a foundation that supports optimal health. It is an easily understood tool to help today's families eat well and prevent disease at the same time. Of course, if an individual has food allergies and sensitivities, modifications to Nature's Food Pyramid need to be made for those conditions.

The whole pyramid model is present on the next page, followed by an explanation of each proportional level. Nature's Food Pyramid is based upon research and the writings of Robin C. Hyman, DC, who we thank for freely sharing this important work.

NATURE'S FOOD PYRAMID

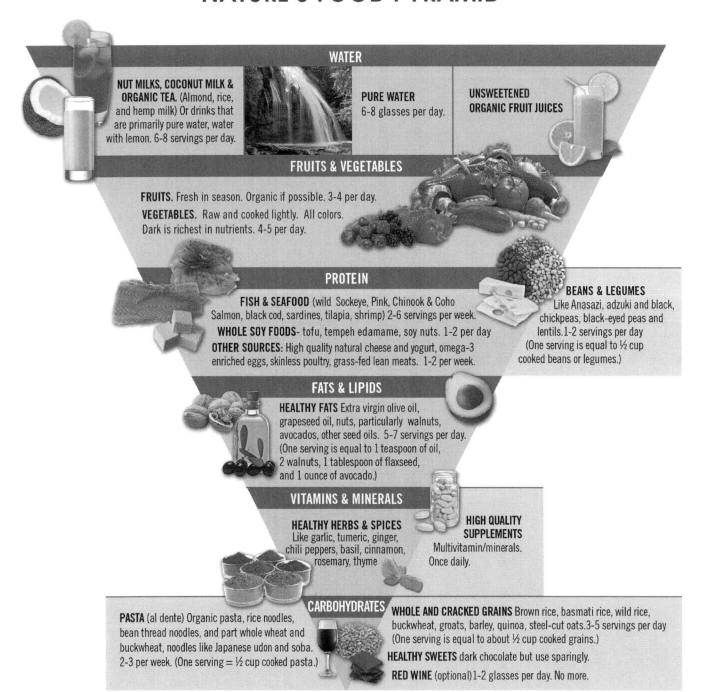

WATER

NUT MILKS, COCONUT MILK & ORGANIC TEA. (Almond, rice, and hemp milk) Or drinks that are primarily pure water, water with lemon. 6-8 servings per day.

PURE WATER 6-8 glasses per day.

UNSWEETENED ORGANIC FRUIT JUICES

FRUITS & VEGETABLES

FRUITS. Fresh in season. Organic if possible. 3-4 per day.
VEGETABLES. Raw and cooked lightly. All colors. Dark is richest in nutrients. 4-5 per day.

PROTEIN

FISH & SEAFOOD (wild Sockeye, Pink, Chinook & Coho Salmon, black cod, sardines, tilapia, shrimp) 2-6 servings per week.
WHOLE SOY FOODS- tofu, tempeh edamame, soy nuts. 1-2 per day
OTHER SOURCES: High quality natural cheese and yogurt, omega-3 enriched eggs, skinless poultry, grass-fed lean meats. 1-2 per week.

BEANS & LEGUMES Like Anasazi, adzuki and black, chickpeas, black-eyed peas and lentils. 1-2 servings per day (One serving is equal to ½ cup cooked beans or legumes.)

FATS & LIPIDS

HEALTHY FATS Extra virgin olive oil, grapeseed oil, nuts, particularly walnuts, avocados, other seed oils. 5-7 servings per day. (One serving is equal to 1 teaspoon of oil, 2 walnuts, 1 tablespoon of flaxseed, and 1 ounce of avocado.)

VITAMINS & MINERALS

HEALTHY HERBS & SPICES Like garlic, tumeric, ginger, chili peppers, basil, cinnamon, rosemary, thyme

HIGH QUALITY SUPPLEMENTS Multivitamin/minerals. Once daily.

CARBOHYDRATES

PASTA (al dente) Organic pasta, rice noodles, bean thread noodles, and part whole wheat and buckwheat, noodles like Japanese udon and soba. 2-3 per week. (One serving = ½ cup cooked pasta.)

WHOLE AND CRACKED GRAINS Brown rice, basmati rice, wild rice, buckwheat, groats, barley, quinoa, steel-cut oats. 3-5 servings per day (One serving is equal to about ½ cup cooked grains.)
HEALTHY SWEETS dark chocolate but use sparingly.
RED WINE (optional) 1-2 glasses per day. No more.

Eat Well...The Natural Way. The Optimum Anti-Inflammatory Pyramid: Nature's Food Pyramid

WATER BASICS

Water is the vital link to life that no one can do without. It is the body's transportation system, distributing nutrients and essential amino acids throughout the body. Without this transportation system, the body would simply stop working.

Since the dawn of civilization, scientists have been trying to find some stable material substance that is behind everything. This is an old concept dating back to Thales of Miletus in the sixth century BC. Thales was looking for something that subsists, something behind everything, something that is permanent and something that is unchanging. This substance is water! Water is a ubiquitous chemical substance, composed of hydrogen and oxygen that is essential for the survival of all life forms.

In a scientific experiment, we must control something in order to measure things against it. We must find a matrix that connects everything with everything else. We pose the scientific question: What is physical life? The answer is water, amino acids, fatty acids, carbohydrates, minerals, enzymes, electricity, and magnetism. In this sea of bioelectromagnetochemical soup, water is the thread or matrix that connects everything.

Change is the most constant thing in nature. This scientific observation was first made by Heraclitus of Ephesus in the sixth century BC. The statement of Heraclitus *panta rhei*, i.e., "everything in life is in a state of flux," is a scientific reality that will always remain constant. Thus, water fits the observations over the millennia that have innate qualities of constancy and change. Water composes about 60 percent of the human body and is the elixir of life. Without water, none of the bioelectromagnetochemical properties in life can be sustained.

The water we ingest should be the purest possible, with the energetic vitality left intact or reintroduced. Generally, two-thirds of an ounce of water per pound of body weight is considered the ideal water formula.

This equates to roughly one quart per fifty pounds of body weight. Naturally, under more extreme climates this may need to be altered. Additionally, to prevent any possibility of a hyponatremic (low sodium) condition, the proper addition of a healthy source of sodium such as a vegetable (celery) or high-quality sea salt is advised.

Drinking water comes from surface water and groundwater. Surface water includes rivers, lakes, and reservoirs. Groundwater is pumped from wells that are drilled into aquifers. These sources of drinking water contain some naturally occurring contaminants. Microbiological and chemical contaminants can enter the water supply. These contaminants can be the result of human activity or can be found in nature.

Due to potential contamination of all sources of bottled water in some states, water must be approved by the state's Commission on Environmental Quality. The Environmental Protection Agency (EPA) has issued drinking water standards or maximum contaminant levels (MCLs) for 87 discrete contaminants. (See www.epa.gov/ogwdw/consumer/pdf/mcl.pdf for more information.)

In establishing these standards and the health risks associated with them, the EPA assumes that the average adult drinks two liters of water each day throughout a 70-year lifespan. The EPA generally sets MCLs at a level that will limit an individual's risk of cancer from a contaminant to between 1 in 10,000 and 1 in 1,000,000 over a lifetime. The resulting law is called the National Primary Drinking Water Regulations.

Additionally, there are 15 potential contaminants are included in the National Secondary Drinking Water Regulations, with non-enforceable guidelines concerning contaminants that may cause cosmetic effects (such as skin or tooth discoloration) or aesthetic effects (such as taste, odor, or color) in drinking water.

More detailed information about government regulations may be found on the United States Environmental Protection Agency website at www.epa.gov/ogwdw/consumer.

Types of Water

Purified water is water that has been produced by distillation, deionization, reverse osmosis, or other suitable processes. The water must contain no more than 10 parts per million (ppm) total dissolved solids (TDS) as stipulated by the United States Pharmacopeia, 23rd Revision, January 1, 1995.

High-Quality Purified Water That Is Oxygen-Rich. There are a number of good water purification processes on the market that produce healthful oxygen-rich water, the type best for the body. Eco-Water and the Rain Fresh Water Purification Processes are examples.

Rain Fresh® Water Purification Process. (http://rainfreshwater.com/index.html). Rain Fresh® Bottled Water Company produces high quality purified water that is oxygen-rich with a refreshing taste. You may find more information about the purification process at these websites: www.rainfreshwater.com and www.ecowater.com.

Ionized water. Home tap water contains a mixture of minerals, salts, and other substances, some of which are good for you and some of which are not. After many of the harmful elements are filtered out, a home water ionizer uses the electrodialysis process to separate the remaining minerals in the water into healthy alkaline minerals and acidic minerals. During the process, some water molecules are split, releasing hydrogen and charged particles.

The charged water ions, called hydroxyl ions, are short lived, but they combine with the minerals in the water to produce mineral ions, referred to in chemistry as hydroxides. Medical research suggests that alkaline water may get its antioxidant properties from these charged mineral hydroxides.

Alkaline water may be the best way to get your minerals; it is associated with health benefits that include reduced rates of heart disease, healthy weight loss, improved digestive health, maintenance of bone density, and improved athletic performance. Studies have shown that minerals in alkaline water are 30 percent easier to absorb than food-based minerals. The higher pH in alkaline water helps fight metabolic acidosis. Alkaline water contains anti-aging antioxidants, hydrates better than plain water, and tastes better than regular water.

Alkaline water has been used in Asia as a health supplement for years, and Asian countries rank highest in world health surveys. Used properly, alkaline water should be combined with a proper diet, exercise, and healthy lifestyle to produce optimum results.

Distilled water is water that has been purified by distillation. The distillation process uses a rapid high-temperature environment (boiling) to separate out the solids and draw off the water as steam; the water then condenses back to its liquid form. One of the disadvantages of this process is that if nitrate is present, it is concentrated by the distillation process. Nitrate in drinking water at levels above the national standard poses an immediate threat to young children. Excessive levels can result in a condition known as blue baby syndrome. If untreated, this condition can be fatal. Boiling water contaminated with nitrate actually increases the nitrate concentration and potential risk.

Spring water is water derived from an underground formation from which water flows naturally to the surface of the earth. Many factors, both natural and manmade, influence the purity levels of a spring. The composition of the soil and rocks may add naturally occurring but unwanted substances to the water, such as radon, fluoride, or minerals. These minerals are in inorganic form and cannot be assimilated by our bodies as such.

Mineral water is water that contains no less than 250 parts per million (ppm) total dissolved solids (TDS), coming from a source tapped at one or more bore holes or springs, originating from a geologically or physically protected underground water source. No minerals may be added to this water. The minerals have been dissolved by water leaching as it flows over and through beds of sediment and rock. Because these minerals are naturally occurring, there is no mechanism to regulate the types or quantities of minerals. These minerals are inorganic, and our bodies need organic minerals from quality food sources.

Arm Your Home with Oxygen-Rich Safe Drinking Water!

We urge you to have your home water tested. Water coming into your home is regulated with *minimum standards* by the government and municipalities. Your municipality or water provider must report your water content annually in a Consumer Confidence Report, or CCR. You may find this information on the Internet as well. Understanding the report is a different matter altogether!

Once the water leaves the main and flows into your pipes, the content of the water may change dramatically. This is because the condition of your pipes and the material your pipes are constructed of can further contribute to contaminants. According to the EPA, household plumbing remains a main cause of lead contamination in homes built before 1986.

Essential Information

Call the EPA's Safe Drinking Water Hotline (800-426-4791) to see whether your municipality provides free or inexpensive testing or to find a certified testing lab in your area. Visit www.epa.gov/safewater/labs for further guidance. Ultimately, you may not need a water filter, but it is always wise to check.

For an objective resource, check out *Consumer Reports* (www.consumerreports.org). The magazine conducted a review of various types of water filters on the market in 2010, and they also address how to decipher your water report.

More than just good-tasting water might be at stake. Dangerous contaminants such as lead, chloroform, arsenic, nitrate, nitrite, radon, and *E. coli* bacteria are common in tap water. Bottled water, often advertised as a "pure" and "natural" alternative to tap water, is generally safe. However, it is actually less regulated by the Environmental Protection Agency than municipal water supplies. Indeed, some bottled water is nothing more than filtered tap water.

A flood of new filters—everything from simple carafes to permanently mounted systems—can make removing impurities from your drinking water almost as easy as turning on the tap. Some models that connect to the plumbing are now simple enough that they can be installed by the homeowner. In addition, across types, more filters now feature electronic indicators that signal when it is time for replacement.

Drinking Water from Private Wells: A Risk to Children

A word of caution from the Committee on Environmental Health and Committee on Infectious Diseases: drinking water for approximately one-sixth of U.S. households is obtained from private wells. These wells can become contaminated by pollutant chemicals or pathogenic organisms and cause illness. Although the Environmental Protection Agency and all states offer guidance for construction, maintenance, and testing of private wells, there is little regulation. With few exceptions, well owners are responsible for their own wells. Children may also drink well water at childcare or when traveling. Severe illness can result from children's ingestion of contaminated water. (See *Pediatrics* 2009; 123:1599–1605.)

Improve Your Water Supply

- Read the label of your bottled water. "Spring" water comes from one or more underground sources, and some bottled water may come from a "municipal source" or from a "community water system," and it may have had additional treatment. The best option is water that says "bottled at source spring water."
- Avoid plastic bottles with the following recycling codes: #1 PET, #3 PVC, #6 PS, and #7 Polycarbonate, which may leak suspected carcinogens and hormone disruptors.
- Look for safer plastic bottles, such as #2 HDPE, #4 LDPE, and #5 PP, but ideally glass bottles.

Know Your Water Source

- Find out if the pipes in your home or apartment building are made of lead or contain lead solder.
- Send tap water samples to your local EPA-certified laboratory for testing, or buy a water testing kit.
- If your water is supplied by a public system:
  ° Ask your supplier what chemicals and parasites are tested for and how the water is treated.
  ° Obtain a Consumer Confidence Report on your water quality from your public water authority.

- If your water supply is a private well:
  - ° Test your water yearly for pesticides, metals, coliform bacteria, and other possible contaminants.
  - ° Avoid using pesticides, fertilizers, and other chemicals near your well's supply source as they can pollute your groundwater.
- Install water treatment filters or conditioning systems. Several types are available, depending on what contaminants are present. A reverse osmosis filter will remove fluoride, chlorine, and many other contaminants. Learn more about what filter to use here: http://www.ewg.org/tap-water/getawaterfilter.
- Flush your pipes by running cold water for at least one minute.
- Do not use hot water from the tap for cooking or drinking, as toxins are more likely to leach into hot water.
- Make sure formula is prepared with safe water, since boiling increases the lead concentration. Infants are at particular risk of lead poisoning because of the larger amount of water they consume relative to their body size.
- If necessary, install shower/faucet filters, since babies can swallow water when bathing.
- Immediately dispose of household chemicals like batteries, fluorescent bulbs, used motor oil, etc., at your municipal hazardous waste depot. Do not leave them around your home where they may contaminate your water supply.

Source: www.healthychild.org/live-healthy.

The benefits of reverse osmosis–treated water versus a carbon-only filtration system are shown in the following table.

Comparison of Carbon Only Versus
Combination Reverse Osmosis And Carbon

Tap Water May Contain	Carbon Clock or Activated Carbon	TFC Reverse Osmosis/Carbon Combination
Bad Taste	improves	improves
Odor	improves	removes
Turbidity	reduces	removes
Organic Compounds	removes	removes
Chlorine and THMs	removes	removes
Bacteria	can control growth	removes
Viruses	will not remove	removes
Cysts	removes some	removes
Parasites	removes some	removes
Arsenic	will not remove	removes
Heavy Metals**	removes some	removes
Dissolved Solids***	will not remove	removes
Fluoride	will not remove	removes
Sulfates	will not remove	remove
Nitrates	will not remove	removes
Radioactivity	removes	removes
Asbestos	removes	removes

*Organic compounds include pesticides, herbicides, and insecticides.

**Heavy metals include iron, lead, cadmium, and aluminum.

***Dissolved solids include sodium, calcium, magnesium, and inorganic minerals.

If using reverse osmosis, it is important to know which minerals are lost. They can be replaced with ½ teaspoon of Celtic sea salt per gallon of water or tablets that may be purchased at your local health food store, grocery, or pharmacy.

Drinking Tips for Healthy Hydration

Start your morning right—morning is the time you are fullest of toxins and have gone the longest without water. Reach for a big glass of water first thing, even before coffee. Water in the morning really gets the blood flowing!

- Drink a glass of water when you get up and another when you go to bed.
- Take regular water breaks.
- Avoid relying on any beverage that may have high dissolved and/or suspended substances. Until relatively recent times, we did not have the choice of drinks we have now. What our body runs on is water, not sodas, etc.
- Drink water before and after eating; ideally drink a glass of water half an hour before you eat your meal and half an hour after the meal.
- You can drink water with meals as well and anytime your body feels like it.

If you like to drink cold water, the following is applicable to you. It is nice to have a cold drink after a meal; however, a cold beverage will solidify any oily stuff you have just consumed. It will slow down digestion. Once this "sludge" reacts with the acid, it will break down and be absorbed by the intestine faster than the solid food. It will line the intestine. Very soon, this will turn into fats. It is best to drink hot soup or warm water after a meal.

It is very important to balance your sodium intake with your water consumption. Take one-fourth of a teaspoon of salt per quart of water, or every four to five glasses of water. Be sure to get sea salt. The best is Celtic sea salt or Himalayan sea salt, both of which are readily available at any health food store.

Drinking water prior to eating and after eating supports the digestive process. The stomach depends on water to help digest food, and lack of water makes it harder for nutrients to be broken down and used as energy. The liver, which dictates where all nutrients go, also needs water to help convert stored fat into usable energy. If you are dehydrated, the kidneys turn to the liver for backup, diminishing the liver's ability to metabolize stored fat. The resulting reduced blood volume will interfere with your body's ability to remove toxins and supply your cells with adequate nutrients.

Keep a water bottle by your side at all times. Use a quality purified bottled water or at least water filtered by reverse osmosis. Carry it with you everywhere—to the gym, in your car, to your office. Start by adding water to your daily regimen for one week, then incorporate more as needed. The point is not to wait until you are thirsty to drink. A feeling of thirst is an emergency body response indicating the early stages of dehydration have begun. By that time, we have lost 2 percent of body weight in fluids.

Keep water flowing before, during, and after a workout. Don't forget to balance your water intake with sodium intake. Drink at least one liter of water for every 60 minutes of exercise. During exercise, it is recommended to replenish fluid at least every 20 minutes.

Drink more if it is hot. During exercise, i.e., playing sports on a hot summer day, you can lose up to two liters per hour of fluid. Pure water and a balanced salt intake are your best bets to keep healthy and hydrated.

For more information about water in general, the ionization process, alkaline and acidic water, and effects on the body, go to www.lifeionizers.com.

So many water options are available to consumers today. The important point is that you are aware of the quality of the water that you and your family drink. Further, that you make an educated choice about the type of water you consume. We hope this overview has helped you in making those choices.

FIBER: FRUITS AND VEGETABLES

Fruits and vegetables are major contributors of essential nutrients, including folate, magnesium, potassium, dietary fiber, and vitamins A, C, and K, as well as being associated with a reduced risk of many chronic diseases. Evidence indicates intake of at least two and a half cups of vegetables and fruits per day is associated with a reduced risk of cardiovascular disease, including heart attack and stroke. Some vegetables and fruits may be protective against certain types of cancer.

Remember to eat your vegetables and fruits in as fresh a state as possible, as it is in this raw state that the more heat-sensitive nutrients are best available. Cooking is great for the release of animal proteins and nutrients from animal and meat sources, but plant-based food should be eaten as close to raw as possible.

Most vegetables and fruits, when prepared without added fats or sugars, are relatively low in calories. Eating them instead of higher calorie foods can help adults and children achieve and maintain a healthy weight. Proper servings and healthy choices are given below.

What to Eat

Vegetables

How much: Four to five servings per day minimum (one serving is equal to 2 cups salad greens, ½ cup vegetables cooked, raw, or juiced)

Healthy Choices: Lightly cooked dark leafy greens (spinach, collard greens, kale, Swiss chard), cruciferous vegetables (broccoli, cabbage, Brussels sprouts, kale, bok choy, and cauliflower), carrots, beets, onions, peas, squashes, sea vegetables, and washed raw salad greens

Why: Vegetables are rich in flavonoids and carotenoids, with both antioxidant and anti-inflammatory activity. Go for a wide range of colors, eat them both raw and cooked, and choose organic when possible.

Fruits

How much: Three to four servings per day (one serving is equal to one medium size piece of fruit, ½ cup chopped fruit, ¼ cup of dried fruit)

Healthy choices: Raspberries, blueberries, strawberries, peaches, nectarines, oranges, pink grapefruit, red grapes, plums, pomegranates, blackberries, cherries, apples, and pears—all lower in glycemic load than most tropical fruits

Why: Fruits are rich in flavonoids and carotenoids, with both antioxidant and anti-inflammatory activity. Go for a wide range of colors, choose fruit that is fresh in season or frozen, and buy organic whenever possible.

PROTEIN

Proteins are the major structural component of the cell, the building blocks of all cells in the body. They function as enzymes, hormones, and other important molecules. They are one of the major macronutrients and an important source of calories. However, both protein and non-protein energy (from carbohydrates and fats) must be available to prevent protein-energy malnutrition (PEM).

Proteins are made up of amino acids. If the amino acids are not present in the right balance, the body's ability to use protein will be affected. If amino acids needed for protein synthesis are limited, the body may break down body protein (like muscle) to obtain needed amino acids. Protein deficiency affects all organs and is especially important during growth and development. Thus, adequate intake of *high-quality* protein is essential for good health.

The most logical source of protein is from a high-quality animal source. Animal-based protein includes all the essential amino acids needed by the body. The body does not need to break down (catabolize) animal protein to each individual amino acid in order to rebuild its cells, thus conserving energy. Plant-based proteins need to be catabolized further and then rebuilt back to human tissue. This is a more inferior process, especially when the body may not be communicating properly between the higher brain centers and the tissue levels.

What to Eat

Fish and Seafood

How much: Two to six servings per week (one serving is equal to 4 ounces of fish or seafood)

Healthy choices: Wild Alaskan salmon (especially sockeye), herring, sardines, and black cod (sablefish)

Why: These fish are rich in omega-3 fats, which are strongly anti-inflammatory. If you choose not to eat fish, take a molecularly distilled fish oil supplement that provides both EPA and DHA in a dose of two to three grams per day.

Cooked and Asian Mushrooms

How much: Unlimited amounts

Healthy choices: Shiitake, enokidake, maitake, oyster mushrooms (and wild mushrooms if available)

Why: These mushrooms contain compounds that enhance immune function. Never eat mushrooms raw, and minimize consumption of common commercial button mushrooms (including crimini and portobello).

Whole Soy Foods (Always Organic)

How much: One to two servings per day (one serving is equal to ½ cup tofu or tempeh, 1 cup soy milk, ½ cup cooked edamame, 1 ounce of soy nuts)

Healthy choices: Tofu, tempeh, edamame, soy nuts, soy milk

Why: Soy foods contain isoflavones that have antioxidant activity and are protective against cancer. Choose whole soy foods over fractionated foods like isolated soy protein powders and imitation meats made with soy isolate.

Beans and Legumes

How much: One to two servings per day (one serving is equal to ½ cup cooked beans or legumes)

Healthy choices: Beans like Anasazi, adzuki, and black, as well as chickpeas, black-eyed peas, and lentils

Why: Beans are rich in folic acid, magnesium, potassium, and soluble fiber. They are a low-glycemic-load food. Eat them well-cooked, either whole or puréed into spreads like hummus.

Other Sources of Protein

How much: One to two servings a week (one portion is equal to 1 ounce of cheese, 8 ounces of dairy, 1 egg, or 3 ounces cooked poultry or skinless meat)

Healthy choices: High-quality natural cheese and yogurt, omega-3 enriched eggs, skinless poultry, grass-fed lean meats

Why: In general, try to reduce consumption of animal foods. If you eat chicken, choose organic, cage-free chicken, and remove the skin and associated fat. Use organic, reduced-fat dairy products moderately, especially yogurt and natural cheeses such as Emmental (Swiss), Jarlsberg, and true Parmesan. If you eat eggs, choose omega-3 enriched eggs (made by feeding hens a flax meal-enriched diet) or organic eggs from free-range chickens.

Protein Tips

- On a diet of 2,000 calories a day, daily intake of protein should be between 80 and 120 grams.
- Eat less protein if you have liver or kidney problems, allergies, or autoimmune disease.
- Decrease your consumption of animal protein except for fish and high-quality natural cheese and yogurt.
- Eat more vegetable protein, especially from beans in general and soybeans in particular.
- Become familiar with the range of whole-soy foods available and find ones you like.

FATS AND LIPIDS

Fats and lipids serve as a carrier to absorb fat-soluble vitamins A, D, E, and K and carotenoids. They are also a source of antioxidants and numerous bioactive compounds, and they serve as building blocks of membranes as well as playing a key role in biological functions. Fats and lipids are necessary in the diet because they are the most important component in the cell wall. They help to hold the proper charge in the phospholipid bilayer. Artificial fats cannot hold a proper charge. This is a problem because the cell must let the right nutrients into the cell and allow the waste products to leave the cell. A faulty cell wall causes leaky cells and thus promotes disease.

What to Eat

Healthy Fats

How much: Five to seven servings per day (one serving is equal to 1 teaspoon of oil, 2 walnuts, 1 tablespoon of flaxseed, 1 ounce of avocado)

Healthy choices: For cooking, use extra virgin olive oil, grapeseed oil, and expeller-pressed organic nut and seed oil. Other sources of healthy fats include nuts (especially walnuts), avocados, and seeds—including hemp seeds and freshly ground flaxseed. Omega-3 fats are also found in cold-water fish, omega-3 enriched eggs, and whole soy foods. Organic, expeller-pressed, high-oleic sunflower or safflower oils may also be used, as well as walnut and hazelnut oils in salads and dark roasted sesame oil as a flavoring for soups and stir-fries. If you use butter, go with organic only, but not for cooking. Ghee is clarified butter and can be made by heating butter and removing the solids.

Why: Healthy fats are those rich in either monounsaturated or omega-3 fats. Extra virgin olive oil is rich in polyphenols with antioxidant activity and canola oil contains a small fraction of omega-3 fatty acids.

Fats and Lipid Tips

- On a diet of 2,000 calories a day, 600 calories can come from fat—that is, about 67 grams. This should be in a ratio of 1:2:1 of saturated to monounsaturated to polyunsaturated fat.
- Reduce your intake of saturated fat by eating less butter, cream, high-fat cheese, unskinned chicken and fatty meats, and products made with palm kernel oil.
- Use extra virgin olive oil or grapeseed oil as a main cooking oil. Organic, high-oleic, expeller-pressed versions of sunflower and safflower oil are also acceptable.
- Avoid regular safflower and sunflower oils, corn oil, cottonseed oil, and mixed vegetable oils.
- Strictly avoid margarine, vegetable shortening, and all products listing them as ingredients. Strictly avoid all products made with partially hydrogenated oils of any kind. Include in your diet avocados and nuts, especially walnuts, cashews, almonds, and nut butters made from these nuts.
- For omega-3 fatty acids, eat salmon (preferably fresh or frozen wild or canned sockeye), sardines (packed in water or olive oil), herring, and black cod (sablefish, butterfish); omega-3 fortified eggs; hemp seeds and flaxseeds (preferably freshly ground). You may also take a fish oil supplement. Look for products that provide both EPA and DHA, in a convenient daily dosage of two to three grams.

VITAMINS AND MINERALS

Vitamins and minerals are key to building and maintaining the body, maintaining health and energy, and enhancing the immune system. However, the presence and quality of such nutrients in foods depend on how the food was grown, handled, packed, transported to market, and, finally, prepared by the consumer.

The fruits and vegetables in which these vitamins and minerals are found are only as good as the soil they were grown in. Today's commercial farming methods have depleted the soil. While it takes roughly 70 nutrients and trace elements to prepare soil for growing, commercial farming does not replace all these elements before growing crops. Usually only about three are replaced.

Organic produce, on the other hand, is grown with the time-honored principles that have been passed down through many generations. These principles maintain the fertility of the soil and yield produce that has up to ten times the nutritional value of commercially grown food.

While we understand that city dwellers may have more difficulty finding organic produce, it is far more readily available today than it was a few years ago. It is worth the extra effort to buy organic, as an ounce of (disease) prevention is worth a pound of cure.

The most essential vitamins and minerals and their food sources are given in the following table:

Sources of Vitamins and Minerals

Calcium	Dairy foods, salmon, sardines, seafood, green leafy vegetables. Found in: almonds, asparagus, blackstrap molasses, brewer's yeast, broccoli, buttermilk, cabbage, carob, cheese, collard greens, dandelion greens, dulse, figs, filberts, goat's milk, kale, kelp, mustard greens, oats, parsley, prunes, sesame seeds, tofu, turnip greens, whey, and yogurt.
Copper	Almonds, avocados, barley, beans, beet roots, blackstrap molasses, broccoli, dandelion greens, garlic, lentils, liver, mushrooms, nuts, oats, oranges, organ meats, pecans, radishes, raisins, salmon, seafood, soybeans, and green leafy vegetables.
Folic acid	Barley, beans, beef, bran, brewer's yeast, brown rice, cheese, chicken, dates, green leafy vegetables, lamb, lentils, liver, milk, oranges, organ meats, split peas, pork, root vegetables, salmon, tuna, wheat germ, whole grains, whole wheat, and yeast.
Iron	Eggs, fish, liver, meat, poultry, green leafy vegetables, whole grains, and enriched breads and cereals. Found in: almonds, avocados, beets, blackstrap molasses, brewer's yeast, dates, egg yolks, kelp, kidney and lima beans, lentils, millet, parsley, peaches, pears, dried prunes, pumpkins, raisins, rice and wheat bran, sesame seeds, and soy beans.
Omega–3	Fish, shellfish, canola oil, soybeans and soybean oil, plant leaves, and flaxseed oil.
Protein	Legumes, grains, nuts, seeds, vegetables, beef, pork, chicken, fish, and tofu.
Selenium	Depending on soil content, selenium can be found in meat and grains, Brazil nuts, brewer's yeast, broccoli, brown rice, chicken, dairy products, garlic, liver, molasses, onions, salmon, seafood, tourla, tuna, vegetables, wheat germ, and whole grains.

Sources of Vitamins and Minerals

Vitamin A	Green and yellow fruits and vegetables, animal livers, fish liver oils. Found in: alfalfa, apricots, asparagus, beets, broccoli, cantaloupe, carrots, Swiss chard, dandelion greens, garlic, kale, mustard greens, papaya, parsley, peaches, red peppers, sweet potatoes, spinach, spirulina, pumpkin, yellow squash, turnip greens, and watercress.
Vitamin B6	Brewer's yeast, carrots, chicken, eggs, fish, meat, peas, spinach, sunflower seeds, walnuts, wheat germ, avocado, bananas, beans, blackstrap molasses, brown rice, grains, cabbage, and cantaloupe.
Vitamin B12	Blue cheese, cheese, eggs, clams, herring, kidney, liver, mackerel, milk, seafood, and tofu (not found in vegetables; available only from animal sources).
Vitamin C	Green vegetables, berries, citrus fruits, asparagus, avocados, beet greens, broccoli, Brussels sprouts, cantaloupe, collard greens, currants, grapefruit, kale, lemons, mangoes, mustard greens, onions, oranges, papayas, parsley, green peas, sweet peppers, persimmons, pineapple, radishes, rose hips, spinach, strawberries, Swiss chard, tomatoes, turnip greens, and watercress.
Vitamin E	Cold-pressed vegetable oils, whole grains, dark leafy vegetables, nuts and seeds, legumes, dry beans, brown rice, cornmeal, eggs, desiccated liver, milk, oatmeal, organ meats, sweet potatoes, and wheat germ.
Zinc	Fish, legumes, meats, oysters, poultry, seafood, and whole grains. Significant sources include: brewer's yeast, egg yolks, lamb chops, lima beans, liver, mushrooms, pecans, pumpkin seeds, sardines, seeds, soy lecithin, soybeans, and sunflower seeds.

Vitamin and Mineral Amounts to Sustain Optimal Health

The three most essential elements necessary to good health are a healthy diet, exercise, and a good attitude toward life in general. People who are large or have a more active or stressful lifestyle require more of the essential nutrients than those who are small or inactive.

The Federal Drug Administration (FDA) has developed a list with amounts of average RDAs (Recommended Daily Allowances). The list of nutrient amounts in the table below is different than the RDA amounts. The RDA amounts are considered the minimum amounts required to sustain life, while the amounts listed below are the minimal amounts required to sustain optimal health.

This information *does not* replace the advice of a nutritionally trained health-care professional acquainted with your particular health status. Dosage will vary with height, weight, age, and general health condition.

Vitamin Amounts to Sustain Optimal Health

Vitamin	Daily Amount for Optimal Health
Vitamin A	10,000 IU (International Units)
Vitamin B1 Thiamin	50 mg–200 mg (milligrams)
Vitamin B2 Riboflavin	50 mg–200 mg
Vitamin B3 Niacin/Niacinamide	100 mg
Vitamin B5 Pantothenic Acid	100 mg–250 mg
Vitamin B6 Pyroxidine	50 mg–200 mg
Vitamin B12	300 mcg (micrograms)
Vitamin C	3000 mg
Vitamin D	400 IU–1000 IU
Vitamin E	600 IU
Vitamin K	100 mcg

Vitamin Amounts to Sustain Optimal Health

Vitamin	Daily Amount for Optimal Health
Beta Carotene	15,000 IU
Bioflavonoids (mixed)	500 mg
Biotin	300 mg
Choline	100 mg
Folic Acid	800 mg
Hesperidin	100 mg
Inositol	100 mg
Niacin	100 mg
Niacinamide	100 mg
PABA	50 mg
Rutin	25 mg

Mineral Amounts to Sustain Optimal Health

Mineral	Daily Amount for Optimal Health
Calcium	800 mg–1200 mg
Chromium	150 mcg–200 mcg
Copper	3 mg
Iodine	225 mcg–1mg
Iron	18 mg
Magnesium	750 mg–1,000 mg
Manganese	2 mg
Molybdenum	30 mcg
Potassium	99 mg
Selenium	200 mcg
Zinc	30 mg–50 mg

Optional Supplements for Optimal Health

Optional Supplements	Daily Amount for Optimal Health
Coenzyme Q10	30 mg
Garlic	As directed on label
L-Carnitine	500 mg
L-Cysteine	50 mg
L-Lysine	50 mg
L-Methionine	50 mg
L-Tyrosine	500 mg
Lecithin	200-500 mg
Pectin	50 mg
RNA-DNA	100 mg
Silicon	As directed on label

Vitamin and Mineral Tips

The best way to obtain all of your daily vitamins, minerals, and micronutrients is by eating a diet high in fresh foods with an abundance of fruits and vegetables. In addition, supplement your diet with a high-quality multivitamin/mineral supplement to fill in the micronutrient gaps in your diet. Make sure that such a supplement includes the following antioxidant cocktail:

- Vitamin C, 200 milligrams a day
- Vitamin E, 400 IU of natural mixed tocopherols (d-alpha-tocopherol with other tocopherols, or better, a minimum of 80 milligrams of natural mixed tocotrienols and tocopherols)
- Selenium, 200 micrograms of an organic (yeast-bound) form
- Mixed carotenoids, 10,000–15,000 IU daily
- Folic acid, at least 400 micrograms
- Vitamin D, 2,000 IU
- No iron (unless you are a female and having regular menstrual periods)
- No preformed vitamin A (retinol)

Take these supplements with your largest meal. Women should take supplemental calcium, preferably as calcium citrate, 800–1200 milligrams a day, depending on their dietary intake of this mineral. Men should avoid supplemental calcium.

Other Dietary Supplements

If you are not eating oily fish at least twice a week, take supplemental fish oil, in capsule or liquid form (2–3 grams a day of a product containing both EPA and DHA). Look for molecularly distilled products certified free of heavy metals and other contaminants. Also, talk to your doctor about going on low-dose aspirin therapy, one or two baby aspirins a day (81 or 162 milligrams).

If you are not regularly eating ginger and turmeric, consider taking these in supplemental form.

You could also add CoQ10 to your daily regimen; take 60–100 milligrams in a soft gel form with your largest meal.

Healthy Herbs and Spices

There are many spices and herbs that are very healthy and contain a variety of vitamins, minerals, and antioxidant compounds.

What to Eat

How much: Unlimited amounts

Healthy choices: Turmeric, curry powder (which contains turmeric), ginger and garlic (dried and fresh), chili peppers, basil, cinnamon, rosemary, thyme, and curcumin.

Why: Use these herbs and spices generously to season foods. Turmeric and ginger are powerful natural anti-inflammatory agents.

Tea

Another good source of anti-inflammatory and antioxidant compounds is tea; tea is healthy and it tastes good as well.

What to Drink

How much: Two to four cups per day

Healthy choices: White, green, oolong teas

Why: Tea is rich in catechins, antioxidant compounds that reduce inflammation. Purchase high-quality tea. Learn how to brew it for maximum taste and health benefits.

CARBOHYDRATES

Carbohydrates—sugars and starches—are necessary for supplying energy to the body in the form of glucose. Glucose is the primary energy source for the brain, central nervous system, digestive system, and red blood cells. Fibers, on the other hand, promote the healthy elimination of waste and decrease the risk of certain chronic diseases such as coronary heart disease and diabetes.

Complex carbohydrates include fruits, vegetables, and grains, while simple carbohydrates are processed sugars and starches. The most preferred sources of carbohydrates are the sugars, starches, and fibers found in fruits, vegetables, grains, and milk products. Each meal should include a balance of carbohydrates, fat, and protein.

The liver is the main organ responsible for handling the metabolism of the foods we eat. It performs functions of carbohydrate, fat, and protein metabolism to sustain life. Our bodies can break down carbohydrates into the necessary metabolites to produce ATP. However, when too much carbohydrate is provided, the excess is converted to fats (triglycerides and cholesterol), while a "sugar spike" is experienced. Human bodies have much more efficient mechanisms to produce ATP from proteins and fats called gluconeogenesis.

Good Sources and Choices of Carbohydrates

WHOLE AND CRACKED GRAINS

What to Eat

How much: Three to five servings a day (one serving is equal to about ½ cup cooked grains)

Healthy choices: Brown rice, basmati rice, wild rice, buckwheat, groats, barley, quinoa, steel-cut oats. (They need to be certified gluten free.)

Why: Whole grains digest slowly, reducing the frequency of spikes in blood sugar that promote inflammation. *Whole grains* is defined as grains that are intact or in a few large pieces. It does not mean whole wheat bread or other products made from flour.

Gluten-Free Pasta (al dente)

How much: Two to three servings per week (one serving is equal to about ½ cup cooked pasta)

Healthy choices: Organic pasta, rice noodles, bean thread noodles, and part whole wheat and buckwheat noodles like Japanese udon and soba.

Why: Pasta cooked al dente (when it has "tooth" to it) has a lower glycemic index than fully cooked pasta. Low-glycemic-load carbohydrates should be the bulk of your carbohydrate intake to help minimize spikes in blood glucose levels.

HEALTHY SWEETS

Best Natural Sweeteners: Honey: local, raw, and unfiltered (has enzymes that help digestion of starches and protein). Maple syrup: grade B. Molasses: unfiltered. Dates: dried or fresh (have high fiber and minerals). Figs: fresh or dried and unsulfured (high fiber and minerals). Raisins: not for cancer. Prunes: not for cancer. Brown Rice: syrup (low in sugar and high in minerals). Agave nectar: from cactus, low sugar, and high in minerals.

NOTE: Never use artificial sweeteners. They are the most acidic residue foods! Use Stevia as the only sweetener in cases where there is cancer and an overgrowth of yeast.

RED WINE

How much: Optional, no more than one to two glasses per day

Healthy choices: Organic red wine

Why: Red wine has beneficial antioxidant activity. Limit intake to no more than one to two servings per day. If you must drink alcohol, then choose wine, but if you do not drink alcohol, do not start.

Carbohydrate Tips

On a diet of 2,000 calories a day, adult women should consume between 160 to 200 grams of carbohydrates a day. Adult men should consume between 240 to 300 grams of carbohydrates a day. The majority of this should be in the form of unrefined, unprocessed foods with a low glycemic load.

Reduce your consumption of foods made with wheat flour and sugar, especially bread and most packaged snack foods (including chips and pretzels). Eat more whole grains such as brown rice and quinoa. The grain needs to be intact or in a few large pieces and not processed. These are preferable to whole-wheat flour products, which have roughly the same glycemic index as white flour products.

Eat more beans, winter squashes, and sweet potatoes. (If not fighting yeast overgrowth. Cook gluten-free pasta al dente and eat it in moderation. Finally, avoid products made with high-fructose corn syrup.

Keep in mind that these are general recommendations to promote optimum health. Always consult your health-care provider and/or nutritionist for your individual dietary recommendations and requirements.

CHAPTER 3

Preparing Your
Home for Healthy Cooking

EMF FUNDAMENTALS: YOUR MICROWAVE,
WI-FI, AND LOW-DOSE RADIATION

According to Andrew Weil, MD, author of *8 Weeks to Optimum Health and Spontaneous Healing*, "Electromagnetic pollution (EMF) may be the most significant form of pollution human activity has produced in this century, all the more dangerous because it is invisible and insensible."

We are all surrounded by a protective field of energy called our *biofield,* which is critical to our overall well-being. If your biofield is out of tune, stress can hit you full force, causing fatigue, anxiety, depression, unclear thinking, and serious disease. In today's fast-paced, high-tech world, it's easy for your biofield to lose its ability to protect you.

Electromagnetic Pollution: Why Is EMF A Pollutant?

Electromagnetic pollution (or EMF pollution) is a term given to all the manmade, fabricated, and manufactured electromagnetic fields (EMFs) of various frequencies that fill our homes, workplaces, and public spaces.

When we call something in our environment a pollutant, we are implying that it is somehow harmful to nature and to ourselves. There is plenty of scientific evidence to support the idea that some types of electromagnetic radiation are harmful to us and to nature. To view some of this evidence, see EMF Health Effects (http://www.emwatch.com/EMF%20Effects.htm).

The Whole Spectrum

The electromagnetic spectrum includes several different classes of radiation: low frequency, radio waves, microwaves, infrared, visible light, ultraviolet light, X-rays, and gamma rays. Wave frequency is what differentiates one class of radiation from another. When we refer to electromagnetic pollution, we are generally speaking of frequencies below (oscillating slower than) visible light waves. Of course, X-rays and gamma rays (which oscillate faster than visible light) are highly dangerous, but we have not filled our homes and workplaces with these rays. We knew they were dangerous, so we have been careful.

What Other Kinds of EMF Waves are Dangerous?

We did not realize that low-frequency electromagnetic radiation (including the 50/60 Hz frequency commonly used for power supplies) was dangerous to our health, so we have not been very careful about that. In addition, although we knew that radio and microwave energy was dangerous at high intensity (for example, inside your microwave oven), we thought it was safe at lower intensities. It now appears we were wrong about that.

It's not surprising, really. Think about sunlight. We always knew it was dangerous at high intensity (sunburn) but we have only recently realized that there may be long-term dangers from frequent, prolonged, but less-intense exposure (skin aging, wrinkles, and skin cancer). It is the same with radio and microwave energy and with low-frequency radiation too. Low intensity over a long period (generally several years) still takes its toll.

Unfortunately, some of these waves do not get absorbed by the skin as sunlight does. They penetrate the body. Some of them penetrate 12" concrete walls. That is why this kind of energy can cause health problems anywhere in your body.

Where Does this EMF Pollution Come From?

Unfortunately, electromagnetic pollution is all around us. Here is a short list of the main culprits:

- Cell (and other mobile) phones
- Computers and related equipment
- Electrical appliances (including televisions)
- Electronic equipment
- Cell phone masts
- Radio and TV transmitters
- Microwave ovens

- House wiring
- High- and low-voltage power lines
- Information networks
- Cars, motorcycles, buses, trains, planes

Practically every new invention adds to the pollution. In fact, collectively, we have all been adding to EMF pollution for over 100 years. The rate of increase is rising exponentially. Electromagnetic pollution has now reached the critical level at which it can seriously damage your health.

EMF Pollution—A Call to Action!

Solving your own personal EMF pollution problem is usually much easier than you expect, especially if you deal with it sooner, rather than later and before your health is compromised. We can avoid becoming victims of EMF pollution. There are many ways we can reduce electromagnetic exposure for ourselves, our families, and others around us. Effective protection depends on knowledge and information.

EMF Protection and Safety

Every year, more research is published about the hazard of electromagnetic pollution, and more evidence is collected. The conclusion that electromagnetic fields can adversely affect your health is now well-founded.

EMF protection begins with good information. If you are aware of EMF risks and EMF protection strategies, you can make better choices to keep yourself and your loved ones safe. If you cannot make all the recommended changes, do what you can. Every bit helps.

General EMF Protection Rules

Rule #1: Reduce Your Exposure to Electromagnetic Radiation by Increasing Your Distance

This is the most important rule for EMF protection, and it is often the easiest to apply. How much to increase your distance depends on the type of EMF hazard. For example, to halve the field intensity, you might have to move farther away by a distance of:

- 25 meters for power lines and cell towers
- 30 cm (15 inches) for your computer monitor
- 5 cm (2 inches) for the electric clock next to your pillow
- 2.5 cm (1 inch) for the cell phone pressed to your ear

Many people understand that they can improve their EMF safety by moving a hundred meters farther away from power lines or cell towers, but they do not realize that they might be able to achieve an even bigger improvement in their personal EMF safety by moving their computer to the floor instead of on the desk, or by sitting farther away from their TV.

Rule #2: If You Can't Avoid the EMF Exposure, Try to Keep It Short.

It can be quite appealing to watch our appliances at work, to hang around office printers and photocopiers for a chat, or to stand next to the oven while it cooks our dinner. In all these cases, and in many others, it would be better for your health to follow this rule and keep it short.

Rule #3: If It Does Not Need to Be Turned On, Switch It Off.

EMF radiation often comes from devices that are left on unnecessarily, for example charger units (for batteries, cell phones, laptops, etc.), computers, and printers. Switching off also contributes to the health of the planet and your wallet. EMF protection protects the body from power lines and substations.

Become aware of all major EMF sources in your environment. First, look at the location of the buildings you occupy. Power lines that are more than four hundred meters away are unlikely to have a health impact. Closer than that and you may want to check the EMF strength with a meter. Local power lines (bringing power to your building) can also be a cause of significant electromagnetic exposure. Note the position of electricity transformers or substations serving your building. The electromagnetic radiation from local substations may extend for five to ten meters. Do not allow children to play in this area. Four hundred meters is also a good distance to keep from cell towers, assuming that you know they are there. (They are getting harder to spot.)

EMF Protection from TV and Radio Masts

While you are looking around the area, take a note of how far away you are from TV and radio masts. These can be much more powerful than cell towers. Several studies have linked increased cancer and leukemia rates to proximity to TV masts, especially the very large and powerful ones, which seem to affect cancer rates up to three to five kilometers away. Unfortunately there is no effective protection except to apply Rule #1.

Home, Sweet Home—with EMF Protection

In the home, electromagnetic radiation originates from house wiring and from electrical appliances of all kinds. House wiring makes a very significant contribution to many peoples' overall electromagnetic exposure, but it's an aspect seldom considered. Some companies offer EMF house surveys. See if you can find one in your area. Alternatively, you can do the job yourself with a suitable gauss meter.

EMF Protection From Home Appliances

Some very common household appliances have quite high EMFs. Increase your distance from these devices and keep your exposure short.

If you make frequent or prolonged use of an appliance, it may be worth finding one with a very low rating. For example, handheld hairdryers often produce high strength EMFs. Yet if you only use it for a few minutes a day, it may contribute little to your overall exposure.

Protection From EMF Radiation in the Bedroom

Switch off electric blankets when not required. Use the lowest setting possible. Keep electric clocks and radios as far away as possible from a sleeping person. Preferably keep a distance of 60 centimeters (2 feet) or more for devices. Even battery-operated clocks and clock radios should not be right next to your head.

Note Where the Main Electricity Enters Your House and the Main Switch Box Location

If it is in a bedroom, place the bed(s) far away (at least 1.5 meters). The magnetic portion of the EMF will easily penetrate walls, so think about what is on the other side of the wall too.

Protection From Cell Phones

Cell phones are shaping up as a major biological hazard, perhaps as significant as smoking cigarettes. Use alternatives (landline phones) where possible.

Do not use cell phones for long conversations or keep others talking on their cell phone for more time than is necessary. Use of an air-tube headset, or at least use the speaker-phone –function so that you can avoid holding the cell phone right next to your head while you talk is recommended.

Children need to be protected from cell phone use because their developing brains are especially vulnerable to cell phone EMFs and their skulls are thinner. Children under ten should not use cell phones for making telephone calls, and older children need strict guidelines.

Workplace EMF Protection

If you spend a lot of time working in an office or factory, try not to sit within 1.5 meters of any major item of electrical equipment—for example, heaters and air conditioners, file servers, or printers. Keep a similar distance from neon lights or major electrical wiring junction boxes.

If you work at a computer for much of the day, position it as far away from you (especially your head) as cables allow. If possible, do not use a CRT monitor but use an LCD monitor instead. Keep it as far away from you as comfort and cables allow.

Try to avoid working in an environment that is pervaded by wireless devices—networks, Wi-Fi, modems and cordless telephones. Do not take their safety for granted. Radio and microwave radiation is probably even more dangerous than low frequency (VLF) radiation.

Sources: www.emf-health.com/qlink-overview.htm EMF Safety and Health, www.emwatch.com/EMF%20Protection.htm

POTS, PANS, METALLURGY, MICROWAVES, AND SUCH

Metals have different properties that influence cooking outcomes. Additionally, nonstick surfaces applied to the metals of pots and pans may have a direct impact on health. Microwave cooking has other properties we should be informed about to make educated food preparation decisions.

When the health risks associated with making Teflon first became known, many cooks trashed their nonstick cookware and went back to using their stainless steel pots and pans. What many people did not realize was that even stainless steel is not immune to controversy regarding health impacts. (EarthTalk, *The Environmental Magazine*, www.emagazine.com/earthtalk/thisweek.)

Nonstick Frying Pans: Frying pans with nonstick surfaces were introduced by DuPont in 1956 under the Teflon brand name. The durability of the early coatings was poor. Improvements in manufacturing have made these products a kitchen standard. Nevertheless, the surface is not as tough as metal, and the use of metal utensils can permanently mar the coating and degrade its nonstick properties. Who hasn't used a Teflon pan that shows permanent scrapes and marring?

Nonstick Pan Caution: Nonstick frying pans featuring Teflon coatings must *never* be heated above about 465°F/240°C, a temperature that can be easily reached in minutes. At higher temperatures, nonstick coatings decompose and give off toxic fumes.

Stainless Steel Cookware Combines Several Metals: It is a mixture of nickel, chromium, and molybdenum. If your cookware becomes dinged and pitted, negligible metals may get into your food.

Anodized Aluminum Cookware: The electrochemical anodizing process locks in the cookware's base metal, aluminum, so that it can't get into food. Anodized aluminum has had the naturally occurring layer of aluminum oxide thickened by an electrolytic process to create a surface that is hard and nonreactive. It is used for sauté pans, stockpots, roasters, and Dutch ovens. (http://en.wikipedia.org/wiki/Cookware_and_bakeware#cite_note-Williams_8-5)

Uncoated and Unanodized Aluminum: This type of cooking pan can react with acidic foods to change the taste of the food. Sauces containing egg yolks or vegetables such as asparagus or artichokes may cause oxidation of unanodized aluminum. We recommend you avoid aluminum pans.

Cast-Iron Cookware: A good choice is that old standby, cast iron, which is known for its durability and even heat distribution. Cast-iron cookware can also help ensure that eaters in your house get enough iron—which the body needs to produce red blood cells—as it seeps off the cookware into food in small amounts. Iron is considered a healthy food additive by the U.S. Food and Drug Administration.

Ceramic Cookware: For those who like the feel and heat distribution properties of cast iron but dread the seasoning process, ceramic enameled cookware is a good choice. The smooth and colorful enamel is dishwasher-friendly and somewhat nonstick and covers the entire surface of the cookware to minimize cleanup.

Copper Cookware: One other surface favored by chefs for sauces and sautés is copper, which excels at quick warm-up and even heat distribution. The cooking surfaces of copper cookware are usually lined with tin or stainless steel, since copper can leak into food in large amounts when heated.

Sources for Cookware

- Le Creuset (www.lecreuset.com)
- Lodge Cast-Iron Products (www.lodgemfg.com)
- Salad Master Cookware (www.saladmaster.com)
- All-Clad (www.all-clad.com)
- You may also want to visit your local camping store
- Baking: You still need to avoid nonstick here and opt for stainless steel, cast iron, or glass or ceramic like Mercola Healthy Cookware (www.mercola.com) or Pyrex (www.pyrex.com).
- If you want to go the extra mile to ensure that no BPAs or other chemicals from plastic are bleeding into your food, ONYX makes a stainless steel ice cube tray, stainless steel drinking straws, and stainless steel popsicle molds.
- Raw Food World also carries glass smoothie straws (www.rawfoodworld.com).

Microwave Oven Cooking Considerations

Over 90 percent of American homes have microwave ovens that are routinely used for meal preparation. Because microwave ovens are so convenient and energy efficient, as compared to conventional ovens, very few homes or restaurants are without them.

In general, people believe that whatever a microwave oven does to foods cooked in it does not have any negative effect on either the food or them. Of course, if microwave ovens were really harmful, our government would never allow them on the market. Or would they? Regardless of what has been "officially" released concerning microwave ovens, you would do well to follow the following guidelines:

Food For Thought

- Do not heat foods in plastic containers or covered by plastic wrap; microwaving can drive plastic molecules into your food.
- Use only glass or ceramic containers, and cover foods with a paper towel or waxed paper.
- Avoid using plastic wrap products in your microwave. Repeated for good reason!
- Unevenly heated foods may contain hot spots that can scald your mouth and throat.
- Be especially careful when heating foods for babies or young children.
- Special care must be taken when cooking or reheating meat, poultry, fish, and eggs to make sure they are prepared safely.
- Microwave ovens can cook unevenly and leave "cold spots" where harmful bacteria can survive. It is important to use a food thermometer. Test food in several places to be sure it has reached the recommended safe temperature to destroy bacteria and other pathogens that could cause food-borne illness.
- Food nutrient levels may be impacted by microwaving, just as with other forms of cooking. Studies show that some food nutrient levels increase and others decrease their nutritional value levels. For more information, go to Dr. Andrew Weil's website at www.drweil.com/drw/u/QAA400107/microwaving-nutrients.

There are no right or wrong answers. Only facts and information can guide you in your healthful decision-making process.

Sources: *The Environmental Magazine: EarthTalk,* www.emagazine.com/earthtalk/thisweek; http://www.fsis.usda.gov/factsheets/microwave_oven

CHAPTER 4

The Right Food: Organics, Shopping, Gardening, and Eating Out

Why Organics?

Beyond toxins, there are poisons! Pesticides are poisons and are also carcinogens. Take time to be an educated eater and know what you are putting in your body and your children's bodies. Visit www.whatsonmyfood.com for an eye-opening account of the chemicals found on our food.

Reading the Label

The United States has a National Organic Program (NOP), as well as an Organic Foods Production Act (OFPA). What we can look for on the shelves is the green and white circle that states that a product is USDA Organic.

What many do *not* know is that if a label claims that the product is organic, the product must consist of at least 95 percent organically produced ingredients. That means that the other 5 percent may consist of nonorganic products (though there is a specific list food producers must adhere to). Their reasoning is because some of the products are not available in organic form. We must ask, then: Do we need to be consuming them?

When an ingredient is made with 100 percent organic ingredients, the company may list that figure on the label. However, it's important to note that both 100 percent organic *and* 95 percent organic foods may use the green label claiming CERTIFIED ORGANIC. For more detailed information, visit www.usda.org.

If a farmer's production is less than five thousand dollars per year, that farmer is not required to certify organic. This does not mean that he or she does not use the same organic methods as the certified sources do. Find a local farmer who grows organically, or even help set up a co-op in your area.

The Dirty Dozen

For many families, cost is a major prohibiting factor in choosing that organic apple versus the traditional apples on the next row, especially in the current state of our economy. Both apples look shiny, both look healthy, and it is difficult to warrant, sometimes even afford, the higher cost.

The Dirty Dozen is a list of the 12 most pesticide-contaminated items of produce. If you must limit your organic selections, try at the very least to buy the organic versions of these. According to Organic.org, the top 12 are as follows:

Peaches	**Nectarines**	**Grapes**
Apples	**Strawberries**	**Spinach**
Sweet Bell Peppers	**Cherries**	**Lettuce**
Celery	**Pears**	**Potatoes**

We are an immediate gratification society. It makes sense that if we do not see an immediate reaction, such as an allergy present, then we do not truly believe in a negative response from the pesticide-treated products. We caution against this flippancy, as much of the damage is cumulative from many years of toxic exposure.

We would be misleading you if we told you that it is not more expensive to eat healthy. It is, in fact, a big expense. In the long run however, healthier eating practices may well lead to lower costs in health complications. The question to ponder is: How much is your health and that of your family worth to you?

STOCK YOUR "FREE" PANTRY

If you have already read the Tips and Tricks section, you may have a large pantry full of black Xs, or you may have opted to throw away such temptations. You may be wondering how to refill the pantry shelves with better choices for your special diet. We have compiled a list of some excellent manufactured products that work well with special diets. Each item will have unique allergen information, but most of the manufacturers list the allergen information on their websites. Do your homework before you shop to reduce the time spent in the aisles of your grocery store.

New products are being introduced more and more frequently, as the need for such foods is definitely on the rise. So be sure to check your local health-food store or super-market for any new products, and *be sure to read each label carefully*. Check our Label Lingo—Label Watch section in this chapter for the guide on how to understand labels.

MANUFACTURED PRODUCTS FOR SPECIAL DIETS

Crackers

Mary's Gone Crackers

Dr. Schar Table Crackers & Snack Crackers

Glutino Crackers

Foods Alive Flax Crackers & Hemp Crackers

Back To Nature Gluten-Free Rice Crackers

Orgran Crackers

Cookies and Bars

Enjoy Life Brands

Orgran Brands

Enny's Organics

Schar Cookies

AllerEnergy Bars

Kinnikinnik

Boomi Bars

Pamela's

Nana's Cookies

Glutino

Annie's Naturals

Lucy's Cookies

Gopal's Energy Bars

NuGoFree

Larabars

Kind Bars

Muffins, Breads, Waffles, Bagels, and Pizza Crusts

Udi's

Rudi's

Food For Life

Enjoy Life

Gillian's Gluten-Free Breads and Buns

Ener-G Brands

Van's Waffles

French Meadow Bakery

Trader Joe's

Canyon Bakehouse Breads

Yeast-Free Breads and Wraps/Tortillas (check individual labels)

Ener-G Breads

Food For Life

French Meadow Bakery

Trader Joe's

Fruit Juices and Fruit Sauces

Sprout's Organics

Trader Joe's Organics

Ceres Juices

Evolution Fresh Juices

Newman's Own

Biotta

Walnut Acres

Naturally Preferred

Lakewood Organics

Mountain Sun Pure

R.W. Knudsen

Sunsweet (w/pulp)

Central Market Organics

Chips

Boulder Canyon

Terra Chips

Kettle Organics

Tostitos Blue Corn

Lundberg Rice Chips (Sea Salt)

Garden of Eatin'

Pirate's Booty

Snack Mixes, Nuts, and Seeds

K&W Non-GMO Organic Popcorn

Now Foods Organic Popcorn, nuts & seeds

Purcell Mountain Farms Rainbow Popcorn

Jaffe Bros.

Gourmet Nut

Nuts Online

Dried Fruit

Bare Fruit

Newman's Own

"Best of All" Dried Fruits

Jaffe Bros.

Eden Foods

Sunsweet Organic Prunes

Frozen Fruit and Vegetables

Diamond Organics

Cascadian Farms

Lunch Meats/Bacon

Boar's Head "All Natural"

Applegate Farms

Rice, Grains, and Beans

Lundberg Farms

Eden Organics

Westbrae Foods

Ancient Harvest Quinoas

Honest to Goodness (goodness.com)

Lotus Foods (find on tropicaltraditions.com)

Wild Harvest Organic

Gluten-Free Pastas

Lundberg Farms Rice Pastas

Ancient Harvest Quinoa Pastas

Orgran Pasta

Tinkyada Rice Pastas

Schar Pastas

Jovial Pastas

EnerG Foods Pastas

Muir Glen Pasta Sauces

Nondairy Milks and Creams

Good Karma Rice Milk

Pacific Foods (Almond, Rice, Hazelnut, MimicCreme Brands

Almond Breeze

Vance's Dari-Free (potato based)

Westbrae (rice)

Hemp and Seven Grain)

Soya too Rice and Soy Whips

Broths & Soups:

Imagine Brand

Pacific Foods

Home Meal Deliveries/Pick-Ups

Healthy Chef

NuLife Foods

My Fit Foods

Cheeses

Galaxy Foods Vegan Cheeses

Daiya Cheese Shreds

Baking, Spices, and Extracts

Eden Foods

Simply Organic

Frontier Spices and Extracts

Frontier Baking Soda and Powder

Olive Nation for Spices and Extracts

Madagascar (Nielsen Massey)

Rumford Baking Powder

Clabber Girl Baking Soda

Bob's Red Mill Baking Soda

Mountain Rose Herbs

Candy and Gum

Natural Candy Store online

Flours and Flour Mixes

Bob's Red Mill

Gluten-Free Pantry

Lucy's Almond Flour

Pamela's

Arrowhead Mills

NOW brands

Ener-G Brands

Tom Sawyer Gluten-Free Products

Oils and Shortenings

Spectrum Cold-Pressed and
Expeller-Pressed Oils

Spectrum Shortening

Pure Nature Products

Puritans Pride Coconut Oil

Tropical Traditions

Santiago Cold-Pressed Olive Oil

Eliki Olive Oil

Middle Earth Organic Olive Oil

Miscellaneous Ingredients That May Be Useful in Your Gluten-Free Kitchen

Knox Gelatin

Kombu

Miso

Himalayan Sea Salt

Real Salt

Bragg's Organic Apple Cider Vinegar

Organic Sunbutter

Tahini

Rice Cakes (Lundberg Farms)

Cream of Tartar

Filtered Water

Carbonated (Soda) Water

Stocking the Cupboards

Other items that can contain allergens as well as harmful chemicals that we may not think about are cleaning and cosmetic items. Pay close attention to the ingredients list on those bottles as well, as you may be surprised at the contents! Some friendly options are listed below.

Shampoos and Conditioners

Giovanni

Worry-Free

Abba

Natural Sprout

Nature's Gate

Mill Creek

Lotions

Kiss My Face

Avalon

Alba

Nature's Gate

Sibu

Toothpastes

Tom's

Kiss My Face

CUSTOMIZE YOUR "FREE" PANTRY SHOPPING LIST

You can download this shopping list at our website, www.foodforthoughtbook.com. The list is a Microsoft Word document, allowing you to customize it for your family's shopping needs.

Food for Thought, The Free Food Cookbook The "Free" Pantry Shopping List www.foodforthoughtbook.com	
Produce	
☐ Organic Apples _____ Pears	☐ Organic Celery
☐ Avocado	☐ Organic Bell Peppers
☐ Bananas	☐ Organic Greens
☐ Beets	☐ Organic Lettuce
☐ Organic Berries _____ Strawberries _____ Blueberries _____ Raspberries _____ Other	☐ Organic Mushrooms
☐ Broccoli _____ Cauliflower	☐ Organic Potatoes (white and/or sweet)
☐ Carrots	☐ Organic Spinach
☐ Organic Cherries	☐ Garlic
☐ Organic Nectarines _____ Peaches _____ Pineapple	☐ Onion
☐ Organic Grapes	☐ Asparagus
☐ Lemons _____ Limes	☐ Green Beans
☐ Cabbage	
☐ Zucchini _____ Yellow Squash	
Spices	
☐ Basil	☐ Oregano
☐ Cilantro	☐ Parsley
☐ Dill	☐ Rosemary
☐ Lemongrass	☐ Sage
☐ Mint	☐ Thyme

Food For Thought

Flours & Baking Goods

☐ Gluten-Free All-Purpose	☐ Egg-Replacer Powder (Ener-G, Orgran, etc.)
☐ Almond Flour	☐ Baking Soda
☐ Amaranth Flour	☐ Baking Powder
☐ Arrowroot Powder	☐ Cream of Tartar
☐ Brown Rice Flour	☐ Vanilla Extract
☐ Buckwheat Flour	☐ Vanilla Bean Paste
☐ Cassava Flour (or Tapioca Flour)	☐ Baker's Chocolate (100% Cocoa)
☐ Corn Starch (Non-GMO)	☐ Carob Powder
☐ Garbanzo or Garfava Flour	☐ Gluten-Free Baking Mixes
☐ Potato Starch Flour	☐ Enjoy Life Chocolate Chips
☐ Sorghum Flour	☐ Sweet or White Rice Flour

Sweeteners

☐ Stevia Plain	☐ Yacon Syrup
☐ Stevia Flavors	☐ Yacon Powder
☐ Raw Honey	☐ Coconut Nectar/Crystals
☐ Organic Grade B Maple Syrup	☐ Brown Rice Syrup
☐ Blackstrap Molasses	

Dairy, Dairy Substitutes & Alternative Products

☐ Almond Milk	☐ Daiya Cheese Shreds
☐ Coconut Milk	☐ Coconut Kefir
☐ Hazelnut Milk	☐ Coconut Yogurt
☐ Hemp Milk	☐ Almond Yogurt (Amande)
☐ Rice Milk	☐ Hummus Dip
☐ Rice VEGAN Cheese	☐ Organic Pastured Eggs
☐ Earth Balance Buttery Spread	

Food for Thought, The Free Food Cookbook The "Free" Pantry Shopping List www.foodforthoughtbook.com	
Grocery	
☐ Beans (dry or canned, like Eden Organics Canned)	☐ Rice or Quinoa Pastas
☐ Lentils	☐ Muir Glen Pasta Sauce
☐ Brown Rice or Wild Rice (like Lundberg)	☐ Dry Cereals (like Orgran, Erewhon, Nature's Path)
☐ Quinoa (Ancient Harvest)	☐ Gluten-Free Oats
☐ Muir Glen Diced Tomatoes	☐ Gluten-Free Soups (Amy's)
☐ Muir Glen Stewed or Whole Tomatoes	☐ Organic Raw Apple Cider Vinegar (Braggs)
☐ Jarred Artichokes	☐ Condiments (Annie's, Eden Organics)
☐ Broths/Stocks (Imagine or Pacific Foods)	☐ Organic Dry Spices
☐ Nut butters (Sunbutter, Almond butter)	☐ Gluten-Free Bread (Udi's, Ener-G, Rudi's, etc.)
☐ Gluten-Free Crackers	☐ Olives
☐ Barbecue Sauce (Annie's Naturals)	☐ Kombu
☐ Frozen Prepared Meals	
☐ Gluten-Free (Rice) Tortillas	
Raw Nuts, Seeds & Dried Fruit	
☐ Almonds	☐ Sunflower Seeds
☐ Cashews	☐ Chia Seeds
☐ Hazelnuts	☐ Flax Seeds
☐ Pecans	☐ Organic Heirloom Popcorn Kernels
☐ Walnuts	☐ Organic Unsulphured Dried Figs or Dates
☐ Pine nuts	☐ Organic Raisins
☐ Sunflower Seeds/Pepitas	☐ Other Unsulphured Dried Fruit
☐ Sesame Seeds	

Food For Thought

Cold-Pressed or Expeller-Pressed Oils

☐ Almond Oil	☐ Olive Oil
☐ Avocado Oil	☐ Sesame Oil
☐ Coconut Oil	☐ Walnut Oil
☐ Grapeseed Oil	☐ Spectrum Organic Shortening (Palm Oil)
☐ Hemp-Seed Oil	

Meat, Poultry & Seafood

☐ Organic Free-Range Chicken: Whole	☐ Organic Pork: Chops
☐ Ground	☐ Ground
☐ Breasts	☐ Tenderloin
☐ Legs/Thighs	☐ Bacon
☐ Organic Free-Range Turkey : Whole	☐ Sausage (Nitrite Free)
☐ Ground	☐ Wild-Caught Salmon (sockeye)
☐ Breast	☐ Wild-Caught Cod
☐ Grass-Fed Organic Beef:	☐ Wild-Caught Tuna
☐ Ground	☐ Wild-Caught Scallops
☐ Steaks	☐ Wild-Caught King Crab
☐ Lamb	☐ Wild-Caught Shrimp
☐ Buffalo	☐ Lunch Meat (Nitrite Free)

Sweets & Treats

☐ Breakfast Bars (Boomi Bar, Larabar, Kind, etc.)	☐ Cereal & Fruit Bars (Glutino)
☐ Gluten-Free Cookies	☐
☐ Dairy-Free Ice Cream	☐
☐ All-Fruit Sorbet	☐

LABEL LINGO AND LABEL WATCH

Consumer Protection Role of the FDA

First and foremost, the Federal Drug Administration (FDA) is a regulatory agency charged with enforcing the Federal Food, Drug, and Cosmetic Act and related public health laws. The FDA has investigators and inspectors who cover the country's more than 120,000 FDA-regulated businesses. These employees are located in district and local offices over 100 cities across the country, from Puerto Rico to Alaska and Maine to Hawaii. These investigators and inspectors visit more than 20,000 facilities a year, seeing that products are made right and labeled truthfully. FDA offices can be found in your state. The FDA has an excellent set of literature that you can access, either in your own state or through a district office for your state. Make yourself acquainted with its websites, location, and telephone number. Review the titles and reference materials available that relate to your interests and your particular food needs at: http://www.fda.gov/Food/LabelingNutrition.

Food Labeling Laws

Foundation Principles: The United Stated Department of Agriculture (USDA) enforces federal laws governing the labeling of food for meat and poultry, and the Food and Drug Administration (FDA) enforced labeling laws for all other foods. The current goal of the Food and Drug Administration and the United States Department of Agriculture is the continued development of the overall labeling strategy that will provide consumers with information they want and need. The Federal Trade Commission (FTC) is also interested in food labeling because of its responsibility for regulating food advertising.

Listing of Ingredients in Order of Predominance: Government regulations called *Standards of Identity* define the composition of many foods, state which optional ingredients may be used, and specify those ingredients, which must be declared on the label. For more, see www.fda.gov/food/labelingnutrition/default.htm.

The Nutrition Facts Food Label: An Overview

The information in the main or top section (see 1–4 and 6 on the sample nutrition label below), can vary with each food product; it contains product-specific information (serving size, calories, and nutrient information). The bottom part (see 5 on the sample label below) contains a footnote with Daily Values (DVs) for 2,000- and 2,500-calorie diets. This footnote provides recommended dietary information for important nutrients, including fats, sodium, and fiber. The footnote is found only on larger packages and does not change from product to product.

In the sample Nutrition Facts label below, we highlight certain sections to help you focus on those areas. A full explanation of each section may be found on the FDA's website, The Nutrition Facts Label. (www.fda.gov/food/labelingnutrition/default.htm.)

Food For Thought

Naming of Ingredients: Most ingredients must be listed on the label by the specific name of the ingredient. However, there are some exceptions to this rule. For example, under the law, spices, flavorings, and colors may be declared in the ingredient statement without naming the specific ingredient used. Furthermore, any of a series of generic or collective names can be used instead of the specific name and/or common reference for an ingredient or product. For example, "whey" can be declared when it is reconstituted whey. Some consumers are confused by chemical names, while others want some specific information about specific ingredients and specific food items because they may be sensitive or have an intolerance/toxicity to specific ingredients.

For example, persons with celiac disease who have a malabsorption problem for Gliadin in wheat, barley, rye, oats, millet, buckwheat, triticale, etc. need to know if those individual ingredients are included. In addition, they need to be aware of additives, preservatives, emulsifies, thickeners, and excipients and any minute amount of a protein from a grain. Without definitive ingredient labeling information to identify protein sources that are toxic, the celiac must then avoid these products and make other selections.

Sample label for
Macaroni & Cheese

① **Start Here** ➡

Nutrition Facts

Serving Size 1 cup (228g)
Servings Per Container 2

② **Check Calories**

Amount Per Serving

Calories 250   Calories from Fat 110

	% Daily Value*	⑥
Total Fat 12g	18%	
Saturated Fat 3g	15%	
Trans Fat 3g		
Cholesterol 30mg	10%	
Sodium 470mg	20%	
Total Carbohydrate 31g	10%	

③ **Limit these Nutrients**

Quick Guide to % DV

Dietary Fiber 0g	0%
Sugars 5g	
Protein 5g	
Vitamin A	4%
Vitamin C	2%
Calcium	20%
Iron	4%

④ **Get Enough of these Nutrients**

• **5% or less is Low**

• **20% or more is High**

⑤ **Footnote**

* Percent Daily Values are based on a 2,000 calorie diet.
Your Daily Values may be higher or lower depending on
your calorie needs.

	Calories:	2,000	2,500
Total Fat	Less than	65g	80g
Sat Fat	Less than	20g	25g
Cholesterol	Less than	300mg	300mg
Sodium	Less than	2,400mg	2,400mg
Total Carbohydrate		300g	375g
Dietary Fiber		25g	30g

Changes in Ingredients: Some consumers want to require that food labels be flagged in some way when a change is made in the ingredients used. This is because once a product has been used for some time, the consumer might not realize that an ingredient change was made or that changes may be made with each batch number. For example, a salad dressing that uses tomato soup as a base may use wheat flour or wheat starch as a thickener for one batch and cornstarch for the next without label notation and/or ingredient identification.

Nutrition labeling is required by regulation if vitamins, minerals or protein are added to the food or if nutrition claims are made. The nutrition label may contain up to 28 items of information, such as the amount of vitamins, minerals, calories, protein, carbohydrate, and fat present.

In addition, the label may contain other information that the manufacturer wants represented, for example, brand name, price, vignettes or product photographs, serving directions, a code number related to the date of manufacture, recipe suggestions, offer to send information, premium offers, product guarantee, product coupons, advertising/benefit claims, ethnic symbols, universal product code, patent numbers, storage directions, and name and address of the container manufacturer.

Container, Production, and Storage Problems: A totally gluten-free product may become contaminated because the box in which the product is sold is put together with a wheat-containing glue or the surface has been treated (sealed for freshness) with a grain product that may turn out to be wheat. In the production process, a machine belt may have been dusted with wheat flour so that drying shells will peel off the belt without tearing. Such processes can contaminate a totally gluten-free product such as a corn taco shell and make it unfit for use by the celiac. Similarly, a bakery that produces excellent gluten-free bread and pastry products may not clean machines or have a clean air facility that has been cleaned of wheat flour dust; thus, all or most of their products become contaminated. Grains in storage and grains being shipped often of necessity must be sprayed with a pesticide to prevent vermin. But a product such as wild rice, an excellent gluten-free grain for celiacs, becomes toxic with the addition of pesticides, which may not be a problem for the individual with a fully functioning immune system. But for the celiac, with a compromised immune system, toxicity and illness will follow ingestion of this pesticide-contaminated grain.

The Current Law: Actions possible under current laws include changes calling for more complete optional ingredient labeling of all foods subject to FDA's standards of identity; expanded use of quantitative amounts on the ingredient labeling; and additional nutrition labeling information of the amount of sugars, sodium (salt), cholesterol, and fatty acids present in a given food. Without a fulfillment of this regulation, there will still be products that are labeled with one detail that may actually mean another. For example, 2 percent Milk is *not* low fat. It has a fat content up to 60 percent.

FOOD ADDITIVES TO AVOID

Eliminate unnecessary and unhealthy chemicals found in the standard American diet. For more detailed explanation of each additive and the scientific research behind each one, go to the FDA website listed at the end of this section. Several other sites are also noted.

The following list contains ingredients to avoid and other names they can hide behind.

Avoid	Also Called, Function, and Foods Found In
Acesulfame-K	Sunette, Sweet One, Sweet 'n Safe (see below)
Aspartame or other artificial sweeteners	Equal, Nutrasweet, Canderel, Acesulfame-K, Acesulfame potassium, Aspartame, Cyclamate, High-fructose corn syrup, Saccharin, Sorbitol, Sucralose. Aspartame is believed to be carcinogenic and accounts for more reports of adverse reactions than all other foods and food additives combined. *Aspartame is a neurotoxin and carcinogen.* Acesulfame-K, a relatively new artificial sweetener found in baking goods, gum, and gelatin, has not been thoroughly tested and has been linked to kidney tumors. *Found in: diet or sugar-free sodas, Jell-O (and other gelatins), desserts, sugar-free gum, drink mixes, baking goods, tabletop sweeteners, cereal, breath mints, pudding, Kool-Aid, iced tea, chewable vitamins, toothpaste*
BHA and BHT	Butylated hydroxyanisole and butylated hydroxytoluene are preservatives found in cereals, chewing gum, potato chips, and vegetable oils. This common preservative keeps foods from changing color, changing flavor, or becoming rancid. Affects the neurological system of the brain, alters behavior, and has potential to cause cancer. BHA and BHT are oxidants, which form cancer-causing reactive compounds in your body. *Found in: potato chips, gum, cereal, frozen sausages, enriched rice, lard, shortening, candy, Jell-O, butter, meats, cereals, baked goods, snack foods, dehydrated potatoes, beer*

Monosodium glutamate	MSG, MSG Accent, Glutamate, Monopotassium Glutamate, Calcium diglutamate, monoammonium glutamate, magnesium diglutamate. Glutamic Acid: MSG is an amino acid used as a flavor enhancer. MSG is known as an excitotoxin, a substance that overexcites cells to the point of damage or death. MSG affects the neurological pathways of the brain and disengages the "I'm full" function, which explains the effects of weight gain.*Found in: soups, salad dressings, chips, frozen entrées, and many restaurant foods, especially Chinese food (Chinese restaurant syndrome), many snacks, cookies, seasonings, most Campbell Soup products, frozen dinners, lunch meats*
	There are more than forty food ingredients besides monosodium glutamate that contain processed free glutamic acid (MSG). Each, according to the FDA, must be called by its own, unique, "common or usual name." These include "autolyzed yeast," "maltodextrin," "hydrolyzed pea protein," and "sodium caseinate." Unlike monosodium glutamate, they give the consumer no clue that MSG is present.
Autolyzed Plant Protein	Autolyzed yeast, Aginomoto.
Calcium Caseinate	Casein, sodium caseinate, calcium caseinate.
Caramel Coloring	Caramel coloring is made by heating a solution of various sugars, often together with ammonium compounds, acids, or alkalis. It is the most widely used (by weight) coloring added to foods and beverages, with hues ranging from tannish-yellow to black. Caramel coloring may be used to simulate the appearance of cocoa in baked goods, make meats and gravies look more attractive, and darken soft drinks and beer. Caramel coloring, when produced with ammonia, contains contaminants, 2-methylimidazole and 4-methylimidazole. *Found in: colas, baked goods, pre-cooked meats, soy and Worcestershire sauces, chocolate-flavored products, beer.*
Citric Acid	When processed from corn.
Gelatin	Gelatin is a protein that is formed when skin or connective tissue is boiled. Although allergic reactions to gelatin are rare, they have been reported. Many vaccines contain porcine gelatin as a stabilizer. Allergy to gelatin is a common cause of an allergic reaction to vaccines. Individuals who have experienced symptoms of an allergic reaction after consuming gelatin should discuss this with their health-care provider before getting vaccinated. If a patient has a severe allergy to gelatin, vaccines that contain gelatin as a component should be avoided.

High-fructose Corn Syrup (HFCS)	HFCS is a highly refined artificial sweetener, which has become the number one source of calories in America. It is found in almost all processed foods. It packs on the pounds faster than any other ingredient; corn syrup increases your LDL ("bad") cholesterol levels and contributes to the development of diabetes and tissue damage, among other harmful effects. *Found in: most processed foods, breads, candy, flavored yogurts, salad dressings, canned vegetables, cereals.*
Hydrolyzed Plant Protein (HPP)	A hydrolyzed vegetable protein is a flavor enhancer added to many processed foods. *Found in: soups, sauces, seasonings.*
Hydrolyzed Vegetable Protein (HVP)	Flavor enhancer: HVP consists of vegetable (usually soybean) protein that has been chemically broken down into the amino acids of which it is composed. HVP is used to bring out the natural flavor of food (and, perhaps, to enable companies to use less real food). It contains MSG and may cause adverse reactions in sensitive individuals. *Found in: instant soups, frankfurters, sauce mixes, beef stew.*
Natural Flavoring	Natural flavor under the Code of Federal Regulations is: "the essential oil, oleoresin, essence or extractive, protein hydrolysate, distillate, or any product of roasting, heating or enzymolysis, which contains the flavoring constituents derived from a spice, fruit or fruit juice, vegetable or vegetable juice, edible yeast, herb, bark, bud, root, leaf or similar plant material, meat, seafood, poultry, eggs, dairy products, or fermentation products thereof, whose significant function in food is flavoring rather than nutritional."
Natural Meat Tenderizer	Fruit juice can be used to tenderize meat. Marinating meat in pineapple juice or papaya juice will break down the meat fibers, and the flavor of the juice normally cooks off during grilling. It is from these fruits that many processed tenderizers are made. It is important to find a pure juice and not a pineapple or papaya drink or punch. (Read more: What Is a Substitute for Meat Tenderizer? www.eHow.com)
Potassium Bromate	An additive used to increase volume in some white flour, breads, and rolls, potassium bromate is known to cause cancer in animals. Even small amounts in bread can create problems for humans. *Found in: breads.*
Sodium Caseinate	Thickening and whitening agent. Casein, the principal protein in milk, is a nutritious protein containing adequate amounts of all the essential amino acids. People who are allergic to casein should read food labels carefully, because the additive is used in some "nondairy" and "vegetarian" foods. *Found in: ice cream, ice milk, sherbet, coffee creamers, some nondairy and vegetarian foods.*

Food For Thought

Sulfur Dioxide	Sulfur additives are toxic and the FDA has prohibited their use on raw fruit and vegetables in the United State. Adverse reactions include bronchial problems, particularly in those prone to asthma, hypotension (low blood pressure), flushing tingling sensations, or anaphylactic shock. It also destroys vitamins B1 and E. Not recommended for consumption by children. The International Labor Organization says to avoid E220, or sulfur dioxide, if you suffer from conjunctivitis, bronchitis, emphysema, bronchial, or cardiovascular disease. *Found in: beer, soft drinks, dried fruit, juices, cordials, wine, vinegar, potato products.*
Sodium Sulfite	Preservative used in winemaking and the production of other processed foods. According to the FDA, approximately one in one hundred people is sensitive to sulfites in food. Individuals who are sulfite-sensitive may experience headaches, breathing problems, and rashes. In severe cases, sulfites can actually cause death by closing down the airway altogether, leading to cardiac arrest. *Found in: wine, dried fruit.*
Sodium Nitrate	Sodium nitrite. Used as a preservative, coloring, and flavoring in bacon, ham, hot dogs, luncheon meats, corned beef, smoked fish, and other processed meats. This ingredient, which sounds harmless, is actually highly carcinogenic once it enters the human digestive system. There, it forms a variety of nitrosamine compounds that enter the bloodstream and wreak havoc on a number of internal organs: the liver and pancreas in particular. Sodium nitrite is widely regarded as a toxic ingredient, and the USDA actually tried to ban this additive in the 1970s but was vetoed by food manufacturers who complained they had no alternative for preserving packaged meat products. Why does the industry still use it? Simple: this chemical just happens to turn meats bright red. It is actually a color fixer, and it makes old, dead meats appear fresh and vibrant. *Found in: hot dogs, bacon, ham, luncheon meat, cured meats, corned beef, smoked fish, any other type of processed meat.*
Senomyx	Substance 951. Wheat extract labeled as artificial flavor. Has not undergone the FDA's usual safety approval process for food additives. The company Senomyx is reinventing food and flavor by genetically engineering taste bud receptor cell triggers. Foods of the future will contain "flavor enhancers" that fool human taste buds into perceiving the sensations of sweetness, sourness, saltiness, and bitterness.

Trans Fat	Partially hydrogenated oils. Used to enhance and extend the shelf life of food products and is among the most dangerous substances that you can consume. Found in deep-fried fast foods and certain processed foods made with margarine or partially hydrogenated vegetable oils, trans fats are formed by a process called hydrogenation. Oils and fat are now forbidden on the Danish market if they contain trans fatty acids exceeding 2 percent, a move that effectively bans partially hydrogenated oils. *Found in: margarine, chips and crackers, baked goods, fast foods.*
Yeast Nutrient	Yeast nutrient assists the wine yeast in producing a complete and rapid fermentation. It is recommended for use in all fermentations. Yeast nutrient provides a singular source of nitrogen for the yeast to utilize during the fermentation process. *Found in: wine, wine products.*
Yeast Extract	Yeast extract is the common name for various forms of processed yeast products made by extracting the cell contents (removing the cell walls). They are often used to create savory flavors and umami taste sensations. Monosodium glutamate (MSG) is used for umami. Yeast extract, like MSG, often contains free glutamic acid. *Used as food additives or flavorings, or as nutrients for bacterial culture media (http://en.wikipedia.org).*
Food colorings (Blue, Red, Green, Yellow)	Your food should not have a number sign next to any of the ingredients. Studies show that artificial colorings found in soda, fruit juices, and salad dressings may contribute to behavioral problems in children and lead to a significant reduction in IQ. Animal studies have linked other food colorings to cancer. Watch out for these: Blue #1 and Blue #2 (E133). Banned in Norway, Finland, and France. May cause chromosomal damage. *Found in: candy, cereal, soft drinks, sports drinks, pet foods.* Red dye # 3 (also Red #40, a more current dye) (E124). Banned in 1990 (after eight years of debate) from use in many foods and cosmetics. This dye continues to be on the market until supplies run out! Has been proven to cause thyroid cancer and chromosomal damage in laboratory animals, may also interfere with brain-nerve transmission. *Found in: fruit cocktail, maraschino cherries, cherry pie mix, ice cream, candy, bakery products, more* Yellow #6 (E110) and Yellow Tartrazine (E102). Banned in Norway and Sweden. Increases the number of kidney and adrenal gland tumors in laboratory animals, may cause chromosomal damage. *Found in: American cheese, macaroni and cheese, candy; carbonated beverages, and lemonade.*

Olestra	Olestra, commonly referred to as Olean, is an artificial fat substitute. It reduces the body's ability to absorb fat-soluble carotenoids (such as alpha and beta-carotene, lycopene, lutein, and canthaxanthin) from fruits and vegetables, but an occasional serving would not be a problem. Olestra enables manufacturers to offer greasy-feeling low-fat snacks, but consumers would be better off with baked snacks, which are safe and just as low in calories. Products made with olestra should not be called "fat free," because they contain substantial amounts of indigestible fat. *Found in: potato chips, snacks, other low-calorie products.*
Potassium Bromate	Flour improver. This additive has long been used to increase the volume of bread and to produce bread with a fine crumb (the part of the bread that isn't the crust) structure. Most bromate rapidly breaks down to form innocuous bromide. However, bromate itself causes cancer in animals. The tiny amounts of bromate that may remain in bread pose a small risk to consumers. Bromate has been banned virtually worldwide except in Japan and the United States. It is rarely used in California because a cancer warning might be required on the label. In 1999, the Center for Science in the Public Interest petitioned the FDA to ban bromate. Since then, numerous millers and bakers have stopped using Bromate. *Found in: white flour, bread, rolls.*
Sodium nitrite	Preservative, coloring, flavoring: Meat processors love sodium nitrite because it stabilizes the red color in cured meat (without nitrite, hot dogs and bacon would look gray) and gives a characteristic flavor. Adding nitrite to food can lead to the formation of small amounts of potent cancer-causing chemicals (nitrosamines), particularly in fried bacon. Nitrite, which also occurs in saliva and forms from nitrate in several vegetables, can undergo the same chemical reaction in the stomach. Companies now add ascorbic acid or erythorbic acid to bacon to inhibit nitrosamine formation, a measure that has greatly reduced the problem. While nitrite and nitrate cause only a small risk, they are still worth avoiding. *Found in: bacon, ham, frankfurters, dry cured meats, luncheon meats, smoked fish, corned beef, and fish.*

Partially Hydrogenated Vegetable Oil/ Trans fats	Fat, oil, shortening, stick margarine. Vegetable oil, usually a liquid, can be made into a semi-solid shortening by reacting it with hydrogen. Partial hydrogenation reduces the levels of polyunsaturated oils and creates trans fats, which promote heart disease. A committee of the U.S. Food and Drug Administration (FDA) concluded in 2004 that on a gram-for-gram basis, trans fat is even more harmful than saturated fat. Ideally, food manufacturers would replace hydrogenated shortening with less-harmful ingredients. The Institute of Medicine has advised consumers to consume as little trans fat as possible, ideally less than about 2 grams a day (that much might come from naturally occurring trans fat in beef and dairy products). Harvard School of Public Health researchers estimate that trans fat had been causing about 50,000 premature heart attack deaths annually, making partially hydrogenated oil one of the most harmful ingredients in the food supply. *Found in: crackers, fried restaurant foods, baked goods, icing, microwave popcorn*

Please take this information with you when you go shopping. Remember to read labels and shop as wholesome and organic as possible. The more whole, natural foods you eat, the better off you are—eat foods that do not contain preservatives, chemicals, fillers, artificial flavors, or artificial colors.

FREE FOOD is FREE of chemicals! Only feed your body food that it will be able to recognize and know what to do with!

Sources:

Laurentine Bosch, producer, "Food Matters," www.drmercola.info, 'Food Matters'. www.foodmatters.tv.com, www.altmedangel.com, www.naturalnews.com, and www.bestofmotherearth.com.

Appetite Journal, www.elsevier.com/locate/appet. Article "Glutamate: Its Applications in Food and Contributions to Health."

Truth in Labeling, www.truthinlabeling.org.

Health and Nutrition Secrets That Can Save Your Life, by Russell L. Blaylock, MD.

FAAN, Food Allergy and Anaphylaxis Network, http://www.foodallergy.org.

Center for Science in the Public Interest, Summary of All Food Additives, www.cspinet.org/reports.

Food and Drug Administration website, http://www.fda.gov/food/default.htmusda.

www.mpwhi.com/senomyx_sweeter_than_sweet.htm

SHOPPING SOURCES

You know what to eat and the types of foods you need to cook with. Now where do you get this stuff? These are some great places where you can find the healthy choices we have been discussing. See the Addendum for a list of food products by vendor and product type. You may also order online from many of these vendors.**Healthy Choice–Friendly Vendors**

HEALTHY CHOICE–FRIENDLY VENDORS

Bountiful Baskets

www.bountifulbaskets.org

Central Market

Austin, Texas

www.centralmarket.com

Costco Wholesale Corp.

Seattle, Washington

www.costco.com

Kroger

Cincinnati, Ohio

www.kroger.com

Sprouts

Arizona Based

www.sprouts.com

Trader Joes

www.traderjoes.com

800-746-7857

Whole Foods

Austin, Texas

www.wholefoods.com

Sunflower Shoppe (Texas)

Ft. Worth and Colleyville

www.sunflowershoppe.com

Azure Standard

www.azurestandard.com

Find your local farmer at Local Harvest

www.localharvest.org

Finding a local farmer can be a fantastic way to get quality affordable produce and food supplies. If a farmer produces under $5000 in product, he or she is not required to certify organic products. This does not mean that the farm does not use organic methods of farming. Get to know your local farmer and ask questions. Most of them will be dedicated to their product and happy to answer your questions.

GET GROWING WITH CONTAINER GARDENING

The hungriest appetites can be satisfied with just a four-by-eight-foot apartment balcony, patio, deck, and/or a patch of yard! Grow organic vegetables, fruits, and herbs at low cost and with high nutrient quality. It is easy, fun, and rewarding.

Container gardening is especially great fun for children and as a family project. Learn and experience together how real organic fruits, veggies, and herbs grow. You will be surprised at how easy it is to get children to eat what they grew. No more begging, "Eat your vegetables and fruits!"

Here are some simple tips and steps to convert a *minimal* amount of time into an abundance of organic foods, just outside of your kitchen. You really can enjoy the fruits of very little labor. So let's get growing!

Top Tips for Successful Bounty

The following five tips can lead to an easily set-up and maintained container garden. There is nothing quite as rewarding as a salad made from vegetables fresh from your own container garden!

Sunlight, Sunlight, Sunlight. More Is Better:

Get your vitamin D outside! Sunlight is the most important factor to consider. Too little and your plants will not be able to convert sunlight into enough energy to produce a crop. Note, though, that some herbs may do fine in low sun areas. Decide on where to place your containers after you have tracked the sun and shade patterns of your garden space. This will help you to plan your garden for best sun exposure. Know that plants that have flowers will need a lot of sunlight. In areas with warm sunny conditions, consider tomatoes, cucumbers, eggplants, peppers, and squashes. High-quality fruit needs lots of sun to photosynthesize the levels of sugars needed for quality fruit with size, yield, and great taste. For a thorough list of plants that will thrive in your location and for further information, it is best to consult with your local independent nursery. At the Kotsanis Institute, we like the book *The Vegetable Gardener's Container Bible,* by Edward CUP Smith; *Dr. Earth Gardening Guide;* and the magazine *Container Gardening,* from which content for this summary is sourced. Other resources include *The Ultimate Container Gardener,* by Stephanie Donaldson, and of course Neill Sperry's books on gardening.

Container Size Matters

The greater soil volume a plant has, the greater nutrient pool the root system can access. This directly influences the size and quality of vegetables and herbs. For example, we know that tomatoes need a minimum of five gallons of soil to grow to full size. Bottom line, vegetable plants will produce larger and more bountiful crops in bigger containers

The type of container also makes a big difference. Terra cotta containers breathe with the soil and maintain steady temperatures. Redwood and cedar planter boxes are good choices since they also breathe and retain moisture. There is a huge selection of plastic containers on the market, and while they will work fine, they do require more watering than pots that have thicker absorbent materials. It is important to use mulch to maximize moisture retention if you use plastic containers. Plants in small containers will dry out quickly, so watch these carefully. Keep a close eye on all plants and water as needed. You have several choices in watering techniques, including self-watering containers.

Organic Soil, the Source of Life:

Soil is not dirt! It is a living thing abundant with beneficial living organisms that promote life for all plants. It directly and indirectly influences the health of all plants and animals that we consume. Treat it with respect and reverence. Healthy soil will yield healthy crops. Choose high-quality organic potting soil such as Dr. Earth Potting Soil, which contains pro-biotic beneficial soil microbes plus Ecto and Edo Mycorrhizae, which help seedlings and transplants get off to a great start. Other brands are also available. Just ask your local organic planting expert. Make sure you avoid potting soils that contain chemicals such as synthetic plant nutrients that are typically found in many bagged commercial potting soils.

Feed Soil with Nature—Free of Artificial and Petroleum-Based Products:

Vegetables, fruits, and herbs need soil that is rich in nutrients and microbes. This means you need to feed your soil a lot of fertilizer to promote their fullest yield potential. Containers limit the roots' ability to reach out to deeper soil for more nutrients. For this reason it is important to use the best organic fertilizers to feed the roots. One such technique is to create your own organic tea fertilizer. Put your leftover fruits and vegetables in a glass container. Fill it with water. Set it outside for 1 week to decompose. It is "ready when smelly." Feed your plants. They will love you for it!

Expose Leaves to Sunlight. Support Your Plants:

Some vegetables, fruits, and herbs need support to keep their leaves exposed to as much sunlight as possible. Allowing open air space helps minimize exposure to fungal and other diseases. Lots of air also aids beneficial insects, enabling them to access blossoms. Ask your nursery professional for a recommendation for plants specific to your needs and location.

Germinating What?

Yes, seeds! It's easy, inexpensive and takes just 10 minutes to get started. Get some small paper cups. Poke a hole in the bottom for drainage. Fill with organic potting soil. Create a hole in the soil, about an inch into the soil. Put seed into the hole. Fill hole with soil. Water thoroughly. Place cup in full day of sun. *Note:* follow the directions on each seed package, as individual plants have their own unique germination timelines. Make sure you water frequently. Watch it sprout.

Milk Carton Gardening

If you were ever in Girl or Boy Scouts or other character-building organizations as you were growing up, you were probably introduced to milk carton gardening. For an inexpensive project, you can start small and do it with your family. Try the following project.

Take a quart or gallon carton and cut the top off. For drainage, poke nail holes in the bottom of the container or cut slits on the corners. Fill the carton with soil, leaving a 3-inch space between the soil and the top of the carton. Plant the seeds according to the directions on the package. Place the carton in optimal sunlight or as directed. Water as needed and watch your plant grow!

A Mini-Garden in Your Patch of Yard or the Side Garden

Easy Prep Work: Choose your patch of yard. It may have weeds all over. Just put a big plastic bag over the whole patch of ground. Secure it with bricks, boards, or rocks so it does not blow away. Let the sun do the work for you over the next two to three months. The sun creates a sauna over the ground, burning off the weeds, plants, and their root systems. Start this process in early April for June plantings.

Easily Grow Fruit-Bearing Bushes and Trees

Select a container that has one-inch-thick walls (20 to 50 gallons) and holes in the bottom for drainage. Fill the container one-fifth full with natural organic compost. Add organic soil on top of the compost up to within an inch of the top.

So Many Options

There is an endless array of container gardening options. These are just a few that can introduce you to this quick and easy way to become a successful container gardener. Whether you choose to create a balcony container garden, a hanging garden, a bucket garden, or design a tasty and tasteful container garden for your entryway, we encourage you to give it a try!

References and Sources:

The Vegetable Gardener's Container Bible by Edward CUP Smith

Dr. Earth Gardening Guide

Container Gardening magazine

The Ultimate Container Gardner by Stephanie Donaldson

Neill Sperry's books on gardening

FOOD HANDLING, PREPARATION, AND STORAGE

You can have the purest food, but you will ruin it all if you don't handle it properly. So here are a few food handling and prep basics to remember.

First, work on a clean surface in a clean kitchen in a clean house. Dirt on your countertop and dust in the air can find its way into what you cook. Keep your home free of dust, chemicals, and toxins, and minimize exposure to electromagnetic fields. Too much Wi-Fi or cell phone use can start to get into your skull through a little heat induction; perhaps not much from occasional sources, but enough of it can add up.

Second, the surface you prepare your food on is important. Granite countertops are all the rage, but a lot of granite in newer homes actually contains small amounts of radiation and radon. Synthetic granite is better if you must go that way.

Wash your food. Veggies should be lightly scrubbed and washed. If you want to make extra sure your food is free of contaminates, you can wash it in hydrogen peroxide or apple cider vinegar.

No plastic! BPA can leach out of water bottles or anything plastic. Moreover, certainly do not put plastic in a microwave, even containers that are labeled BPA-free. Use Pyrex whenever possible. Pyrex is fantastic because it can go from freezer to oven safely.

Nonstick pans can also leach hazardous toxins into your food, and then into your body. So stay away from Teflon and aluminum. A long-time favorite cooking surface is cast-iron pans.

We should also note that whenever possible, cooking in an oven or on a stove is much preferred to doing it all in a microwave. Microwaves can alter the molecular structure of water in small ways that may not be good for you._

Food Storage

Proper food storage starts as soon as you select the food at the store. This goes for both the big weekly grocery runs and the quick trips. The order that you pick out your foods, as well as how you arrange them in your cart, is also important. After all, you don't want your ice cream thawing by the time it reaches checkout, do you? On the other hand, you don't want your piping-hot deli item cooling its heels next to the frozen fish. Then the food must be handled carefully and make it home safely. Finally, check the product dating on the foods you purchase and use.

Filling Your Cart

- Shop for shelf-stable items such as canned and dry goods first.
- Buy refrigerated and frozen foods and hot deli items last—right before checkout.
- Do not choose meat, fish, poultry, or dairy products that feel warm to the touch or have a damaged or torn package.
- Place leaking packages in plastic bags.
- Choose only pasteurized dairy products.
- Choose only refrigerated eggs and make sure that they are not cracked or dirty.
- Check sell-by and use-by dates on packages.
- Buy intact cans that are not bulging, leaking, or dented on the seam or rim.

Handling Food Safely at Home

Many cases of food poisoning occur each year due to improper handling of foods in the home. Once you purchase food, go directly home. If it's a hot day out, then you have less time to get your perishables to proper storage. If a straight route home is not possible, then keep a cooler in the car to transport perishable items. Once you are home, immediately put your cold perishables into the refrigerator or freezer.

Hot perishable foods picked up from the deli department need to be kept warm and consumed within two hours. If you purchase hot deli foods to eat later, then place the food in small portions in shallow containers and refrigerate or freeze as soon as possible. Perishable foods should be kept at room temperature no longer than two hours.

Bacteria multiply rapidly at temperatures between 40 and 140 degrees Fahrenheit. Unfortunately, the harmful bacteria that cause most cases of food poisoning cannot be seen, smelled, or tasted. Therefore, it is important to keep cold foods cold (40°F or below), and hot foods hot (140°F or above). Follow these other rules for handling food safely:

- Keep everything clean: hands, utensils, counters, cutting boards, and sinks.
- Always wash hands thoroughly in hot, soapy water before preparing foods and after handling raw meat, poultry, or seafood.
- Do not let raw juices from meat, poultry, or seafood touch ready-to-eat foods, either in the refrigerator or during preparation.

Food Product Dating

Dates are printed on many food products. After the date expires, must you discard that food? In most cases, no. A calendar date may be stamped on a product's package to help the store determine how long to display the product for sale. It is not a safety date.

Product dating is not required by federal regulations, although dating of some foods is required in fifteen states. Calendar dates are found primarily on perishable foods such as dairy products, eggs, meat, and poultry. Coded dates might appear on shelf-stable products such as cans and boxes of food.

There are several types of dates:

- **Sell-by date**: tells the store how long to display the product for sale. You should buy the product before the date expires.
- **Best if Used By (or Before)**: recommended for best flavor or quality. It is not a purchase or safety date.
- **Use-by date:** the last date recommended for the use of product while at peak quality. The date has been determined by the manufacturer of the product.
- **Closed or Coded Dates**: packing numbers for use by the manufacturer in tracking their products. This enables manufacturers to rotate their stock as well as locate their products in the event of a recall.

In addition to the above, there are a few caveats. First, do not buy or use infant formula and baby food past its use-by date; federal regulations require a date on those products. Next, as long as a product is wholesome, a retailer may legally sell fresh or processed meat and poultry products beyond the expiration date on the package.

Pantry Storage

Naturally, different kinds of food require different ways of being stored. Shelf-stable foods such as canned goods, cereal, baking mixes, pasta, dry beans, mustard, and ketchup can be kept safely at room temperature. To keep these foods at their best quality, store them in clean, dry, cool (below 85°F) cabinets away from the stove or the refrigerator□s exhaust. Pease note that extremely hot (over 100°F) and cold temperatures are harmful to canned goods.

Never use food from cans that are leaking, bulging, badly dented, or with a foul odor; cracked jars or jars with loose or bulging lids; or any container that spurts liquid when you open it. Don't even taste such foods, it could be contaminated with botulism. Throw out any food you suspect is spoiled.

In general, most canned foods have a long "health life" and, when properly stored, are safe to eat for several years.

- Low-acid canned goods: two to five years (canned meat and poultry, stews, soups except tomato, pasta products, potatoes, corn, carrots, spinach, beans, beets, peas, and pumpkin)
- High-acid canned goods: twelve to eighteen months (tomato products, fruits, sauerkraut and foods in vinegar-based sauces or dressings)
- Some canned hams are shelf stable, but do not store ham or any foods labeled "keep refrigerated" in the pantry. Such foods must be stored in the refrigerator.

FREEZING FOOD

Freezing is a quick and convenient method to preserve fruits and vegetables and their nutrients if done properly. Freezing retards the growth of bacteria, molds, and yeasts, but once food is thawed, microorganisms may continue to grow. Foods frozen at peak quality will taste better than foods frozen near the end of their useful life, so quickly freeze items you don't plan to use in the next day or two.

Natural enzymes can change the flavor, color, texture, and nutritive value of foods over time. Freezing slows this activity but does not stop it. To prevent further enzyme activity, vegetables need to be blanched in boiling water or steamed before freezing. Some nutrient loss does occur during such blanching, but by comparison the nutrient losses from enzymatic activity are far greater.

Enzymatic browning in light colored fruits can be prevented by using ascorbic acid mixtures; lemon juice is fine, or lemon juice and sugar for fruits. However you need to prepare your food for freezing. If fruits and vegetables are not properly packaged, air can cause changes that affect flavor. You should also freeze your fruits and vegetables at the lowest possible freezer setting, though at least 0°F, since the water in these foods will expand upon freezing, breaking the cell walls and sometimes causing them to be soft and mushy once thawed.

Any food that has been cooked may be frozen. Furthermore, unused portions of foods that were previously cooked, frozen, and then thawed in the refrigerator may be refrozen. Food kept continuously frozen at 0°F will always be safe, but quality sutters with lengthy freezer storage. Note that it is okay if any food product dating on the packaging expires after the food is frozen. Remember, also, to place frozen foods in the cart last when shopping to minimize thawing, then take them directly home and place in your freezer.

Packaging and Freezer Burn

Moisture from food can evaporate, causing the food to become dry and tough and develop off-flavors. This is called freezer burn, and it can be prevented with proper packaging. Use moisture and vapor-proof or resistant packaging, such as "can or freeze" glass jars, plastic freezing containers, heavyweight aluminum foil, plastic coated freezer paper, and plastic wraps or bags. It is perfectly safe to freeze foods in their supermarket wrappings, but use them within a month or two as many supermarket wrappings are air-permeable. Write the date on packages and use the oldest items first.

If frozen food does get freezer burn, it is still safe to eat; it will merely be dry in spots. Just cut freezer-burned portions away either before or after cooking the food.

Defrosting

Freezing to 0°F inactivates but does not destroy microbes—bacteria, yeasts, and molds—present in food. Once thawed, however, these microbes can again become active, multiplying under the right conditions to levels that can lead to food-borne illness.

Never defrost foods outdoors, in a cold room in the house such as the basement, or on the kitchen counter. These methods encourage growth of harmful bacteria.

There are three safe ways to defrost food: in the refrigerator, in cold running water, and in the microwave. Food thawed in the refrigerator is safe to refreeze without cooking. It is important to plan ahead, because food takes longer to thaw in the refrigerator.

Most frozen vegetables can be cooked without thawing. Corn on the cob, though, should be partially defrosted. Cook your vegetables in about half a cup or less of water until just tender; this should take about half as long as if they were fresh. Frozen fruits should be thawed at room temperature in their original package; if faster defrosting is required, simply submerge in lukewarm water or partially defrost in the microwave. A few ice crystals remaining is okay for vegetables, but fruits should be completely thawed or they will be limp or mushy.

For a complete guide to freezing specific vegetables and canning specific fruits, see the U.S. Department of Agriculture's Complete Guide to Home Canning, available at www.uga.edu/nchfp.

REFRIGERATING FOOD

We keep food in the refrigerator to preserve its freshness and quality, and to keep it safe. Cold temperatures keep food fresh and inhibit the growth of most bacteria. However, microorganisms that contribute to food spoilage can still grow and multiply slowly over time, so there is a limit to the length of time various foods will stay fresh in the refrigerator. Eventually, food will begin to look or smell bad and should be thrown out. Use the following temperature and storage tips to help keep perishable food safe.

Refrigerated Temperature

Set the refrigerator to maintain a temperature of 40°F or below, and keep a refrigerator thermometer inside in order to check the temperature periodically. You may also need to adjust the control seasonally. For example, a refrigerator set for 40°F in the summer may be too cold for the winter, resulting in frozen lettuce or milk. You also don't want to overload the refrigerator, as you need room for the air to circulate freely and cool all foods evenly.

Refrigerator Storage

Leave meat and poultry products in the store wrap before using, since repeated handling can introduce bacteria into the product or spread bacteria around the kitchen. Store opened food in foil, leak-proof plastic bags, or airtight containers to keep it from drying out. Place meat, poultry, and fish in the coldest part of the refrigerator. Store eggs in their original carton on a shelf, not in the door.

Defrost frozen meats or marinate meats in the refrigerator where they will remain safe—never on the kitchen counter. You also need to clean the refrigerator regularly to remove spoiled foods so that bacteria can't be passed to other foods.

Shelf Stable Foods

Before opening, shelf stable foods should be safe unless the can or packaging has been damaged. After opening, store products in tightly closed containers. The storage of many shelf stable items at room temperature is a quality issue, unless the product is contaminated (bugs in flour, for example). Some foods must be refrigerated after opening, such as tuna or chili.

Bakery Items

Bakery items containing custards, meat, or vegetables and frostings made of cream cheese, whipped cream, or eggs must be kept refrigerated. Bread products not containing these ingredients are safe kept at room temperature, but eventually they will mold and become unsafe to eat.

Fresh Produce

Raw fruits are safe at room temperature, but after ripening they will mold and rot quickly. So for best quality, store ripe fruit in the refrigerator or prepare and freeze.

Some dense raw vegetables, such as potatoes and onions, can be stored at cool room temperatures. Refrigerate other raw vegetables for optimum quality and to prevent rotting. After cooking, all vegetables must be refrigerated or frozen within two hours.

Cold Storage Guidelines

The following chart should give you an idea about how long you can store something either frozen or refrigerated. Of course, if any food starts to smell or look bad before these times, you should always discard it!

Cold Storage Guidelines		
Product	Refrigerator: 40°F or below	Freezer 0°F or below
Salads		
Egg, chicken, ham, tuna, and macaroni salads	3 to 5 days	Does not freeze well
Hot dogs		
Opened package	1 week	1 to 2 months
Unopened package	2 weeks	1 to 2 months
Bacon and Sausage		
Bacon	7 days	1 month
Sausage, raw, from chicken, turkey, pork, beef	1 to 2 days	1 to 2 months
Hamburger and Other Ground Meats		
Hamburger, ground beef, turkey, veal, pork, lamb, and mixtures	1 to 2 days	3 to 4 months
Fresh Beef, Veal, Lamb, and Pork		
Steaks	3 to 5 days	6 to 12 months
Chops	3 to 5 days	4 to 6 months
Roasts	3 to 5 days	4 to 12 months
Fresh Poultry		
Chicken or turkey, whole	1 to 2 days	1 year

Chicken or turkey, pieces	1 to 2 days	9 months
Soups and Stews		
Vegetable or meat added	3 to 4 days	2 to 6 months
Leftovers		
Cooked meat or poultry	3 to 4 days	2 to 6 months
Chicken nuggets or patties	3 to 4 days	1 to 3 months
Pizza	3 to 4 days	1 to 2 months

Eggs and Egg-based Products

Raw eggs in shell	3 to 5 weeks	Do not freeze. Instead, beat yolks and whites together, then freeze.
Raw egg whites	2 to 4 days	12 months
Raw egg yolks	2 to 4 days	Yolks do not freeze well

Cold Storage Guide for Eggs and Egg-based Products

Raw egg accidentally frozen in shell	Use immediately after thawing	Keep frozen, then refrigerate to thaw
Hard-cooked eggs	1 week	Do not freeze
Egg substitutes, liquid: unopened	10 days	12 months
Egg substitutes, liquid: opened	3 days	Do not freeze
Egg substitutes, frozen: unopened	After thawing, 7 days, or refer to use-by date	12 months
Egg substitutes, frozen: opened	After thawing, 3 days, or refer to use-by date	Do not freeze
Casseroles with eggs	3 to 4 days	After baking, 2 to 3 months
Eggnog: commercial	3 to 5 days	6 months
Eggnog: homemade	2 to 4 days	Do not freeze
Pies: pumpkin or pecan	3 to 4 days	After baking, 1 to 2 months
Pies: custard and chiffon	3 to 4 days	Do not freeze
Quiche with filling	3 to 4 days	After baking, 1 to 2 months

Food Temperature Control

Temperature control is important too. Follow food-safety guidelines to ensure that your food stays out of the "danger zone," and store food at temperatures at which bacteria are least likely to grow.

Food Temperature Guidelines

165°F and higher	Most bacteria die within several seconds
141°F to 164°F	Holding hot foods and sauces. Bacteria are not killed, but they do not multiply either.
40°F to 140°F **Food Temperature Danger Zone**	Bacteria thrive and multiply. Limit exposure of perishable foods to one hour or less.
33°F to 39°F	Refrigerated food storage. Bacteria aren't killed. They multiply, but relatively slowly. Food is safe here for a limited time.
32°F and lower	Frozen food storage: Bacteria are not killed, but they do not multiply either.

It is also important to note that refrigerated leftovers not only lose their nutrient value as they sit, they also increase the likelihood of growing potential harmful bacteria. Try to eat your food as fresh as possible, or freeze it.

Sources:

USDA Food Safety Unit—Kitchen Companion on Food Safety; Food Marketing Institute

SCHOOL LUNCHES AND A LETTER TO TEACHERS

School lunches are by far the biggest challenge for a child on a special diet. The obstacles abound. Face those obstacles head-on with clarity and coolness. Here are some simple solutions to conquering them confidently.

Obstacle #1: What to Pack

School lunches are the most challenging because you are throwing in an extra element to an already limited choice pool. The meal you send must be safe to keep at the temperatures you are able to manage and must be able to be eaten without being cooked or reheated (in most cases). Many schools have arranged for such situations now by providing refrigerators, but not everyone has this option. For those that do not provide this perk already, arrangements can often be made on an individual basis, but many school-age kids feel awkward having to do anything different than their peers.

Purchase the right food storage containers. Some good choices are Pottery Barn Kids Spencer Ice Pack Lid Food Storage or Fit Fresh Containers. Another favorite of ours is the well-known Thermos, which is now BPA free. Your storage containers may carry an initial investment, but they are an invaluable necessity to making your school lunch packing a success.

Do not get into a lunch funk. Use some of these great ideas to pack the perfect school lunch any day of the week:

The BACKPACKER'S CRACKER SNACKER: GFCF Crackers (try Back To Nature's new gluten-free selections) with rice vegan cheese slices and fresh fruit.

P.E. PERFECT PASTA SALAD: Make a simple cold pasta salad with gluten-free pasta and a healthy dressing.

ALL A's PARFAIT: Layer dairy-free yogurt with fresh fruit and enjoy like granola.

MATH-WHIZ MUFFIN MEAL: Send a gluten-free muffin with some butter spread or nut butter.

SAVE THE FISHIES SUSHI: See the recipe for Hawaiian Ham Sushi.

PEP RALLY PEPPERONI PANINI: Grill up a Panini on your favorite gluten-free bread, with rice vegan mozzarella, Applegate Farms pepperoni, and organic pizza sauce.

Obstacle #2: Peer Pressure

Peer pressure has many faces. Both children and parents alike can feel an innate sense of pressure not to stray from the pack, fearing that it will draw even more attention to the already awkward social challenges of ASD or attention deficit disorder. Mothers may fear sending "special" food with their child, wanting to protect them from bullying or ridicule. Your special student may even refuse to eat anything different than what their peers are eating.

Food For Thought

Your child's health is of the utmost importance, and we know we can all agree on that! Even if your child does not suffer immunological symptoms, such as allergies, diet may strongly affect his or her mental health. That special diet may be the difference between getting Cs and getting As! It is important to keep your focus on the reason your child needs specific foods and to keep reminding yourself and your child (and anyone else that may need to hear it) that your child's special diet is for health reasons and should not be taken lightly.

Make sure that you are sending your special eater off to a successful eating environment by practicing some of the following tips:

1) At-home pep talk: Be sure to communicate openly with your child about the "whys" of their special diet. Explain to them the positive changes that you have seen in them. Talk with them about whether they feel different when they have eaten certain foods. Feed them the assurance that they need to confidently eat whatever food is necessary for them to reach their personal best and feel their best, too.

2) Communication station: It may be important to check in every now and then to be sure that your child isn't feeling awkward about his or her special food. Be sure that your child knows that you are there to listen and help with any situation that may arise.

3) Talk to other parents: In some situations, it may be helpful to contact the other parents in the class, even a quick e-mail, to let them know that your child is on a special diet for medical reasons. Ask them to please be sure to communicate directly with you or with the teacher if they ever plan on bringing special treats to the classroom for a birthday celebration or other occasion so that you can make arrangements to send something for your child on that day.

4) Power of positivity: Be sure to put a positive spin on the situation for your child's sake. Explain that your child is working toward a goal, reassuring him or her that the situation may not be permanent. Get as creative as you like as it pertains to your child. Here are some fun examples of positive spins:

- Your little man's great-great-great-grrrrrrrreat-grandfather was a very famous pirate who courageously sailed to new lands; and the blood of a pirate, even a great-great-great-grrrrrrrreat-grandson-pirate, must be fed a very special diet indeed. Arrhhh, keeps away the scurvy!
- H.R.H., your little princess must eat only the finest of foods, because that is what a real princess must do; after all, she is royalty.
- Athletes? Who knew that you were in a special training program with a highly prestigious medical trainer (wink, wink), working on a strength-building regime that will surely get your game in record-breaking shape.

Use the summer months to prepare your tot for the challenges he or she might face in the school year to come. Train! You will find that the more effort you put into preparing your special dieter, the less you will have to worry when sending him or her off to school with a GFCF-filled lunchbox.

Every mother worries about peer pressure, but in the life of an ASD parent, that worry is exponentially greater. Like all of your obstacles, this too can be conquered, and if anyone can do it, it is you.

Obstacle #3: School Staff

Be sure to communicate clearly and openly with the school staff, not just your teacher, but also the school nurse. They should be more than accommodating.

A tougher concept for some teachers to grasp is the fact that gluten and other sensitivities can be present beyond just food. Children may have sensitivities to chemicals in cleaning agents or hand sanitizers, and even some daily school supplies.

See www.autismspot.com and www.greatertots.org, Kendra Jean Finestead's blog, for more about school lunches and working with the school system.

A LETTER TO TEACHERS

Many teachers are aware that gluten and other sensitivities exist, but we have found that few are aware of the wide range of actual school supplies in which gluten can be found. We wanted to include this sample letter that Kendra Jean Finestead leaves with her daughter's teacher at the "meet the teacher" night before the beginning of the school year, along with the list of school supplies that her daughter cannot use.

Dear teacher and trusted caregiver,

Our daughter has some medical speed bumps that provoke her system to being highly sensitive to gluten (found in wheat, barley, rye, and some oats) and to any dairy products. I am providing a separate list for her food sensitivities, but many people do not realize that these ingredients are not only found in food. The following supplies COULD cause a negative reaction in Molly, and we greatly appreciate you monitoring her exposure to them.

We are providing all Molly-friendly supplies and marking them clearly as such, so please use ONLY those which we have established as "safe" for her to use.

If you should ever have a question, please feel free to call us, or simply error on the side of caution.

Much appreciation,

Kevin and Kendra Finestead

MOLLY'S NO-NO LIST

COLORS & PAINTS

NO Elmer's finger paints

NO Ross finger paints

All Crayola paints are fine.

Dick Blick, Lakeshore, and Palmer paints are fine, as well as Prism, Prismatone, Ross paints (OTHER THAN FINGER PAINTS), and Sargent Art Paints.

DOUGHS & GLUES

NO Play-Doh

NO Crayola fun doh

NO RoseArt Fun Dough

NO RoseArt modeling clay

NO Ross Doh

NO Amoco Super Dough

Please use instead: Colorations (provided), Crayola Magic Modeling Clay, Prang, or Silly Putty.

NO glues or pastes unless listed here.

NO traditional paper mache.

Crafty Dab School & Craft, Crayola Glitter Glue, Elmer's (OTHER THAN FINGER PAINT), and Ross glues (OTHER THAN FINGER PAINT) are gluten-free.

Scotch tape and Post-It Notes are okay.

Blick's Mix Instant Papier Maché is gluten-free, or simply let me know ahead of time and I can make you some gluten-free mix.

TIPS, TRICKS, AND HAPPY-KID EATING GAMES

You have the right food, but you've gotten mixed up as to which box in your pantry should or should not be eaten by whom, you've run out of time to prepare the meal properly, or your kids simply refuse to touch it. What's a mother to do? Here are some tips you can use to keep you and your family on the right path and make the preparation of meals a bit easier on yourself, and a few tricks you can use to make the eating more fun for the kids so they won't just sit and stare at their plates.

X MARKS THE SPOT: The very first thing we recommend to any parent faced with special diet challenges is to grab your heavy-duty permanent marker and draw a large black X on the visible side of any box, bag, or package in your pantry, fridge, or freezer that has ingredients in it that are now "off limits" for your special family member. With so much information to learn at once, it is impossible to retain the information of every food label of every product, so marking the box will help you avoid re-reading the same label again and again.

CHART IT: If you are anything like us, the thought of having to keep up with a chart or food consumption log is enough to make you want to hire a full-time feeding assistant! Nevertheless, it is extremely important to write down results and reactions to the new foods you are introducing. Food logs can help you to find patterns in flavors and textures that your child is responding well or poorly to so that you can create more successful meals. It is also an important tool for your doctors and nutritionists, so that if your child is having a reaction, you may be able to pinpoint nutritionally what the culprit is. Kendra has a two-step system that works well at her house. She outlines it below.

I created a binder that I write all of her meals and snacks in at the end of the day or week.

We bought a large chalkboard for our dining room wall. When I have a free second during the day, I jot down what she has eaten so that I don't have to pull the binder out each meal. Every couple of days, I will sit down and open the binder and write in a more detailed history.

FREEZE: Your freezer is your friend. To stretch your dollar as far as you can, keep frozen portions on hand of your favorite ingredient essentials by freezing chopped or puréed fruit or veggies, broths, or even fat from cooking into ice cube trays. Once the food is frozen, you can pop the cubes out and store them in a ziplock bag or freezer safe container. Fruit is perfect for adding into smoothies or for baking, and savory foods like stocks and fats are fantastic to have pre-portioned for individual meals.

You can also freeze baked goods, like muffins. The ingredients that a special diet can require are not cheap, so don't throw away the muffins you couldn't get to; freeze half of your batch and pull them out at a later date.

DOUBLE UP: Make a large batch of an entrée and freeze the other half for the following week. Any time you can cut down in the kitchen is going to cut down on your workload and your stress level!

TEAM EFFORT: Cooking is an adventure. Make it fun for both you and your children by letting them be a part of the planning. Make each meal a work of art, not just another regimen and another battle. Make it exciting! Let them help you in the preparation, even if it does mean just having them fetch the butter or wash the veggies. This can make it fun for them and then they will have enough personally invested in the meal to actually want to eat it just to see how their efforts came out. It really is all in how you sell it.

SPROUTS FOR YOUR "Little Sprout": We are hearing more and more moms tell us they are learning to sprout and for beneficial reasons. Sprouting your beans, seeds, grains, and some nuts is a practice that can be very helpful to the proper digestion and assimilation of those foods, especially to sensitive systems that do not process foods completely. Sprouting, or even simply soaking beans, grains, nuts, or seeds sufficiently, neutralizes anti-nutrients, like phytic acid and other enzyme inhibitors, which are protestants to the food in nature. By breaking down that protective layer, you are essentially breaking down the defensive wall between you and that food's nutritional content. What was a "sleeping" seed (or nut or bean) actually "wakes up" and becomes a living plant that is much easier to digest.

Sally Fallon, author of *Nourishing Traditions,* offers fantastic information on sprouting. In her book, Fallon explains: "We must warn against over-consumption of raw sprouted grains as raw sprouts contain irritating substances that keep animals from eating the tender shoots. These substances are neutralized in cooking. Sprouted grains should usually be eaten lightly steamed or added to soups and casseroles."

POSITIVELY POSITIVE: Make sure your glass is always more than half full! To ensure that you keep your cool in the kitchen, it is vital to remain positively positive. Don't think about your special diet in terms of *restrictions,* spending time wishing for all of the items you *can't* have. Think of all the items you *can*. This was one of the first revelations I had when we started our own special diet. I was standing in the middle of my kitchen, glaring and sneering at the list I had stuck to the side of my fridge. That list was all of the items that our daughter could *not* eat. I was racking my brain to come up with meal ideas. Every item I would think of making from my old arsenal would be knocked down by that list. It was like a tennis match between me and that list. I'd serve and that list would return with a vengeance—and with some *mean* top spin! Ouch.

But then something inside me awakened and rallied, and I dominated the match. I literally ripped the list right off of the fridge and jammed it confidently into the recycling bin.

I decided to change my approach. Instead of posting a list of all of those "can't haves," I decided to make a list of all of the things she *could* have. Guess what? The new list was actually fun to make and was even much *longer* than the "can't" list.

DISABLE YOUR ENABLER: Eating is a behavior. Behaviors are trained. Most importantly, behaviors are train*able*! If you find yourself saying, "My child will never eat that," or "Little Bobby *only* eats XYZ Brand of chicken nuggets and that is just how it is," then it's time to own up, Mom and Dad! Your two-year-old does not go to the grocery store, pick up a box of XYZ Chicken Nuggets, walk through the self-checkout, and swipe their bankcard—you do. The fact is that your child will eat what you train them to eat. It will not always be easy, but it is possible. Think of it as just another challenge in life that you can conquer and walk away from, saying, "Been there, done that, bought the T-shirt."

EATING GAME IDEAS

JIMMY'S BUFFET: Set up buffet-style choices with finely chopped veggies, fruits, and/or salsas. You will be amazed at what your kiddo will try when it is all their idea.

RAINBOW OF FUN: Declare each day of the week a particular color day—make Monday Yellow Day, Tuesday Purple Day, and so on. Each day, have your little one pick a fruit and a vegetable to eat that corresponds with that color.

PICTURE MENUS: Let your little one "order" from their own menu. Create a digital version, just like a menu at a restaurant, or go the extra mile with a magnet or Velcro board and picture pieces. Check out your local teacher's supply store or Christian bookstore to find cutouts and magnets in different food shapes. If you can't find them pre-made, make your own!

GOOGLY FOOD: Make funny faces with your little one's food. This seems so simple, but it works like a charm! I have a collection of cookie cutters, pans, and utensils that I always have on hand to get creative with. You don't have to be an artist to draw a smiley face!

THEME IT OUT: Use the holidays to the fullest. Holiday themes can be a great starting point to getting creative with your next dish. They can also be a fun way to broaden your child's horizons and get him or her to try something new. Another fun idea is to match a theme to the category of food—you can even choose a movie that goes along with your theme. For example, you can watch *Kung Fu Panda* and eat rice noodle chicken soup (loaded with hidden veggies, of course) or watch *Beverly Hills Chihuahua* while you and your tot try chicken and squash enchiladas.

REWARDS: Try sensory rewards to really train your child to enjoy eating healthy. Some examples include getting to play silly putty or getting to ring a bell or a gong when they either take a bite or finish a set goal of number of bites, etc. We have a wildly obnoxious little plush dog that plays the song "Who Let the Dogs Out" while shaking his hips. Our daughter would sit and push that button from dawn to dusk if we let her, so we use it as a fun reward when she eats her given goal of bites or tries a new food without gagging or spitting it out. She gets very excited about this.

USE THE ABA REWARD SYSTEM—Applied Behavior Analysis

Behavior analysis (working with an occupational or speech therapist) is a scientific approach to understanding behavior and how it is affected by the environment. *Behavior* refers to all kinds of actions and skills (not just misbehavior) and *environment* includes all sorts of physical and social events that might change or be changed by one's behavior. The science of behavior analysis focuses on principles (that is, general laws) about how behavior works, or how learning takes place. For example, one principle of behavior analysis is positive reinforcement. When a behavior is followed by something that is valued (a reward), that behavior is likely to be repeated. Through decades of research, the field of behavior analysis has developed many techniques for increasing useful behaviors and reducing those that may be harmful or that interfere with learning. Applied behavior analysis (ABA) is the use of those techniques and principles to address socially important problems and to bring about meaningful behavior change (www.autismspeaks.org).

Include your therapist in your food goals! Many therapists are trained in techniques that train and refine specific behaviors. Eating is a behavior, so elicit the help if you are struggling.

Try not to reward with treats like candy or foods that you are trying to get your child to stop eating. The ultimate goal should not be just to survive getting through the diet; the goal should be to teach your child to really enjoy eating healthy and to truly understand the benefits and the differences in how their body and mind feels when they are fueling it sufficiently.

DINING OUT
RESTAURANTS, HOSPITALS, AND AIRLINES

Restaurants

Adults, children, and teens can be easily introduced to eating out at the same time they are developing skills for eating at home. Most cooks, chefs, and restaurant managers are very willing to assist with making selective and appropriate gluten-free, casein-free, and other allergen-free food menu choices at their place of business. Just saying, "I will need your help in choosing foods from your menu" usually opens the doors to both their kitchen and their friendly cooperation.

Many restaurants post their menus on the Internet, so you can check out what they have in the way of free food choices before you even leave the house. Often you will find nutrients and calorie counts listed for each menu item.

Call or e-mail the restaurant manager with any questions. Do this in advance. In some instances, a visit a few days prior to the restaurant meal can be helpful. Call or visit at a time when the chef or cook is not occupied with heavy meal traffic and ask if he or she can help you, a special needs customer, to become a better patron of their restaurant. A call ahead, an e-mail outlining your diet requirements, and a sharing of literature on your particular condition can be helpful and often will be graciously accepted and appreciated.

Dos and Don'ts of Eating Out
Don'ts

- Don't make a big scene
- Don't "get off" into a litany of all of the food items you or your child can and cannot eat. (People with you really don't want this type of attention and to hear about your food issues. Belaboring your food options can get old fast and makes eating out with you an unpleasant experience. Surely you can plan to address these issues before you go to the restaurant, if you have advanced notice, of course.)
- Don't respond to your friends or family's suggestion of specific restaurants with an immediate "I/we can't eat their food!" Adjust your expectations and remain open. Consider that there may well be foods on the menu you can eat. Call to see if they can make exceptions. Eating is a social event too. Try to remain open to the social aspects of restaurant selection and at the same time find a way to "eat freely" with the group.
- Don't put a damper on the fun of eating out by making the selection of a restaurant all about you or your child's free food requirements. You will find that most restaurants want your business and are willing to prepare something special for you or your family.
- Don't expect every item of a particular menu to be adapted to your requirements. Again, checking out the menu in advance can help set your own expectations.

Dos

- Check out the menu beforehand online or stop by the restaurant.
- Call the restaurant with your questions.
- Ask how you can best order from the wait staff at the time of your meal/dinner.
- Choose wisely. Perhaps a fresh salad, steamed vegetables, fresh fruit, a healthy protein selection (fish, chicken, a low-fat tasty meat).
- Keep a record of your food choices if you frequent the restaurant. Ordering will become simple.
- Take a picture! Our project manager always carries a picture of how she wants her cob salad prepared. Waiters often laugh, yet it makes their job easier and the cooks never have to redo the order. After all, a picture is worth a thousand words.
- Get to know the restaurant manager, chefs, and wait staff of places you frequent. Often they will take an interest in your requirements and will let you know when new selections are available.

With many restaurants you may visit over a period of several months, you are likely to be pleasantly surprised with the interest of their staff in you and the needs represented in your specific version of your free diet. The waiter will memorize your food selections and share immediately that he already has your order—unless there are changes. From time to time, you can expect some new food selections to be added. You might even find that the cook will prepare some new recipes just for you! Moreover, you can expect a telephone call with the message that "there's this new family in today with a father who has similar diet to yours, can you come over and meet him?" You will win new friends and a support group with a friendly approach to restaurant staff and managers.

Fast food chain restaurants can be more of a challenge, but with the interest and support of the manager on duty, food selections that are safe can typically be made. They want to help and they are happy to do so—if the customer can communicate what is needed. They may not know about the wheat starch coatings on French fries and they may not know about the addition of oat products to low-fat content hamburger. But they can ask questions and check out the labels. They can also call their regional offices and headquarter training centers. They are typically most cooperative and want to serve the customer in the best way possible.

For trips across the country, it is often best to call ahead to hotels, restaurants, and resorts to learn if a specific location can accommodate the needs of the gluten-free casein-free or any other free diet. Chefs contacted several days ahead of time will typically be happy to make up special free-food entrées. With a few added snack items and a few free-food purchases from grocery stores along the way, the family trip can be a success for everyone .

For your immediate living area—develop relationships, a set of information resources, and simple food lists with a core group of restaurants, which can then in turn support your dietary needs with appropriate food selections. Your connections with a hotel or two and with several restaurants can then become your support system for eating out. With a bit of planning, communication of the dictates of your gluten-free, casein-free or particular free-food diet, your group of restaurants can be as good as eating at home.

In Hospitals

With the variety and varying services of hospitals and the differing levels of knowledge of the gluten-free, casein-free, and other free-food diet requirements, entrance to a hospital without previous communication and planning can be—and will likely be—a major problem. Most people are admitted to a hospital with the primary diagnosis and an accompanying definition of needs no matter what the procedure or medical problem that has prompted admission.

It is crucial that patients with food-related requirements find a physician with a good understanding of them. Most physicians are not educated in or have minimal exposure to nutrition in medical college. With only a little communication and pre-planning, however, a hospital stay for most patients can be managed very well in terms of both the handling of the disease and the clinical needs of the diet and medications.

Education of hospital personnel about food-related diseases and reactions is necessary and important. Unfortunately, since fewer than one in twenty-five thousand hospital admissions is related to these types of conditions, it is not likely to be achieved or maintained. Thus, it is essential that each person be prepared for several aspects of self-care.

Make sure you make advance preparations through the admitting physician for any special needs related to the illness and for particular nutritional needs—for example, a gluten-free diet as relates to both foods and medications. It is also wise for a family member or friend to be available to provide the information needed to represent the diet requirements for the patient. Preplanning, communication, and monitoring are crucial. Always follow two cardinal rules when being admitted to the hospital:

1. Ask to be admitted as a patient whose primary illness is celiac (or other food related disease or diet requirement).

2. Ask to be admitted as a patient with needs for a strictly specified free diet.

Bring along a diet list and an explanation, which includes an introduction to the gluten-free or other type of diet, to the hospital. It is ideal if a pre-conference can be arranged with the dietician who will be supervising menu choices and meal preparation and with the pharmacist who will be issuing medications.

- Be proactive and be prepared to explain to hospital staff members, including physicians, nurses, pharmacists, and dietitians, about your condition and its dietary needs.
- Expect that most specialists and consulting physicians other than gastroenterologists and your primary care physician may have no reason to know what foods or medications are permissible on your particular diet.
- Do not expect the dietitian or pharmacist to have first-hand knowledge of the special diet.

Keep Your Instructions Simple

In terms of the diet, explain simply and in specific terms what you can have. Omit the listing of what is not acceptable for your dietary intake. Concentrate on a few foods that will work and leave out all of the many items that will cause problems.

With many hospitals working within a system and with outside contractors for food services, expect that some very well-meaning staff member along the way will make the observation that your food tray has been overlooked for the chocolate cake dessert or for the extra toast or the honey-roasted peanuts for snacks today. In addition, they may have been thoughtful enough to add wheat flour–thickened gravy to your blank mashed potatoes. So, what may have started out in the kitchen as a perfect gluten-free meal is now contaminated—at least, for you and your diet needs. Therefore, you may always need to do a quick check of foods served. Just as in your own home, you need to be in charge of what makes up your or your child's intake of food, and you need to choose it wisely.

In addition, in order to feel truly organized, try this plan: pack a toiletry kit with any personal items needed, such as appropriate soaps, toothpaste, lotions, etc. Along with these items, also include a listing of your needs for a gluten-free or other special diet and a copy of all of the medications you are taking by prescription. You can use this kit for trips, overnight visits to family and friends, and a possible hospital or care center stay in your future.

In addition to the dietitian and the dietary department, make certain also that the head nurse for your floor and the nursing department along with the pharmacist and the pharmacy department within the hospital have adequate information on your needs that all items taken by mouth can be free and consistent with your food intake requirements. Selected staff members may not be aware of the differences between such items as gluten-free Tylenol and regular Tylenol, the potential of wheat starch coatings on pills, etc. Critical for the celiac patient is to have access to gluten-free medications as well as gluten-free foods. For some select few, there may be additional needs related to gluten-free items for use on the skin. Thus, both put-ins as well as put-ons will need to be gluten-free.

If you are moving on from the hospital to a care center or rehabilitation facility, be sure to have your admitting physician include in the orders for admission the need for a gluten-free or your special free diet. Once again, communication and pre-planning are crucial in preparing the nursing staff and the dietary department and for the definition of both over-the-counter and prescription medications. The care center or nursing home can do a good job when adequate information has been provided. Without good information, additional problems and concerns may be added unnecessarily and without reason.

On Airlines

If you fail to plan you plan to fail. It may not always be quite that severe, but without planning at the time of ticket purchase, it may not be easy to convert from a regular meal order to gluten-free or an alternate choice that would be appropriate for your particular dietary needs. Of course this only applies to airlines that still serve meals on board. Otherwise, you may need to plan to bring your own food on board.

Of airlines surveyed, virtually all offer lacto-ovo, vegetarian, strict vegetarian, fruit platter, seafood, low-fat, low-cholesterol, low- or no-salt, and kosher meals. A number of the larger airlines also serve Hindu, Muslim, Asian, bland, and low-fiber meals.

Food For Thought

Most overseas flights can handle both gluten-free meals and gluten-free snacks. Some airlines, however, only promise to do gluten-free meals but not snacks, since snack foods are typically large contract items without a great deal of variance and choice allowed from the providers. Thus, for example, a celiac passenger should expect that snack items on most flights would likely not include gluten-free choices. With a bit of planning, however, snack items might be saved from a previous meal or more realistically brought on board as a planned food item for the trip.

For those airlines that do include a gluten-free diet through their catering services, the choices tend to be exact and well done. There can be and usually is a hitch with international flights whose food preparation base is located in another country outside the United States. This problem occurs since those companies are likely to be using the definition of the 5 percent level of tolerance (5 percent of total weight for gluten allowed) approved by the International Codex Alimentarius that is seated in Rome, Italy. All breads, cakes, pastries, and commercial food items may have been prepared to fit that standard.

CHAPTER 5

The Great 8 Food Allergies

A WORD ABOUT THE GREAT 8

Milk	**Fish**
Wheat	**Shellfish**
Eggs	**Peanuts**
Soy	**Tree Nuts**

When Kendra Jean Finestead discovered that her daughter, Molly, had food allergies, her biggest question was "Why?" She asked, "Why now? She has never really had any allergies before this and she is three years old! Why are we just seeing them now?"

The truth is, allergies were showing up. They just did not understand them at the time or recognize them as being allergic reactions. Kendra continues:

We used to giggle and think it was adorable that as a baby and young toddler, Molly would always stick a finger in her ear while she was eating.

We were searching everywhere for answers to why she continued to get horrendous diaper rashes, lasting months, even though we were buying expensive topical ointments and had changed our diaper brands countless times. We had tossed every soap and lotion out and purchased a slew of all-natural products. We were on the waiting list of specialists in the area.

We were consumed by our mission to piece together our puzzle of major motor-skill delay, extreme distractibility, obsessive compulsive behaviors, pain tolerance so high that she walked on a broken leg for almost two weeks before we knew it was broken…the list goes on. Little did we know then that removing the foods her body was recognizing and defending itself against would lead us to such an A-HA life moment.

In this, our first *Food For Thought* book, we introduce an abbreviated explanation of allergies, as this topic is the subject of much research and many books. If you wish to delve beyond what we address here, we encourage you to read *Is This Child Yours? Discovering and Treating Unrecognized Allergies in Children and Adults* by Doris Rapp, MD. Doris is one of the world's authoritative pioneers in allergy and environmental medicine. She is board certified in pediatrics, allergy and environmental medicine and a clinical assistant professor of pediatrics at the University of New York at Buffalo. (See the addendum for a partial list of her books, many of which have been on the *New York Times* best-seller list.)

Allergies are an immune response. The best battle tactics include:

- **Remove the cause for the immune response;** Either through testing or elimination remove the foods that are provoking an immune response.
- **Condition and train your army, your immune system troops:** Think of your immune system as the soldiers of your wellness. They really are there for your benefit, to protect you from internal harm. Give your army the tools it needs to prevail. Eat a diet rich in immune-supportive nutrients, as we have tried to give you with the recipes here. Do not blur your soldiers' and troops' vision with unnecessary chemicals and toxins.

Changing Molly's food changed our lives. She has come so far and improves every day. Her changes were so significant that they inspired me to start a business, Greater Tots Organization, and coauthor this cookbook. Is she perfect? Well, yes, she always was and always will be. Now, though, she's perfect *and* she's reaching goals we never thought possible. It is our mission to give as many families as we can the opportunity to reach their fullest health potential.

The truth is, we are raising a generation that is not as immunologically strong as generations past. That is why it is vital to make health-giving nutritional choices that not only support but build up the immune system. Food allergies and environmental pollution intolerances are extremely common. It is vital to know what your individual system is responding to and to remove those food items or environmental toxins that are damaging your immune system and damaging those soldiers and troops who could be using their energy to fight off more important attackers.

Let's take a look at the top most common culprits, the Great 8 Food Allergies. We will focus on what to look for and substitutes or exchanges.

MILK SOURCES

What to look for:

Artificial butter flavor, butterfat, butter oil

Butter

Buttermilk

Casein

Caseinates (ammonium, calcium, magnesium, potassium, sodium)

Cheese

Cream

Cottage cheese

Cream cheese

Curds

Custards

Ghee

Half and half

Hydrolysates (casein, milk, protein, whey, whey protein)

Lactalbumin

Lactalbumin phosphate

Lactoglobulin

Lactose

Lactulose

Goat's milk

Milk (powder, protein, solids, malted, evaporated, dry, low-fat, nonfat, skim)

Nougat

Puddings

Sour cream

Whey

Yogurt

A "D" on a label next to K, or U, means the presence of milk protein

Other Sources to Look Out For: Natural flavoring, caramel, Bavarian cream, coconut cream, brown sugar, butter, chocolate, lunch meat, dressings, hot dogs, sausages, margarine, high-protein flours, candy, baking mixes (even gluten-free ones), especially pancake or biscuit mixes. Mixes of rice and cheeses must say vegan. Watch out for whipped cream, cookies, crackers, breads, and any baked goods, sherbets (even when the box says 100 percent fruit, check the labels).

DAIRY SUBSTITUTES

Buy the unsweetened versions and sweeten on your own, naturally—or not at all.

Any nondairy milk can be substituted in equal portions. Some varieties have a thicker consistency and others are more watery. You may want to adapt to your own liking. Almost all grocery stores now carry great-tasting alternatives to cow's milk and casein-containing dairy products. Humans are the only animals that drink another animal's milk. Here are the most popular:

MILK

Almond Milk: Delicious and nutritious (almonds are a Super-Food). Almond milk is a fantastic substitute because of its great nutritional benefits! Rich in protein, vitamin E, and magnesium.

Coconut Milk: Again, delicious and nutritious. It is a bit thicker than milk. When using in baking you may want to water it down. Coconuts have many nutritional benefits and may have anticarcinogenic, antimicrobial, antibacterial, and antiviral effects.

Soy Milk: This is probably the most common and readily available milk. However, we do not recommend simply removing cow's milk from the diet and replacing it with soy milk. Soy is being researched quite a bit lately. We now know that 80 percent of soy sources are genetically modified, so if soy milk is the only way you can go, please look for organic and try to rotate it in with other nondairy choices.

Hemp Milk: A high source of protein as well as omega-3 and omega-6 fatty acids, hemp milk is also a source of B12, which has been shown as a very promising supplement for those on the autism spectrum.

Hazelnut Milk: Hazelnuts are strongly anti-inflammatory and immuno-supportive and are a fantastic source of protein, fiber, and Vitamin E.

Rice Milk: Also very readily available, rice milk bakes well. It is thinner than milk.

Here are some good substitutes for other dairy products:

BUTTER

Earth Balance Buttery Spread

Oils (See oil section for cooking and/or baking suggestions)

Organic Valley or Horizon are real butters for those who don't have dairy allergies.

CHEESE

Rice vegan slices, blocks and Parmesan topping (Parmesan contains soy)

Daiya Shreds (in Cheddar and mozzarella)

CREAM

So Delicious Coconut Creamer

MimicCreme Coffee creamer and crème

SoyaToo whipped cream substitutes (in soy or rice base)

WHEAT SOURCES

What to look for:

Bran

Breadcrumbs

Bulgur

Cereal extract

Couscous

Crackers

Cracker meal

Durum, durum wheat, durum flour

Enriched flour

Farina

Gluten

Graham flour

High-gluten flour

High-protein flour

Seitan

Semolina

Soft wheat flour

Spelt

Vital gluten

Wheat (bran, germ, gluten, malt, starch)

Whole wheat berries

Whole wheat flour

Could also be present in: gelatinized starch, hydrolyzed vegetable protein, modified food starch, modified starch, natural flavoring, soy sauce, starch, vegetable gum, vegetable starch

Other Sources to Look Out For:

Baked goods, pastas, donuts, breads, bagels, crackers, baking mixes, spices, extracts, sauces, soy sauce, salad dressings, supplements (multivitamins, etc.).

BUILD YOUR OWN GLUTEN-FREE FLOUR

Use each measure shown below per part (column A, B, and C) to make a **Basic All-Purpose (GF) Gluten-Free Flour Blend**. Mix 2 parts from column A with 1 part from column B and 1 part from column C

Basic All-Purpose GF Flour Blend Portion Guideline		
A (2 parts)	B (1 part)	C (1 part)
brown rice flour	sorghum flour	arrowroot powder
almond flour	sweet potato flour	potato starch
white rice flour	garbanzo bean (chickpea) flour	tapioca flour
buckwheat flour	fava bean flour	teff (not good for baking)
Montina	**quinoa flour**	kodzu root (mix portion)
	GF oat flour	**quinoa flour**
	garfava flour	corn starch
	chestnut flour	
	potato flour	
	coconut flour	
	corn flour (masa)	

You can also combine flours from a single column to equal your serving from that column. For example; Column A flour combinations can be a combination—1 cup of white rice flour (A) *or* ½ cup brown rice flour (A) + ½ cup almond flour (A) = A column measurement.

Portion	Formula	Example
A	2 parts	2 cups rice flour
B	1 part	1 cup quinoa flour
C	1 part	1 cup arrowroot powder

Try different combinations until you find a flour flavor that your family enjoys.

Use in smaller quantities some of the following for added flavor or nutrition (not more than ¼ of your mix):

- Amaranth flour—a complete protein, add in small quantities to mixes or recipes
- Teff flour—high in iron and fiber
- Mesquite pod flour—high in fiber, contains no fat, is naturally sweet
- Hemp flour—very high in fiber, a complete protein and source of omega-3s and omega-6s
- Salba—omega-3s, fiber, antioxidants
- Cassava meal (also called manioc flour)—may be purchased at Latin American-Caribbean Specialty Foods and Spices, 408-375-5850.

KENDRA'S FLOUR POWER

I tested many combinations of flours and this is my favorite combination of taste, texture, and nutritional value. I call it Flour Power because of its nutritional advantages over traditional wheat flour.

2 parts brown rice flour

2 parts almond flour

1 part each amaranth, arrowroot, tapioca

More Flour Mixtures		
Flour	**Yield**	**Recipe**
Blanched Almond Flour	1 cup	1 cup blanched and ground almonds
Simply Rice Flour	1 cup	1 cup brown rice flour
Rice Flour Mix	2 cups	1 cup brown rice flour 1 cup white rice flour
General Baking Mix #1 Carol Feinster, cookbook author	2 cups	1 cup rice flour ½–¾ cup potato starch ¼ cup tapioca starch/flour
General Baking Mix #2 Carol Feinster	9 cups	3 cups garfava bean flour 2 cups potato starch 2 cups cornstarch 1 cup tapioca flour 1 cup sorghum flour
Original Formula Bette Hagman, cookbook author	3 cups	2 cups rice flour 2/3 cup potato starch 1/3 cup tapioca starch/flour
Four Flour Bean Bette Hagman	3 cups	2/3 cup garfava bean flour 1/3 cup sorghum flour 1 cup cornstarch 1 cup tapioca starch/flour

Special Purpose Flour Mixes		
Special Mix	**Yield**	**Recipe**
Pastry mix Mary Schluckebier, home economist	1 cup	1/8 cup potato flour 7/8 cup Ener-G Foods rice flour
Cookie mix Mary Schluckebier	2 cups	¼ cup chickpea flour 1¾ cup sorghum flour ¼ cup sweet rice flour
Bread mix Mary Schluckebier	2 cups	1 cup brown rice flour ½ cup potato starch ½ cup sweet rice flour 1 tablespoon unflavored gelatin
Featherlight Bette Hagman	3 cups	1 cup rice flour 1 cup cornstarch 1 cup tapioca starch/flour 1 tablespoon potato flour
Flour Power Kendra Jean Finestead	3 cups	1 cup brown rice flour ½ cup almond flour ½ cup amaranth flour ½ cup tapioca flour ½ tablespoon arrowroot flour

EGGS

What to look for:

Albumin

Apovitellin

Cholesterol free egg substitute (e.g., Eggbeaters)

Dried egg solids, dried egg

Egg, egg white, egg yolk

Egg wash

Eggnog

Fat substitutes

Globulin

Livetin

Lysozyme

Mayonnaise

Meringue, meringue powder

Ovalbumin

Ovoglobulin

Ovomucin

Ovomucoid

Ovotransferrin

Ovovitelia

Ovovitellin

Powdered eggs

Silici albuminate

Simplesse

Trailblazer

Vitellin

Whole egg

MAY ALSO BE PRESENT IN: Artificial flavoring, lecithin, and natural flavoring. Nougat is also used as a binder in vaccines and other medications. Be sure to ask your pediatrician to see the insert in your vaccines or even flu shots and check the list carefully for all of the names listed above.

SUBSTITUTIONS

Baking Powder and Baking Soda (Mostly for Leavening):

1 egg = 1½ tablespoons baking powder + 1½ tablespoons warm water + 1½ tablespoons oil

1 egg = 1½ tablespoons baking powder + 1 tablespoon warm water + 1 tablespoon apple cider vinegar

1 egg = 2 teaspoons baking soda + 2 tablespoons warm water

1 egg = 2 teaspoons baking soda + 2 tablespoons warm water + ½ teaspoon oil

1 egg = 1 teaspoon baking powder + 1 teaspoon vinegar

Fruit (Mostly Binding and Moisture):

1 egg = ¼ cup applesauce or pureed fruit

1 egg = ¼ cup pumpkin purée or squash purée

1 egg = ¼ cup apricot or prune purée

1 egg = ½ mashed banana

1 egg = ½ mashed banana + ¼ teaspoon baking powder (leavening)

Nuts and Seeds:

1 egg = 3 tablespoons nut butter

1 egg = 1 tablespoon ground flax seed + 3 tablespoons hot water (let stand 10 minutes)

1 egg = 3 tablespoons ground flaxseed + 1/8 teaspoon baking powder + 3 tablespoons water (let stand 10 minutes, leavening)

1 egg = 1 teaspoon psyllium seed husk + ¼ cup water (let stand 5 minutes, binding and moisture)

Soy:

1 egg = 1½ tablespoons lecithin granules + 1½ tablespoons water + 1 teaspoon baking powder (leavening)

1 egg = ¼ cup silken tofu (binding and moisture)

Starches:

1 egg = 2 tablespoons arrowroot + 1 tablespoon water (binding and moisture)

1 egg = 2 tablespoons corn starch + 1 tablespoon water (binding and moisture)

1 egg = 2 tablespoons potato starch + 1 tablespoon water (binding and moisture)

1 egg = 1½ teaspoon Ener-G Egg Replacer + 2 tablespoons warm water (leavening)

Other:

1 egg = 1 teaspoon yeast dissolved in ¼ cup warm water (leavening)

1 egg = 3 tablespoons vegetable oil + 1 tablespoon water (binding and moisture)

1 egg = 3 tablespoons vegan mayonnaise (binding and moisture)

1 egg = 3 tablespoons mashed beans (binding and moisture)

1 egg = 3 tablespoons mashed potatoes (binding and moisture)

Egg White Substitutions:

1 egg white = ¼ teaspoon xanthan gum + ¼ cup water (let stand 5 minutes, then whip)

Egg Yolk Substitutions:

1 egg = 1½ tablespoons lecithin granules + 2 teaspoons water

SOY SOURCES

What to look for:

Bulking agent

Carob

Hydrolyzed vegetable protein (HVP)/ Hydrolyzed soy protein

Lecithin

Artificial and natural flavoring

Bulking agent

Miso*

Monosodium glutamate (MSG)

Protein

Starch

Textured vegetable protein (TVP)

Vegetable broth/gum/starch

*Miso is a paste made from fermented soybeans used as a flavoring agent in Japanese cuisine.

Soy Lecithin: Soy lecithin is an additive derived from the oil of soybeans. Since most allergic reactions are to the actual protein, some people with soy allergies can tolerate soy lecithin. If you or your child has anaphylaxis reactions, steer clear of soy lecithin. Otherwise, use at your discretion. It will definitely be the toughest soy ingredient to avoid, as it is used as an emulsifying agent in many, many products.

Much of soy is also genetically modified (GMO), so it is important if you can or are choosing to eat soy products, you look for non-GMO or (IP) identity preserved by which suppliers guarantee that their products are GMO-free.

Sources:

Soy sauces

Asian foods

Vegetable gums and starches

Broths

Dressings

Frozen meals

Fried snack foods, like potato or corn chips can be fried in soybean oil

Anything emulsified, including nonstick cooking sprays

FISH AND SHELLFISH

- If you have a seafood allergy, avoid seafood restaurants. Even if you don't order seafood, it is safer to always assume that *cross contact* is possible.
- Asian restaurants often serve dishes that use fish sauce as a flavoring base. Exercise caution or avoid eating there altogether.
- Shellfish protein can become airborne in the steam released during cooking and may be a risk. Stay away from cooking areas.

What to look for:

Shellfish
Barnacle
Crab
Crawfish
Krill
Lobster
Prawns
Shrimp

Mollusks
Abalone
Clams
Cockle
Cuttlefish
Limpet
Mussels
Octopus (Calamari)
Oysters
Periwinkle
Scallops
Snails
Squid

Fish
Anchovy
Bass
Bluefish
Carp
Catfish (channel cat, mudcat)
Cod
Eel
Flounder
Grouper
Haddock
Hake

Halibut
Herring
Mackerel
Mahi-Mahi
Marlin
Monkfish (angler fish, lotte)
Orange roughy
Perch
Pickerel (dore, walleye)
Pike
Pollock
Rockfish
Salmon
Sardines
Shark
Smelt
Snapper
Sole
Sturgeon
Swordfish
Tilapia (St. Peter's Fish)
Trout
Tuna (albacore, bonito)
White fish

Can also be found in:

Caviar, surimi (imitation crab made from white fish), aar, alginic acid Alginate (paired with ammonium, calcium, potassium, propylene glycol, sodium) Disodium ionsinate, fish/shellfish flavoring. Fish sauce (used inThai and Vietnamese cooking) fish gelatin, fish oil (like omega-3 supplements, or foods with omega-3s added)

Shellfish can be found in: bouillabaisse, fish sticks, fish sauce, glucosamine, seafood flavorings or extracts, Surimi. Also watch for Worcestershire, imitation fish, barbecue or teriyaki sauces, and salad dressings, like Caesar. In addition, fish oil. (See section on oils for suggestions on fish-free options for getting your essential fatty acids.)

PEANUTS AND TREE NUTS

Peanuts are dangerous and have gotten a lot of hype and the most attention in schools due to the airborne effect of the peanut's protein. A peanut allergy can also be very severe.

What to look for:

- Artificial nuts, beer nuts, ground nuts, mixed nuts, monkey nuts
- Cold-pressed, expelled, or extruded peanut oil or arachis oil
- Goobers. mandelonas, peanuts, peanut butter, peanut flour
- Thai foods such as Pad Thai or Satay
- Chinese foods often use peanuts as an ingredient or fry in peanut oil. Egg rolls are often "glued" together with peanut butter
- African foods, Indonesian foods, Vietnamese foods
- Chili sometimes has peanut butter in it as a thickener
- Muesli and breakfast bars or energy bars
- Enchilada sauce
- Sweets such as marzipan, nougat, ice cream, and chocolate
- Food additive 322
- Natural flavoring

Avoid the following nuts: Almonds brazil nuts, cashews, chestnuts, hazelnuts (sometimes called filberts), Hickory nuts, macadamia nuts, pecans, pine nuts, pistachios, walnut.

Can be found in: Marzipan/almond paste, nougat, Artificial nuts

- Nut butters (such as cashew butter and almond butter)
- Nut oil (both edible and in lotions, shampoos, etc.)
- Nut extracts (such as almond extract)
- Nut milks (almond milk)
- Pesto
- "Creamy" vegan soups (often made with almonds)
- MimicCreme (referred to in some of the recipes in this book)

COCONUTS: Coconuts are considered a tree nut according to the FDA for labeling guidelines, although many manufacturers will list coconut specifically instead of labeling it as such. Use at your discretion, but according to the FAAN, there is no correlation between coconut and tree nuts, and they rarely go hand-in-hand. (View specifics at www.foodallergy.org.)

Nutmeg is not considered a nut for allergy reasons.

FOOD SENSITIVITIES AND ALLERGIES TO CORN

Corn is *not* on the Great 8 list, but it needs to be addressed. First, it is a common allergy and becoming more so. That may be because it is becoming such a genetically modified crop and our bodies are having a hard time deciphering if it is actually corn.

Second, even if you do not have a corn allergy, corn is a starch, and a sugary starch at that. Corn should definitely be limited in your diet for optimal results. Also, pay close attention to the sources of your corn. Much corn is now genetically modified (GMO).

Corn is tricky as an allergen because it is used in so many capacities as a food additive. Like citric acid, for example. It is not always derived from corn, but it often is. Same with xanthan gum, a popular ingredient used in GFCF cooking. It is derived from corn. Corn is also found in some baking powders as well as powdered sugar.

Here is the long list of foods and other items that may contain corn:

Adhesives (envelopes, labels, stickers, tapes, stamps)
Any products that contain cornmeal, corn flour, corn oil, cornstarch, corn sugar, corn syrup, or sorbitol.

Aspirin
Bacon
Baking powder (most)
Bath or body powder
Beer, ale, gin, whisky
Biscuits
Bisquick
Breads (commercial)
Brown sugar
Cake, pancake, and pie mixes
Candied fruit
Candy
Canned fruits (sweetened)
Canned or bottled juice drinks
Capsules
Carob (CaraCoa)
Cereals (presweetened)
Coffee (instant)
Coffee Rich
Confectioner's sugar
Cookies
Corn kernels
Corn cereal
Corn chips
Cornmeal
Corn oil and anything fried in it
Cornstarch
Corn sugar
Corn syrup
Cottage cheese (thickened)

The Great 8 Food Allergies

Cranberry juice (some)
Custards
Doughnuts
Dried fruits (sweetened)
Fritos
Frostings
Frozen fruits (sweetened)
Fruit desserts
Graham crackers
Gravies
Ham (cured)
Hominy
Hot dogs
Ice cream
Infant formulas (Enfamil, Similac, Advance, Portagen, Lofenalac, Isomil, Prosobee, Nursoy
Powder [not liquid], Soyalac [not I-Soyalac], Pedialyte, Hydrolyzed casein, Nutramigen, Progestimil)
Jellies and gelatin mixes
Luncheon meats
Maize
Milk in paper containers
Monosodium glutamate (MSG)
Ointments
Oleomargarine
Orange juice (some frozen or sweetened)
Paper cups, cartons, plates and any liquids contained in them
Peanut butter
Pie fillings
Plastic food wrappers (some)
Popcorn
Puddings
Sandwich spreads
Sauces that have been thickened (like some Chinese sauces)
Sausages
Sherbet
Sticky portion of envelopes and stamps
Sorbitol
Succotash
Suppositories
Tablets (most medicinal)
Tea (instant)
Toothpastes/powders
Vitamins (some)
Yogurt (thickened or sweetened)
Zest soap
(www.adrenalfatigue.org)

Xanthan Gum and Guar Gum

Xanthan gum or guar gum: with a few exceptions, most alternative flour mixes will have a much better taste and texture (and overall probability of success) with the help of one of these two gums, because they help with the leavening that doesn't happen so easily when the protein from the gluten is not present. Other flours do not rise like gluten flour does. Xanthan gum is corn based, so those with corn sensitivities should opt for guar (pronounced "gwar"). With either, a little goes a long way, so measure very carefully.

General Tips for Using Xanthan Gum and Guar Gum in Gluten-Free Cooking:

Bread and pizza dough recipes: 1 teaspoon per cup of gluten-free flour

Cake, muffin, and quick bread recipes: ½ teaspoon xanthan per cup of gluten-free flour

Cookie and bar recipes: ¼ teaspoon per one cup gluten-free flour

I have found that since I have been baking more with almond flour and Kendra's Flour Power, little or no xanthan gum is needed. I try to leave the gums out unless necessary.

FOOD SENSITIVITIES AND ALLERGIES TO SUGAR

In the previous section "Food Myths and Logical Solutions," we mentioned the importance of removing sugar. This bears repeating. It is extremely important to pay close attention to the sugar that your family is consuming

Sugar as We Know It: White sugar is acidic. Sugar is no better than high-fructose corn syrup, as it is just as processed. It is a version of sugar that is concentrated fructose and sucrose. White sugar is *not* a natural sweetener.

Sugar and Cancer: In chapter 4 of *The Kinder, Gentler Cancer Treatment*, Richard Linchetz, MD, explains that "Cancer cells, like most cells, require glucose to derive energy. However, cancer cells…require much more sugar than normal cells just to survive. If they are to maintain their rapid growth pattern, they need that much more sugar. All cells take in sugar through a mechanism that can be conceptualized as a "lock and key" system, where insulin is the key and an insulin receptor is the lock. It turns out that cancer cells have many more "doors" with these "locks and keys" than normal cells. This is understandable because any cancer cell without a mechanism for concentrating sugar will not survive. Only those cells with high concentrations of these receptors will be able to rapidly divide and develop into cancerous tumors. If we think about this process carefully, does it tell us anything about the way we should eat? Of course we should limit (or preferably eliminate) our sugar intake and our intake of anything else that will cause a significant rise in our blood sugar (especially refined carbohydrates, but even sweet fruits and grains can be a problem in some patients).

Sugar and Yeast: Sugar is the main life-source and breeder for yeast. The fact is that many times, disease is congruent with an abnormal shift in the gut bacteria, causing there to be a greater amount of "bad" bacteria than "good" bacteria. This is called dysbiosis. It can also be referred to as yeast-overgrowth.

Dysbiosis can happen for a number of reasons, but whether the cause is excessive exposure to antibiotics, deficiencies in enzymes, or a genetic weakness in your gut lining to protect as it should, the dysbiosis means that there is an overgrowth of "bad" bacteria, like Candida. In researching a number of sites regarding yeast overgrowth, the consensus was that an average approximation of 70 percent of people actually have yeast overgrowth. Why is yeast overgrowth so prevalent?

To answer that question, let's ask, "What do these living micro-organisms eat to get their strength to invade 70 percent of the human race?" The answer is sugar. Sugar, in all of its forms: sugar, honey, syrup, even carrots, fruits, etc. If you think about it, that makes perfect sense. Have you ever tried to eat at a picnic or outdoor barbecue. Those sweet treats attract ants and other pesky bugs quicker than anything!

To get a fairly clear visual of sugar's effect with yeast, perform this simple experiment. Take two bowls or cups. *Fill each with 1 teaspoon of baker□s yeast and fill each with ½ cup of hot water. Add 1 teaspoon of sugar to one of the cups. Watch how much more the cup with the sugar ferments and grows than the cup without any sugar added.*

This is a very simple display, though we all know that most of us consume far more than 1 teaspoon of sugar on a daily basis.

For children on the autism spectrum, this is extremely important to consider due to their vulnerability systemically to this infectious imbalance in gut flora. In a report filed on Pub Med by the *Division of Allergy/Immunology and Infection Diseases, Department of Pediatrics, University of Medicine and Dentistry of New Jersey (UMDNJ)-New Jersey Medical School (NJMS), studies involving children on the Autism Spectrum "indicate dys-regulated innate immune defense in the ASD/Inf+GI children, rendering them more vulnerable to common microbial infection/dysbiosis and possibly subsequent behavioral changes."*

Behaviors that have been associated with yeast overgrowth:

Brain fog

Hyperactivity

Short attention span

Lethargy

Irritability

Aggression

Stomach aches

Headaches

Loss of verbalization

How many grams of sugar you have you eaten today? Moreover, more importantly, how many grams of sugar has your child on a GFCF diet eaten today?

2 Enjoy Life Chocolate Chip Cookies = 12 grams of sugar (or 3 teaspoons)

1 Cup Almond Breeze Original = 7 grams of sugar (or 1.75 teaspoons)

2 Van's Waffles with 2 tablespoons maple syrup = 37 grams of sugar (or 9.25 teaspoons)

These are all technically gluten-free and casein-free options, but if you are still seeing patterns of behavior that match any of the above symptoms of yeast overgrowth, you could be feeding the beast you are working so hard to fight against. If there is yeast present in your child's gut, can you imagine adding 9.25 of those teaspoons to the "bowl"?

Beverages can add lots of sugar to a daily routine. Instead of juices, try making or purchasing unsweetened nut, coconut, or hemp milks and sweeten with Stevia or a small amount of coconut nectar. If you don't want to remove fruits, avoid giving them to your child at the same time as a starch; instead, let them eat fruits by themselves. Starving the yeast will help you get control of the intestinal flora and allow you to heal the leaky gut that is most likely present. When neurotoxins are not escaping into the bloodstream, those related behaviors will diminish.

(See article called "Sugar, Sugar Honey, Honey" on www.autismspot.com.)

Natural Sugars: The only natural sugars are fruits, raw honey, and Stevia. In most of the recipes you will find in this book, we have given alternatives to the sugar source, providing you with a choice for your personal taste. Maple syrup, agave nectar, brown rice syrup, coconut nectar, or coconut sugar; although these are from natural sources, they still undergo varying processes to get them to the state in which we consume them.

If you want the purest and rawest selections, you will want to substitute these sweeteners with raw honey, fruit, or Stevia.

If following the principals of proper food combining, these sweeteners, too, are not suggested in combination with starches or proteins.

If you are battling cancer or yeast overgrowth, it is suggested to avoid all sugars, natural or otherwise, including limiting your starches, as starch turns to sugar in the body. The only exception to this seems to be Stevia. Try NutraMedix Stevia, or we also use the flavored Stevia drops from SweetLeaf.

It is important to inform yourself on all of your options and make choices based on your own individual body, as well as what fits into your own individual lifestyle.

ALLERGENS AND TOXINS BEYOND OUR FOOD

While the scope of our cookbook does not address allergens and toxins beyond food in detail, it is important to check other household products for potential allergens and toxins. Get in the habit of reading labels.

- Soaps
- Lotions
- Shampoos
- Deodorants
- Hairsprays
- Makeup
- Sunscreen
- Insect Repellants
- Cleaning Products
- WATER: Filter your water. You can install an at-home system like those found at www.ecowater.com or www.berkeyfilters.com.

There are many natural products on the market, and they are becoming easier to find as consumers become more enlightened. We encourage you to consider natural alternatives for healthier living.

- The major "bad" ingredients in lotions to avoid include:
- Sodium lauryl sulfate
- Methylparaben
- Propylparaben
- Propylene glycol
- Isopropyl alcohol
- Isopropyl myristate
- Hydrolyzed wheat proteins (for wheat allergy and high gluten sensitivities)

SUPPORT YOUR IMMUNE SYSTEM TROOPS!

The key to recuperating and maintaining your overall health is to create and maintain a healthy immune system, our little troops that have been given the great mission of protecting our bodies. The soldiers of our immune system go to war for us every day.

Imagine for a moment that your soldiers are going out onto a battlefield. How well will those soldiers fight if they are malnourished, disoriented, and fighting through a cloud of fog? This is what inflammation causes for the fighters of our immune systems.

Reducing our intake of inflammatory foods and eating a large majority and variety of anti-inflammatory foods ensures that our body gets the perfect balance needed for wellness and the perfect environment for our soldiers to do what they do best.

Anti-Inflammatory Foods = Immuno-Supportive Foods

Keep your inflammatory food intake at or below 20 percent.

AIM FOR 80

Baked goods
Sugars
Fried foods
Animal proteins
Fast food
Caffeine
Table salt
(Use sea salt)

80 percent anti-inflammatory food *intake.*

Bell peppers
Broccoli
Broccoli sprouts
Cabbage
Cauliflower
Fennel bulb
Garlic
Green beans
Greens
Kale, chard, collards
Leeks
Spinach
Sweet potatoes
Almonds
Flaxseed
Hazelnuts
Pumpkin seeds
Sunflower seeds
Walnuts

Spices like turmeric cumin, cayenne, oregano, parsley, rosemary, licorice

Wild caught fish
Green tea
High-quality (cold-pressed or expeller-pressed and unrefined oils)
Apples
Avocado, blueberries & pineapple, kiwi, lemons and limes
Oranges
Raspberries
Rhubarb
Strawberries
Tomatoes

A recent article in *Discover* magazine pointed out the importance of our immune system troops. At Duke University Medical Center, Susan LaTuga is one of several medical researchers working with microbial ecologists to study the development of the human microbiome—the enormous population of microbes, including bacteria, fungi, and viruses, that live in the human body, predominantly in the gut.

The Trillions of Microbes That Call Us Home—and Help Keep Us Healthy

The human body is a habitat for a huge range of harmless and beneficial microbes, which may be the key to fighting disease without antibiotics.

Your Microbial Menagerie

There are twenty times as many of these microbes as there are cells in the body, up to 200 trillion in an adult. Our skin hosts at least one thousand different species, with more than a million microbes per square centimeter. The largest collection, weighing as much as four pounds in total, clings to your gut. Seen through the prism of the microbiome, a person is not so much an individual human body but a super organism made up of diverse ecosystems, each teeming with troops of microscopic creatures that are essential to our well-being.

Two of the largest human microbiome studies include the Human Microbiome Project, funded by the National Institutes of Health and the European Union's Metagenomics of the Human Intestinal Tract. It is already clear that the microbiome is much more complex and very likely more critical to human health than anyone suspected.

They are discovering that the human body is a complex balance of microbial communities that are interdependent upon each other and their host body. Each one thrives only if all the others do. They work together and help the body as well by priming our immune system, keeping out malevolent pathogens and increasing the efficiency of many of our own biological processes. Understanding and controlling the diversity of our germs, as opposed to assaulting them with antibiotics, could be the key to a range of future medical treatments.

It is the hope of such studies to discover medical treatments that do not involve the overpowering assault of antibiotics, which destroy the good with the bad. Researcher Segre says. "It's remarkable how Americans are so focused on sterilizing our exterior using antimicrobial products. Bugs throughout the body keep us healthy. We need to lose some of that language of warfare." Moreover, of course, we need to take good care of and support our immune system troops.

For more information on our microbial kingdoms and how they support our immune system, you can read the full article, "The Trillions of Microbes That Call Us Home—and Help Keep Us Healthy," by Michael Tennesen, in the March 2011 issue of *Discover* magazine (http://discovermagazine.com/2011/mar/04-trillions-microbes-call-us-home-help-keep-healthy).

THE EAT FREE OATH

Place your right heart over your mouth and repeat after me:

I

[State your name]

Okay, how many of you said the actual words "state your name"?

Now be serious!

I

[State your name]

Hereby pledge the oath of Eating FREEly.

I will remove any foods that don't agree with my body

I will give my body the food it needs, not give my brain the food it wants

I will remove toxins and poisons from my diet

I will limit the inflammatory foods and eat more anti-inflammatory food choices

(or I will limit the "bad guy foods" and chose more "good guy foods.")

I will try something new that I have never tried before

I will have fun with my food

I will have fun with my food

I will have FUN with my food

I

will

FREE my FOOD!

And now, you are ready to begin!

CHAPTER 6

Natures Food Pyramid: Eating Freely

FAMILIES SHARE THEIR THOUGHTS ABOUT FOOD, THEIR CHALLENGES, AND SUCCESSES

NATURE'S FOOD PYRAMID AND EATING FREELY STORIES

Ginger P.: About Her 15-Year-Old Son

My 15 year-old son experienced constipation, joint pain, muscle aches and weakness, mood disorder, headaches, stomachaches, lethargy, acne, Candida.

We went to Dr. K, and he put him on a gluten-free, dairy-free, casein-free diet. He told us to eat an all-natural non-GMO diet with lots of raw fruits and veggies. Lean meats and proteins, no aspartame or artificial sweeteners, no high-fructose corn syrup. We did allergy testing and then removed beef, milk, sugar, pecans, carrots, eggs, soy, red grapes, asparagus, seafood, and sesame seeds.

We started seeing small changes pretty early in the treatment, but the big changes came about six months into it. My son was eating high-fiber, raw foods, fresh fruits, vegetables, non-GMO foods, organic everything. After about six months, his thinking was clearer, his bowels were beginning to normalize, and for the first time in his life he was having a bowel movement every day!

Our biggest change was to stop eating out. We started cooking every meal, buying everything at the farmer's market or local farms and The Sunflower Shoppe. It was very expensive, but when you deduct the amount we were spending at restaurants before, it pretty much balanced out. Getting off sugar was *very* hard, but it was so worth it!

I learned a lot from the website Karina's Kitchen (www.glutenfreegoddess.blogspot.com). I learned to make a "happy flax egg" out of flax seed that would mimic an egg in recipes. It worked better than the egg replacer sold in stores. Another publication that is invaluable to me is the magazine *Living Without.* I have made lots of recipes from it, and they are all great! They also have great ideas, stories, and products that I had never heard of that ended up being life savers for me.

Finally, after Dr. K told us what our son should not eat, I was almost in tears. Allison came in, took me by the hand, and with her caring words and sweet smile said, "You can do this, and I will help you!" I e-mailed her *lots* of ridiculous questions over the course of that year, and she answered them all and never made me feel like a moron. I love all of Dr. K's staff and Dr. K himself.

He definitely saved our child's life!

I only wish that we would have known about Dr. K when our son was young, because we were not able to start treatment until he was 15 years old. We definitely recommend Dr. K to anyone who is in need of better health. He addresses the mind and body and treats it as a whole, not just the parts that are sick.

We will be patients for life!

Jessie H.: About Four-Year-Old Abigail

Abigail is our beautiful, blue-eyed, blonde, curly-haired daughter. She is four years old and is on the autism spectrum. She participated in early childhood intervention and has blossomed. She is currently attending a private school and continues to progress. We are so proud and we love her so much!

In my encounters with other parents who have children on the spectrum, I continued to hear about this GFCF diet. More and more I heard about it and I decided to research it to see if my daughter would benefit. I read a lot of books on the diet and how it helps many children. I have a close family member who tried it with her son and witnessed progress, so I decided to accept the challenge.

My first experience in a health food store was not a pleasant one. When I walked in I was overwhelmed with all the different brands and departments. I asked someone to help me find some foods that were gluten-free and casein-free and they looked at me clueless. I spent an hour studying labels, and I walked out of the store with nothing in my basket. I was overwhelmed. My goal was to research companies that catered GFCF meals at home, and I discovered Kendra from Greater Tots in Dallas, Texas.

Unfortunately, Kendra's company only caters within her state. However I wrote to her and she called me, devoted to help me and Abigail. I was stressed out because I didn't know where or how to start.

My second concern was that Abby was a very picky eater, and I was afraid that she would go on a hunger strike and not eat a thing. Kendra listened to me and was very understanding and supportive. She knew exactly what I had been going through, and she lent an experienced helping hand.

Kendra suggested that I start by eliminating dairy first and then start replacing foods with gluten-free substitutes. She informed me that the transition would be a lot easier for Abby. She offered to give me a list of foods with the brand name to save me the time-consuming hassle of label reading. She went beyond the call of duty to help me get started with no financial incentive; she cares.

The next day I went back to the health food store and was able to select exactly what I needed. I was stress free. I went home and prepared Abby's meal. I was nervous that my little girl would not even try it. Well, she did and loved it! Kendra gave me all the tools and ideas that I needed to start Abby on this journey. It has only been a couple of weeks, but I have seen great improvements. She is a lot happier enjoying life with fewer tantrums. She is starting to explore different foods too!

I am a mother with a lot of faith and hope in my heart. I have a lot of support from my family, especially my wonderful husband, who stands with me whenever I need him. I would like to thank Kendra for her special interest in helping Abigail. Kendra's time and experience to selflessly assist our family has been a blessed opportunity and we will forever be grateful.

Glenn W.: About His Own Success

I am a 52-year-old man who has had numerous food allergies for many years. It has been quite a struggle to find meals and snacks that I can tolerate. Food has never been something to enjoy, just a necessity. With every holiday or family get-together there is food involved. I was never able to participate in the meals or snacks brought to these functions. It is a difficult thing to sit and watch everyone else eating these yummy things.

Something else that is difficult for me is to go grocery shopping. Imagine going down aisle after aisle and finding very few things that I can eat without having stomach problems. When I heard of Greater Tots from a coworker, I was skeptical. I checked out their website and then met with Kendra. I was amazed that she actually understood the struggles I have with food. She took the information I gave her and came up with a menu just for me that excluded all of the items that irritated my system. I now have a list of meals, which by the way are delicious, that she can prepare for me. I like to order weekly so I can always have meals on hand.

Greater Tots saves me time and money and an added benefit is that I am gaining weight and have more energy to face the day!

Tracy S.: About Eight-Year-Old Tracy

I choose to use Greater Tots to provide my eight-year-old daughter's meals for several reasons. First off, I am a single mom of two girls (eight and five). I work full time and my youngest daughter has special needs. My eight–year-old has a large variety of food sensitivities. It was extremely stressful, time-consuming, and costly to run around town trying to find gluten, casein, soy, egg, and dye-free items and come up with recipes that she would like. She has sensory issues, which also makes it very difficult to find foods that she will eat.

We began ordering breakfast, lunch, and snacks for five days a week to cover school days. This has worked out great for her (and me). My stress level has been reduced and it has become a great way for my daughter to be involved in choosing her food items. Kendra actually created a menu just for my daughter that had the food choices in picture form. This really got her excited and now she looks forward to getting her food each week and choosing what she will eat each day.

Greater Tots has been a great resource for my family, and I strongly recommend anyone that struggles with food allergies to utilize their service.

Marisol M.: About Daughter Jada

Health Challenges

Jada was having staring spells, waking up in the middle of the night almost every night either crying or laughing uncontrollably. She was only saying a few words, not really socializing with other children but engaging in parallel play. Jada was having many digestive issues—lots of constipation and sometimes diarrhea, not making good eye contact either.

Diet Recommendation

Dr. K recommended that we go gluten- and casein-free as well as limit carbs and sugar because of a suspected yeast overgrowth.

Improvements

About a week and a half after removing gluten, Jada went from saying a few words here and there to talking in full sentences. She became more social and started playing with other children. She also began sleeping through the night for the first time since birth. Everyone told us she seemed like a different kid. The most dramatic change happened a week and a half after removing the gluten, and the rest took a couple of weeks.

The biggest challenges with the diet were how much she was craving the carbs and starches because of the yeast. It was really hard to get her to eat fruits and veggies.

So I had to get creative!

I would say every mom doing this diet should have a really good blender (like a Vitamix), because I found that if I could blend anything up she would drink it. I also snuck veggies into things like gluten-free pancakes and muffins. Even into oatmeal and brown rice cereal. Once I started sneaking the veggies in while at the same time offering them in small amounts on her plate often, after a while I could give her whatever it was raw and she would eat it. We went from eating maybe one or two veggie choices to about six. I took recipes from www.pecanbread.com and I used the techniques for hiding veggies in food from the cookbook *The Sneaky Chef*. After a while, I kind of knew what I could sneak in and what I couldn't. I am very pleased to say that we all eat so much healthier now, and my seven-year-old son, who also did not like veggies and fruits very much, now eats many more choices of them.

Nicole and Greg C.: About Four-Year-Old Max

Dr. K recommended we put Max on a gluten/casein-free diet about four years ago. It was definitely an overwhelming thought at the time, but integrating it was not nearly as hard as I thought it would be. The diet has significantly improved Max's ability to focus and pay attention to things around him; he is much calmer as well, which makes everything easier to do on a daily basis.

The best advice I can think of for other parents is to remove gluten and casein one at a time. Start with the gluten first and do it gradually. It may take a while to find the gluten-free products that your child likes best, because there are lots to choose from now. Try as many as you need; some are better than others. Once you are completely off the gluten and observe how your child is doing, then remove the casein. Removing everything at once makes trying to find foods that they can eat impossible and then everyone is miserable. It makes you want to give up easily when you go cold turkey.

DON'T GIVE UP! Give the diet a reasonable length of time to implement and observe. This is several months, not weeks! Doing anything over the course of a week is not long enough to see any real results. You are trying to heal the body, and I think it's really worth the effort. I believe the majority of people will feel better on this diet; maybe not every person but the majority.

Eszter, Mark and Anna's Mom

When Mark got off dairy, we had 10 days of aggression and hostility—we did not recognize our own child. After that he started singing, chanting nursery rhymes, and being communicative at once! This was nothing short of a miracle.

As Mark had several food sensitivities, Dr. Kotsanis suggested the GAPS diet to us. GAPS is a form of SCD that uses a lot of probiotic food, and practically everything is home-cooked. Since we have gone on the GAPS diet, his condition has improved immensely. Mark is now:

- Truly bilingual, translating between languages
- Tells stories with 5-10 -word sentences in them
- Picking up information in the natural, unstructured way
- Having fun playing with his twin sister and loves family get-togethers
- Enjoys going to pre-school, where he is "one of the boys" by now
- Growing well physically; Mark is not scrawny or malnourished any more, but tall, strong and active. He has strength to learn and love. His life is not about survival anymore.

Mark's twin sister had food sensitivities as well, though not as severe. After Mark's success, it was easy to have Anna on GAPS too. Her eczema has disappeared completely. Additive- and preservative-free food tastes real good, so the transition was relatively easy the second time around. Or maybe my cooking got better by then!

Tips for Fellow Moms Who Want to Start GAPS

- Batch cooking is key if you do not want to spend endless hours in the kitchen.
- Involve your husband in the process. Have him be the master of the grill.
- Buy a really good knife and a larger freezer; you will need it!

It is comforting to know that I can prevent a whole array of difficulties right from our kitchen. It makes me feel like a superhero!

Jennifer B.: About Eight-Year-Old Reagan

Our autistic eight-year-old daughter, Reagan, has been on the GFCF diet for approximately a year and a half now.

We have noticed several changes in Reagan since she began this diet. She is calmer and has started talking more and more, which is so exciting to us as parents. She has even started to *answer* questions that are asked of her. The diet is challenging, but we would definitely recommend it to others.

A couple of suggestions we would offer to other parents who try the diet are:

1. If you know your child will be having snack time at school or church or will be attending a birthday party, etc., call ahead of time and find out what food will be served and then pack a similar GFCF substitute for your child.

2. Provide your child's grandparents/caregivers with a few GFCF snack items to keep on hand at their homes.

Five Children with Allergies

Food allergies? Our five kids have almost all of them! Gluten, casein, soy, beef, peanuts, eggs, artificial anythings! Our journey to being diagnosed with food allergies was a long, tiring one...I wish I had known about the effects that food allergies can have on a child's digestion, disposition, attention span. Our lives would have been different for our older kids. As it was, it was our fourth child that was first diagnosed with multiple food allergies, so I'll start our story with him!

I thought Max was a healthy, typically developing two-year-old. His quirky behavior and low language development seemed normal to me, because I compared him to his big brother, who did not speak at all until age four. Max used sign language, baby talk, and was so cute. He was even "graduated" from early intervention therapy. I thought everything was fine until he caught the rotavirus (a bad stomach virus), which hit him like a ton of bricks. He was sick for days with it, and when he finally got over it, his tummy aches and bowel movements never returned to normal. His little stomach was now huge; he literally looked like a poor starving African child—skinny little legs and arms, huge distended tummy, pale with dark circles under his eyes. His bowel movements were infrequent and exceptionally painful. We would both cry when he had a B.M.

I kept bringing him to our pediatrician, who thought he had parasites. We ran test after test, all negative. This went on for a year! I didn't know what to do. I knew something was wrong, but the doctor kept saying there was nothing wrong. I don't remember how I ran across Jenny McCarthy's book *Louder Than Words,* but I found it. I read her story about her son Evan and parts of it sounded like Max (and some of my older kids too). Dr. Kotsanis's name and number were listed in the back of her book, and I called right away to make an appointment for Max. We had to wait six weeks for our first appointment, and I knew he would most likely suggest we go dairy free, so I went ahead and weaned all the kids off dairy. They rebelled a little at first, but oh, my goodness.

After six weeks off dairy, I had a different batch of kids at home! Max had improved only just the tiniest bit, but my other kids were transformed—they were no longer puffy-pasty looking in their faces, and their dark circles were gone from under their eyes. I hadn't even considered that they had a milk allergy. Friends would literally pull me to the side and ask me what I had done to the kids (the girls especially) to make them so healthy and beautiful looking in the past month! Now I look at the "before" pictures of them, before we took them off dairy, and they look like little vampires, with their pale, slack, puffed faces with dark circles around their eyes. One of the most amazing benefits, though, was that their math scores went up so high, almost immediately. All of their schoolwork improved dramatically!

Back to Max—poor Max. We got him in to see Dr. K, who diagnosed him with multiple food allergies. It took about two months for Max to really respond to the dietary changes we made for him. He used to walk around with his hand in the peanut butter jar—now we found out he is very allergic to peanuts and was self-medicating with it! We pulled him off gluten, casein, soy, peanuts, beef, anything in a box, all artificial anythings, and fed him an organic (as possible) diet.

At first I started with just organic meats (chicken and buffalo), veggies, and GF/CS breads, and I added about one new recipe a week. I mixed up rice milk and almond milk for him. It was really fun and challenging. The food tastes so much better, and my kids have learned so much about nutrition and cooking. I even have a teenage daughter (with her own food-allergy diagnosis) who wants to go to cooking school in the next couple of years!

Max is transformed. His tummy is usually normal sized (sometimes his yeast will make it distend), his B.M.s are normal, and there is no more crying! He eats and eats now—he used to just pick at his food before (no wonder; his old diet was making him so sick)—and grew two inches the first year on his new diet. His speech is better, his schoolwork is improving, and he is very cheerful and fun! We have him on supplements too, to help him with his absorption of nutrients (as is my older son).

I wish I had known about food allergies back when my oldest son was younger. He was born in '93, back when all these quirky little boys were a relatively new phenomenon. He was a lot like Max—he had lots of food obsessions, only wanting to eat French fries (which I wouldn't give him). I fed him lots of healthy food, like beans and rice and eggs and milk, but he did not thrive. He had significant language issues and interventions, which did not help at all. I could literally write a book about our journey with him! But I'll skip up to age 13, when we changed his diet. He too became a patient of Dr. Kotsanis, who diagnosed him with multiple food allergies. When we changed his diet, his language greatly improved, his math skills went up, he started gaining weight and gaining muscle, and his overall health improved. Oh, I wish I had known about food allergies earlier in his life.

Bobby B.: Gluten-Free—An Amazing Process to Watch

Removing gluten from our daughter's diet was not easy, but it was like opening a window to the world for her. With each new treatment, it is as if we are pulling her out of that window and into society. It's been an amazing process to watch.

LET'S GET COOKING!

RECIPES

CHAPTER 7

Breads, Biscuits, Muffins, and More

Photo Recipes From Left: Island Breeze Muffins (One Topped with Shredded Coconut, One Topped with a Dried Pineapple Round), Nuts About Banana Muffins, Currantly Carrot Muffins, Cinna-Mini Apple Muffins (Topped With Granola).

BREADS, BISCUITS, MUFFINS, AND MORE

Bacon Cheddar Biscuits

Baked Doughnuts Without Eggs

Beverly's Pancakes

Cinna-Mini Apple Muffins

Cinnamon Walnut Coffee Cake

Chocolate Figgy Scones

Currantly Carrot Muffins

Egg-Less English Muffins

Focaccia Bread

For Oats O Haulin' Oats

Hazelnut French Toast Casserole

Island Breeze Muffins

Nuts About Bananas Muffins

Oatmeal's Qrazy Cousin Quinoa

Pistachio Pear Pancakes

Raisin Shine Zucchini Bread

Sammy-Which Bread (Yeast-Free)

Sweet Irish Soda Biscuits

Vanilla Bean Almond Pancakes

Wheat/Gluten-Free Tortillas

Wishful Waffles

Yummy Tummy Breadsticks

Bacon Cheddar Biscuits

Dry Ingredients:

2¼ cups Kendra's Flour Power

1 tablespoon aluminum-free baking powder

1 teaspoon sea salt

¼ teaspoon garlic powder

½ teaspoon Bragg's Sprinkles seasoning

1 tablespoon egg replacer

¼ teaspoon guar gum

Wet Ingredients:

1 cup almond or rice milk

1 teaspoon apple cider vinegar

¼ cup grapeseed oil

¼ cup carbonated water

2 tablespoons Vegenaise (made with grape-seed oil)

Use turkey bacon for a leaner and more nutritionally rich choice. These are a treat for any bread lover who thought they wouldn't be able to eat their favorite biscuits again!

For a nut free version, simply use Bob's Red Mill Gluten-Free Flour.

You can use Vegenaise Spectrum Organic Olive Oil Mayo (if eggs are tolerated) or non-dairy yogurt.

Miscellaneous:

1/3 cup Daiya Cheddar shreds

4–6 slices bacon, cooked and broken into pieces

Preheat oven to 400°F.

Whisk together the dry ingredients in a mixing bowl.

Stir all of the wet ingredients together in a separate bowl.

Incorporate the wet ingredients into the dry ingredients until thoroughly combined.

Fold in the Cheddar shreds and bacon pieces.

Spoon ¼ cup portions onto a lightly oiled or parchment-lined baking sheet.

Bake for 18 to 20 minutes until you have lightly golden brown biscuits.

Baked Doughnuts without Eggs

Wet Ingredients:

¼ cup coconut yogurt

½ cup apple juice concentrate (thawed)

½ cup pure maple syrup

½ cup applesauce

2/3 cup dried cane juice

3 tablespoons grapeseed oil

Dry Ingredients:

1 cup brown rice flour

½ cup potato starch

½ cup tapioca flour

2 teaspoons xanthan gum

1½ teaspoons baking soda

1 teaspoon gelatin powder (or agar flakes)

1½ teaspoons baking powder

½ teaspoon sea salt

2 teaspoons ground cinnamon

¼ teaspoon ground cloves

¼ teaspoon ground nutmeg

Miscellaneous: Cooking spray

This recipe brings a completely new meaning to the phrase "Free Donuts"! This gluten-free, dairy-free, and egg-free take on those donut shop classics gives you all the sweet indulgence and saves you approximately 80 calories, 6 grams of fat, and 3 grams of saturated fat and gives you an added 1.5 grams of protein.

These figures aside, treats like these should be an indulgence and not a daily offering. They are still high in sugar and clearly fall into the 20 percent immune-suppressive/pro-inflammatory category of your daily dietary intake.

TIP: Use a spray pump bottle with oil in it to grease pans.

Preheat oven to 375°F.

Coat pans with cooking spray or brush with melted butter using a paper towel.

Purée yogurt, apple juice concentrate, maple syrup, applesauce, dried cane juice, and oil until mixture is very smooth, about 3 minutes.

Stir flours, xanthan gum, gelatin powder, baking powder, baking soda, sea salt, cinnamon, cloves, and nutmeg together in a large mixing bowl.

Add yogurt mixture to dry ingredients.

Stir until moistened. *Batter will be very soft.*

Divide batter in half if you will be baking in two batches.

Spoon batter into prepared mini-molds, about 2 generous tablespoons per mold. If using muffin tins, fill 2/3 full.

Bake for 20 to 25 minutes, or until tops spring back when touched lightly.

Loosen edges of doughnuts.

Turn onto a wire rack to cool.

Clean pan, spray again with cooking spray, and repeat process if needed. Makes 12.

Beverly's Pancakes

Ingredients:

2/3 cups rice milk
1 teaspoon Ener-G egg-replacer powder
¼ cup brown rice flour
¼ cup potato starch
1 tablespoon tapioca flour
1¼ teaspoons baking powder
¾ teaspoon baking soda
½ teaspoon honey
½ teaspoon sea salt
1 teaspoon gluten-free vanilla extract
1 tablespoon grapeseed oil

Blend rice milk and egg-replacer powder in blender until frothy, about 1 minute.

Add remaining ingredients.

Blend until just mixed.

Place large, nonstick skillet that has been lightly coated with oil over medium heat.

Pour batter into skillet.

Cook until tops are bubbly (2 to 3 minutes).

Turn and cook until golden brown (30 seconds).

Makes about eight 4-inch pancakes.

Let's face it, what kind of gluten-free cookbook would this be without a gluten-free pancake recipe!

Tip: Instead of dousing your cakes in the traditional maple syrup, which will really rack up your inflammatory food points for the day, why not try a nut butter? The favorite at our house is this mixture:

Sunflower seed butter

100% cocoa powder

Vanilla Crème Stevia Drops

TIP: Recipe may be easily doubled.

Cinna-Mini Apple Muffins

NUTS

Dry Ingredients:

2 cups Kendra's Flour Power
1½ teaspoons egg-replacer powder
2 teaspoons ground organic cinnamon
½ teaspoon sea salt
2 teaspoons baking soda
¼ teaspoon guar gum

Wet Ingredients:

4 tablespoons melted Earth Balance soy
    free coconut or grapeseed oil
½ cup brown rice syrup
1 tablespoon organic vanilla extract
¼ cup water
½ cup organic unsweetened apple sauce
½ cup squash (whichever is in season,
    peeled and finely shredded)

Miscellaneous:

¼ CUP DRIED APPLE PIECES

Almond flour is a good source of protein, and fiber and is a heart-healthy food, helping to reduce "bad" cholesterol. It is high in fiber for healthy GI function and a great alkaline source of protein and mono-unsaturated fats that help lower bad cholesterol.

Apples provide us with anti-oxidants like quercitin and cat-echin, which are anti-inflammatory/immuno-supportive and have good fiber content.

3 Cinna-Mini Apple Muffins provides 2.5 grams of fiber, 23 percent RDI of Vitamin E, and 13 percent RDI of magnesium.

Preheat oven to 350°F.

Whisk together dry ingredients in a large mixing bowl.

Stir wet ingredients together in a separate bowl.

Incorporate wet ingredients into dry mixture until thoroughly combined.

Fold in apple pieces.

Spoon batter into lightly greased mini-muffin tins, filling each cup 2/3 full.

Bake for 20 to 22 minutes, or until a toothpick inserted into the center comes out clean.

Cool in pan for 10 minutes and then transfer to a wire rack.

Cinnamon Walnut Coffee Cake

NUTS

THE CAKE

Dry Ingredients:

2½ cups blanched almond flour
1 tablespoon egg-replacer powder
¼ teaspoon sea salt
½ teaspoon baking soda

Wet Ingredients:

¼ cup walnut oil
½ cup water
¼ cup brown rice syrup
1 teaspoon organic apple cider vinegar

Miscellaneous:

½ cup chopped walnuts
½ cup raisins, chopped dates, chopped figs,
   or currants

THE TOPPING:

2 tablespoons ground cinnamon
2 tablespoons melted Earth Balance
   soy-free coconut or grapeseed oil
¼ cup brown rice syrup
½ cup chopped walnuts

Preheat OVEN TO 350°F.

Cream together wet ingredients for the
cake in a mixing bowl.

Whisk together dry ingredients for the cake in
a separate bowl.

Incorporate dry cake ingredients into wet ingredients until completely mixed.

Fold in miscellaneous ingredients.

Spread batter into a greased 8-inch square baking dish.

Almond flour is high in fiber for healthy GI function and a great alkaline source of protein and monounsaturated fats that help lower bad cholesterol.

Apples provide antioxidants like quercitin and catechin and are anti-inflammatory/immuno-supportive, also providing good fiber content.

Figs are rich in calcium, highly alkaline, balancing out the body's pH level and increasing overall immune health.

Walnut oil is a great source of omega-3 fatty acids and ALA alpha-linolenic acid, which the body converts to DHA and EPA to help control immune function, amongst other things.

Apple cider vinegar is a natural bacteria fighter and pH neutralizer. Apple cider vinegar will be added to many of the recipes in this book. It has anti-inflammatory/immuno-supportive properties as well as a balancing effect for tastes and textures in recipes. We use Bragg's Organic Raw Unpasteurized Apple Cider Vinegar.

Mix topping ingredients in a separate bowl.

Spread topping evenly over batter.

Bake for 25 to 30 minutes, or until a toothpick inserted into the center comes out clean.

Cool in pan for 10 minutes.

Chocolate Figgy Scones

Dry Ingredients:

2 cups Kendra's Flour Power
1 tablespoon egg-replacer powder
½ teaspoon sea salt
1½ teaspoons baking soda

Wet Ingredients:

1/3 cup Earth Balance soy-free coconut or
    grapeseed oil
¼ cup brown rice syrup
2 teaspoon vanilla extract
¼ cup and 2 tablespoons carbonated water

Miscellaneous:

½ cup Enjoy Life chocolate chips
¼ cup chopped dried figs, chopped

Preheat oven to 350°F.

Whisk together dry ingredients in a mixing bowl.

Stir wet ingredients together in a separate bowl.

Incorporate wet mixture into dry mixture until thoroughly combined.

Fold in chocolate chips and chopped dried figs.

Spoon batter in ¼-cup portions onto a lightly greased or parchment-lined baking sheet.

Shape into desired scone shapes.

Bake for 20 to 22 minutes, or until a toothpick inserted into the center comes out clean.

Cool in pan for 10 minutes and then transfer to a wire rack.

Almond flour is high in fiber for healthy GI function and a great alkaline source of protein and monounsaturated fats that help lower bad cholesterol.

In one study, mice with an Alzheimer's-like disease were fed an almond-rich diet. After four months, the animals that ate the almond-rich diet did much better on memory tests than those fed the usual chow. The diet also reduced the number of Alzheimer's deposits in the rodent brains. (Source: David Grotto, 101 Foods that Could Save Your Life)

Figs are fantastically anti-inflammatory/immuno-supportive! They are rich in fiber (three figs contain 6 grams), promote regularity, and aid with digestion.

Currantly Carrot Muffins

NUTS

Dry Ingredients:

2 cups Kendra's Flour Power
2 tablespoons egg-replacer powder
2 teaspoons baking soda
½ teaspoon sea salt
1 teaspoon cinnamon

Wet Ingredients:

¾ cup brown rice syrup
¾ cup grapeseed oil
½ cup carbonated water
1 cup organic unsweetened applesauce

Miscellaneous:

2 cups finely grated carrots
½ cup organic currants (or raisins, optional)

Preheat oven to 350°F.

Whisk together dry ingredients in a mixing bowl.

Stir wet ingredients together in a separate bowl.

Incorporate wet ingredients into dry ingredients until thoroughly combined.

Fold in carrots and currants, if using.

Spoon batter into lightly oiled baking cups.

Bake for 20 to 22 minutes, or until a toothpick inserted into the center comes out clean.

Carrots are the richest vegetable in Vitamin A-carotenes, which is directly related to a decreased risk of heart disease. Animal research has shown that diets rich in beta-carotene can reduce the occurrence of emphysema as well as vision/macular degeneration.

Carrots also contain a phytonutrient called Falcarinal, which in a study published in the Journal of Agricultural and Food Chemistry, was touted as a protective agent against colon cancer.

Other research on humans suggests that consuming foods that are high in carotenoids can actually make insulin more effective in our bodies, improving blood-glucose control. (Important for diabetes.)

Currants are rich in iron and Vitamin C and are a great source of fiber and ellagic acid, a phytochemical that that may reduce some cancers. Ellagic acid is shown to cause cell death in cancer cells and may reduce cholesterol. It also contains anthocyanins, which may be anti-inflammatory/immuno-supportive.

(Source: American Cancer Society, www.cancer.org)

Egg-less English Muffins

Dry Ingredients:

2 tablespoons active dry yeast
21/3 cups brown rice flour
2 cups tapioca flour
2/3 cup nondairy milk powder
2½ teaspoons guar gum
1 tablespoon agar flakes or powder
1 teaspoon sea salt

Wet Ingredients:

¼ cup grapeseed oil
½ cup coconut yogurt
2 tablespoons raw honey
1¼ cups warm water (110°F)

Preheat oven to 350°F.

Combine dry ingredients in a mixing bowl.

Add oil, yogurt, raw honey, and water.

Beat on high speed with an electric mixer for 1 to 2 minutes.

Arrange 12 greased muffin rings on baking sheet.

Divide dough into 12 equal portions.

Press dough into rings.

Cover and let stand in warm place for 1 hour. (Dough should be almost even with top of ring.)

Bake for 15 minutes, or until light brown.

Turn each muffin over with a spatula.

Bake for another 10 minutes.

Cool on wire rack, leaving ring on muffins until cool enough to remove.

Enjoy with your favorite spread or for sandwiches. Freeze any extras for later use.

> *Tricks: Stuff these full of fresh vegetables for a gluten-free vegetarian salad.*
>
> *You can also use them to create little pizzas. Again, pile those veggies on for the best nutritional value possible.*

Focaccia Bread

Dry Ingredients:

2 cups Bob's Red Mill All-Purpose Flour

1 tablespoon egg-replacer powder

1 teaspoon guar gum

1½ teaspoons baking soda

1 teaspoon baking powder

½ teaspoon onion powder

½ teaspoon garlic powder

¼ teaspoon agar flakes

¾ -teaspoon sea salt

Wet Ingredients:

1 cup nondairy milk

¼ cup carbonated water

2 tablespoons oil, plus more for
    brushing pan and top of bread

1 teaspoon apple cider vinegar

Preheat oven to 375°F.

This Focaccia bread recipe is such a versatile batter, it will become a staple in your gluten-free, casein-free kitchen!

The best part is that it is a yeast-free bread, which makes it a much less inflammatory choice.

Use it for bread sticks, make deep-dish pizzas, roll it out for thinner pizza crusts, or even roll it up and twist it into large pretzel shapes.

It's the perfect vessel for some nutrient-rich vegetables!

If you have an allergy to agar, you can omit or substitute 1 teaspoon unflavored gelatin.

Whisk together dry ingredients in a large mixing bowl.

Stir together wet ingredients in a separate bowl.

Incorporate wet ingredients into dry ingredients until dough comes together.

Transfer dough to an oiled loaf pan and smooth top with spatula.

Brush or drizzle dough with oil.

Bake for 20 to 25 minutes.

For Oats O HAULIN' OATS

NUTS

You may also cook them ahead and freeze them in serving portions. Take out the night before and hold in the refrigerator.

Ingredients:

Cinnamon-Sugar Oats

½ cup Bob's Red Mill GF Oats

1 cup filtered water

¼ teaspoon sea salt

1–2 teaspoons brown rice syrup

½ teaspoon cinnamon

1–2 tablespoons raisins

Zesty Orange Oats

½ cup Bob's Red Mill GF Oats

1 cup hot water (use caution when handling extremely hot or boiling water)

¼ teaspoon sea salt

1 tablespoon orange juice, fresh squeezed

¼ teaspoon orange zest

Maple Rum Raisin

½ cup Bob's Red Mill GF Oats

1 cup filtered water

¼ teaspoon sea salt

1–2 teaspoons maple syrup

1 tablespoon dark raisins

½ teaspoon rum extract or 1 teaspoon rum (optional)

Many sources will list oats as a grain that contains gluten. If you do not have an allergy to oats, you can purchase certified gluten free oats, such as Bob's Red Mill gluten-free oats.

Oats are a quick and easy source for fiber and a good source of complex carbohydrates that fuel your body and high in protein.

Oats are heart healthy because they lower cholesterol—beta glucan—therefore lowering the risk of heart disease.

Choose the least refined varieties for the best nutritional benefits. Soak your oats for at least an hour for ease of digestion.

For oats on the go, use Bob's Red Mill GF Quick-Cooking Oats. If you have time to let a pot simmer, opt for the rolled oats or even the steel-cut; they take longer but keep more of their nutritional elements.

Tip: Cook ahead and freeze them in serving portions. Take out the night before and hold in the refrigerator.

Bring oats, water, and salt to a low boil over medium high heat.

Reduce heat to medium low and simmer to desired consistency.

Stir in remaining ingredients.

Hazelnut French Toast Casserole

Ingredients:

8 slices GF/CF/EF bread (I use
 Ener-G Yeast-Free Brown Rice Loaf)
½ cup Earth Balance (1 stick)
1 tablespoon tapioca flour
3 cups hazelnut nondairy milk (see recipe)
2 teaspoons vanilla extract
½ cup brown rice syrup
1/3 cup hazelnut butter
¼ cup hazelnut pieces (optional)

Hazelnuts are strongly anti-inflammatory/immuno-supportive and a fantastic source of protein, fiber, and Vitamin E.

Families go "NUTS" for this nutty casserole! It's a take on classic French toast.

Preheat oven to 375°F.

Toast bread just until lightly browned.

Cut toast into ½-inch cubes and toss into a lightly greased casserole dish.

Melt Earth Balance in a large saucepan over medium heat.

Whisk in 1 tablespoon tapioca flour (or arrowroot powder).

Stir in hazelnut nondairy milk, vanilla extract, brown rice syrup, and hazelnut butter.

Simmer over medium heat for approximately 5 minutes, stirring to combine.

Pour liquid over bread cubes and press cubes down in the liquid.

Let Sit for 15 to 20 minutes to absorb the liquid.

Cover and bake for 40 minutes.

Sprinkle the top with hazelnut pieces if desired.

Uncover and continue baking for 10 to 15 more minutes.

Serve piping hot.

Island Breeze Muffins

(NUTS)

Dry Ingredients:

1½ cups almond flour
½ cup coconut flour
2 tablespoons tapioca flour
1 tablespoon egg-replacer powder
½ cup brown rice flour
2 teaspoons baking soda
½ teaspoon guar gum

Wet Ingredients:

¾ cups coconut oil, melted
2 bananas, mashed
½ cup organic chopped pineapple
    (like Native Forest brand)
½ cup raw honey
½ cup organic unsweetened applesauce
1 cup finely shredded zucchini
½ cup carbonated water

Miscellaneous:

Organic unsweetened coconut (optional)

Bananas: These tropical treats are definitely a splurge.

If you are fighting cancer or yeast overgrowth, save these island beauties for a time when your gut and microbes are in a healthier state.

Avocado oil is a very versatile oil. It is rich in Vitamin E and low in acidity and oxidation. It is a monounsaturated fat just like olive oil. It provides those "good fats" that are needed to help nutrient absorption, cell integrity, and nerve transmission.

Pineapple contains bromelain, an anti-inflammatory enzyme that can interfere with growth of malignant cells and tumors.

Preheat oven to 350°F.

Sift together dry ingredients into a mixing bowl.

Stir wet ingredients together in a separate bowl.

Incorporate wet ingredients into dry ingredients until thoroughly combined.

Fold in coconut if desired.

Spoon batter into lightly oiled baking cups.

Bake for 20 to 22 minutes, or until a toothpick inserted into the center comes out clean.

Nuts about Bananas Muffins

NUTS

Dry Ingredients:

2 cups Kendra's Flour Power

2 tablespoons coconut flour

1 teaspoon baking soda

¼ cup flax seed meal

1 tablespoon egg-replacer powder

Wet Ingredients:

¾ cup brown rice syrup

¼ cup organic pure molasses

½ cup Earth Balance soy-free, softened

2 teaspoons pure vanilla extract

3 ripe bananas, mashed

¾ cup coconut milk (unsweetened)

2 tablespoons nut butter (almond, Tahini, sunflower)

¼ cup carbonated water

Miscellaneous:

½ cup chopped raw walnuts

Bananas and banana powder have been used for centuries as a natural remedy for heartburn or GERD, associated with gastrointestinal discomfort.

Use walnuts raw or soaked. Some believe that soaking the nuts allows their nutrients to be more bio-available in our systems. Walnuts are a super-nut!

Preheat oven to 350°F.

Whisk together dry ingredients in a mixing bowl.

Stir wet ingredients together in a separate bowl.

Incorporate wet ingredients into dry ingredients, stirring until fully combined.

Fold in walnuts.

Spoon batter into lightly greased muffin tins, filling 2/3 full.

Bake 20 to 22 minutes, or until a toothpick inserted into the center comes out clean.

Oatmeal's Qrazy Cousin Quinoa

For the next best thing to oatmeal in the morning—or any time of day—try cooked quinoa done up like a traditional bowl of oatmeal. Tips: Put quinoa in a mesh colander and wash thoroughly. Soak for several hours or overnight. For a quicker method, buy quinoa already sprouted (you can find sprouted quinoa in the bins at Whole Foods). Try these variations:

Apple Pie Quinoa

½ cup quinoa

¾ cup filtered water

¼ teaspoon sea salt

½ teaspoon cinnamon

1 tablespoon fresh or dried apples

Nitty Gritty Quinoa

½ cup quinoa

¾ cup filtered water

¼ teaspoon sea salt

½ teaspoon organic sea salt

¼ teaspoon garlic powder

2 tablespoons Daiya Cheddar shreds

Blueberry Almond Quinoa

½ cup quinoa

¾ cup filtered water

¼ teaspoon sea salt

1 teaspoon honey

1–2 tablespoons fresh or dried blueberries

What is quinoa?

Quinoa is an ancient grain that was first noted in history by archaeologists and anthropologists as early as 2000 BC. Native Americans grew it in middle and southern America. It most notably occurred amongst natives in the Andes Mountains of Peru.

Quinoa is a source of complete protein, which means that it supplies all of the amino acids that the body needs in one source. Quinoa is also rich in iron and a good source of saponins, which may have anti-cancer and anti-inflammatory properties.

Bring quinoa, water, and salt to a low boil over medium-high heat.

Reduce heat to medium low and simmer to desired consistency.

Stir in remaining ingredients.

Pistachio Pear Pancakes

NUTS

Dry Ingredients:

1½ cups Kendra's Flour Power

1 teaspoon baking soda

½ teaspoon baking powder

½ teaspoon sea salt

Wet Ingredients

2 tablespoons brown rice syrup or raw honey

1 tablespoons grapeseed oil

½ cup nondairy milk

2 teaspoons vanilla extract

One serving of pistachios contains more fiber than ½ cup of broccoli. They are very high in protein and potassium. Pistachios are also high in resveratrol, known for its cancer-fighting, anti-inflammatory properties.

Pears are high in pectin, even higher than apples. Pectin is the dietary fiber that makes pears an excellent choice for "toning" the intestinal tract.

Miscellaneous:

¼ cup diced fresh pear

¼ cup shelled pistachios, chopped and pan roasted

1-2 tablespoons grapeseed oil

Whisk together dry ingredients in a large mixing bowl.

Stir together wet ingredients in a separate bowl.

Incorporate wet ingredients into dry ingredients until well combined.

Fold in miscellaneous ingredients.

Heat grapeseed oil in a large skillet over medium heat.

Ladle or pour batter into desired size and shape for your pancakes.

Cook until edges begin to look dry.

Flip and cook other side for 2 to 3 minutes.

Transfer cooked pancakes to a plate and repeat until batter is gone.

Raisin Shine Zucchini Bread

NUTS

Dry Ingredients:

2 cups all-purpose flour

2 tablespoons tapioca flour

2 teaspoons baking soda

2 tablespoons egg-replacer powder

1 teaspoon cinnamon

Wet Ingredients:

2/3 cup brown rice syrup, raw honey, or
    organic grade B maple syrup

2 cups finely grated zucchini

1 cup applesauce2/3 cup grapeseed oil

½ cup carbonated water

2 teaspoons apple cider vinegar

Miscellaneous:

½ cup finely chopped walnuts (optional)

1/3 cup dark raisins

Walnuts are a fantastic nut; definitely a power food. It is the richest nut source for omega-6 EFA's and provides the omega-6's in a healthy balance ratio with the omega-3's. A rich source of fiber, Vitamin E, folic acid, and magnesium. Uniquely, walnuts contain a flavonoid called resveratrol, which has shown to have fantastic anti-cancer and anti-inflammatory properties.

In addition, walnuts are a strong source of ellagic acid. Recent animal research studies indicate ellagic acid is good for cancer prevention by means of detoxifying potential carcinogens.

Raspberries are also a good source of ellagic acid.

Preheat oven to 350°F.

Whisk together dry ingredients in a mixing bowl.

Stir wet ingredients together in a separate bowl.

Incorporate wet ingredients into dry ingredients, stirring until fully combined.

Transfer to a lightly oiled loaf pan (or two small loaf pans).

Bake 2 small loaves for 20 to 25 minutes or a large loaf for 40 to 45 minutes, or until a toothpick inserted into the center comes out clean.

Cool for 5 minutes in pan and then transfer to a wire rack.

Sammy-Which Bread (Yeast-Free)

Dry Ingredients:

2½ cups Kendra's Flour Power
1 tablespoon potato starch flour
1 tablespoon baking powder
1 teaspoon sea salt
1 tablespoon egg-replacer powder

Wet Ingredients:

2 tablespoons Sorghum molasses
2/3 cup almond milk or rice milk
¼ cup grapeseed oil
1 teaspoon organic apple cider vinegar

Preheat oven to 350 degrees

Mix together: flour, potato starch, baking powder, sea salt and egg-replacer powder.

Make a well in the center of the dry ingredients.

Pour in the molasses, non-dairy milk, oil, and apple cider vinegar.

Stir until a dough forms.

Transfer to a lightly oiled loaf pan.

Bake for 45 to 55 minutes.

Cool in pan for 10 minutes.

Turn out on to a wire rack to cool completely.

Nut flours and the higher protein flours used in this bread mix provide more nutrition than the gluten breads you are used to.

When you are first making the switch to a gluten-free lifestyle, the cravings for bread and other baked goods will remain; after all, that is how you have eaten your entire life. Eventually, the goal is to move away from wheat breads and inflammatory grains completely. By then, you will be eating so many delicious fruits and vegetables you won't even miss that dry and bulking piece of bread!

153

Sweet Irish Soda Biscuits

Dry Ingredients:

3 cups gluten-free all-purpose flour
1 tablespoon tapioca flour
1½ teaspoons baking soda
1½ teaspoons egg-replacer powder
¼ teaspoon sea salt

A gluten-free and yeast-free take on a classic biscuit.

The yogurt provides healthy probiotics.

Wet Ingredients:

1 teaspoon apple cider vinegar
1 cups plain coconut yogurt
¼ cup brown rice syrup
3 tablespoons carbonated water

Preheat oven to 375°F.

Whisk together dry ingredients in a large mixing bowl.

Make a well in the center.

Pour in wet ingredients.

Stir everything together until well combined.

Scoop out mounds of dough mixture, using an ice cream scoop, and place on a greased baking sheet.

Space them out about 2 inches apart.

Press down on top of each mound with the back of the scoop to make a biscuit shape.

Drizzle the tops with brown rice syrup before baking.

Bake for 20 to 25 minutes.

Vanilla Bean Almond Pancakes

NUTS

Dry Ingredients:

1½ cups blanched almond flour

1 tablespoon arrowroot powder or potato starch flour

1 tablespoon egg-replacer powder

½ teaspoon baking soda

½ teaspoon sea salt

> *Vanilla beans are used to treat many common health conditions. They have anti-inflammatory and even pain relieving properties.*
>
> *Pancetta can have nitrites, so be sure to select your brand carefully.*

Wet Ingredients:

2 tablespoons brown rice syrup or raw honey

1 tablespoon vanilla bean paste

1 tablespoon grapeseed oil

½ cup unsweetened vanilla almond milk

Miscellaneous:

1-2 tablespoons grapeseed oil

Whisk together dry ingredients in a large mixing bowl.

Stir together wet ingredients in a separate bowl.

Incorporate wet ingredients into dry ingredients until well combined.

Heat grapeseed oil in a large skillet over medium heat.

Ladle or pour batter into desired size and shape for pancakes.

Cook until edges begin to look dry.

Flip and cook other side for 2 to 3 minutes.

Transfer cooked pancakes to a plate and repeat until batter is gone.

Vanilla Bean Syrup:

Add 1 teaspoon of vanilla bean paste to ½ cup organic grade B maple syrup to drizzle over pancakes.

Wheat/Gluten-Free Flour Tortillas

Dry Ingredients:

2 cups sorghum or brown rice flour
½ cup tapioca starch or flour
    (can also use arrowroot)
1 teaspoon sea salt
1½ teaspoons xanthan gum

Wet Ingredients:

¼ cup olive oil
5 cups water

Rice-flour tortillas just may be your lifesaver in the gluten-free kitchen. They are a versatile vessel for loads of vegetables, fruits, and proteins, making them a winner in every household!

Try using these for a spinach quesadilla or an avocado, tomato, arugula wrap.

TIP: Do these while doing laundry, helping with homework or baking other foods. They are easy, but they take time.

Mix all dry ingredients in a large bowl.

Add oil and about half of the water.

Beat with electric mixer or fork until smooth (no lumps).

Add remaining water and beat until smooth.
The batter will be very thin (like a too-thin pancake batter).

Heat a very large nonstick skillet or griddle over medium to medium-high heat.

Pour ½ cup batter onto the middle of the skillet using a measuring cup.

Spread batter out into a tortilla-size circle using the back of a large spoon.

Cook for a few minutes, until the edges are dry and the entire top looks like a moonscape; it may or may not bubble a bit like a pancake.

Flip tortilla over quickly using a large spatula. *The cooked side should be firm to crispy and lightly browned. A few really brown spots are okay.*

Cook for a few more minutes until the tortilla stops steaming.

Flip again and cook until tortilla looks completely done (not wet in the middle). *They may puff up or be very crispy and inflexible at this stage. THIS IS GOOD. They need to get crispy on both sides to be done in the middle. They will soften up and get flexible again as they cool.*

When done, flip onto a clean plate.

Continue cooking tortillas and stack them up as they are done. These freeze very well. We stack 4 tortillas in a set and separate sets with wax paper, then freeze all in a ziplock bag. Microwave a stack for 1 to 2 minutes to defrost.

Fill with meat, beans, vegetables, or any safe food and enjoy!

Makes 10 to 12 8-inch tortillas.

Wheat/Gluten-Free Flour Tortillas

We have also tried these with buckwheat flour, but we found they are too soft and break too easily. The recipe may work with bean and other flours. Experiment and feel free to share this recipe with anyone who needs to avoid wheat and gluten.

Tips & Tricks

Even if your children are on an egg, wheat/gluten, potato, and dairy-free diet, they can still enjoy Mexican food by eating corn tortillas. When we discovered our son was also allergic to corn and a few other things, the world as we knew it ended.

Creating a tortilla to meet exacting standards took about eight tries, but we finally have one that gets the "high-five" stamp of approval. Bring on the fajitas and burritos!

To make a good "safe" tortilla, it is all about technique. You will go through a number of practice phases in which you will be sure they have flopped. Be assured your tortillas will be just fine when it is time for eating.

If you have ever cooked wheat flour tortillas, forget everything you know about it and be prepared to make a leap of faith. About the only thing wheat tortillas have in common with these is the circle shape.

You may need to turn the heat down a little for rice flour as it tends to brown more easily than sorghum.

Be BRAVE when you flip. Timid flipping = torn tortillas. You must flip them quickly and with gusto to prevent them from breaking in mid-flip. Broken tortillas can be reattached or used as dippers for salsa.

You may have to pitch a few tortillas until you get a feel for cooking time and flipping. Don't throw them out—the birds love them!

Take "safe" food to restaurants. Take your tortillas to Mexican restaurants. You may also take "safe" hamburger buns and ketchup to burger joints. There is life with food allergies!

Wishful Waffles

NUTS

Dry Ingredients:

1½ cups Kendra's Flour Power
½ teaspoon baking soda
1 teaspoon baking powder
1 tablespoon egg-replacer powder
2 teaspoon raw honey
½ teaspoon sea salt

Wet Ingredients:

1 tablespoon grapeseed oil
2 teaspoons vanilla extract
1 cup nondairy milk
½ cup filtered carbonated water

Varieties:

Strawberries and almond slices

Coconut flakes and Enjoy Life chocolate chips

Apricots and walnuts

Apples and cinnamon granola (Enjoy Life)

Whisk together dry ingredients in a mixing bowl.

Stir wet ingredients together in a separate bowl.

Incorporate wet ingredients into dry, stirring until smooth.

Fold in variety ingredients, whichever desired.

Spoon batter into a heated and oiled waffle iron.

Cook to desired doneness, following manufacturer's instructions.

For a nut-free version, simply use 1 cup all-purpose gluten-free flour plus ½ cup gluten-free oat flour.

Try variations of add-ins and toppings.

One of our favorite tricks is to top these waffles with a fruit and veggie salsa; getting a veggie in at breakfast is always a feat for any mommy!

TIP: Use a spray pump bottle with oil in it to grease pans.

Yummy Tummy Breadsticks

Ingredients:

1 tablespoon gluten-free dry yeast

½ cup brown rice flour

½ cup tapioca flour

1 tablespoon nondairy milk powder (like Vances brand)

2 teaspoons xanthan gum

½ cup Rice Vegan (Galaxy Foods) vegan Parmesan

½ teaspoon sea salt

1 teaspoon onion powder

1 teaspoon unflavored gelatin powder or agar flakes

2/3 cup warm water (105°F)

¼ teaspoon honey

1 tablespoon olive oil

¼ teaspoon vitamin c crystals

1 teaspoon Italian herb seasoning

Cooking spray

> *The perfect addition to bread-sticks? Marinara.*
>
> *Try a Pasta Sauce like Muir Glen's Garden Vegetable variety to sneak in all that extra veggie goodness.*

Preheat oven to 400°F for 5 minutes, then turn off.

Blend yeast, flours, dry milk powder, xanthan gum, Parmesan cheese, sea salt, onion powder, and gelatin powder on low speed with an electric mixer.

Add warm water, honey, olive oil, and vinegar.

Beat on high for 3 minutes. *Dough will be soft and sticky. (Bread machine is not recommended.)*

Place dough in large heavy-duty freezer bag and cut a ½-inch diagonal opening at one corner. (This makes a one-inch circle.)

Coat a large baking sheet with cooking spray.

Squeeze dough out of bag into sheet in 10 strips, each 1-inch wide by 6 inches long. *For best results hold bag upright as you squeeze, rather than at an angle. Also, hold bag with seam on top rather than at side.*

Spray bread sticks with cooking spray and sprinkle with Italian herb seasoning.

Place in warm oven to rise for 20 to 30 minutes, leavening breadsticks in oven.

Turn oven back on to 400°F and bake until golden brown, about 15 to 20 minutes.

Switch position of cookie sheet halfway through baking to assure even browning.

Cool on wire rack. After cooling, store in an airtight container.

CHAPTER 8

Lite Bites and Super Snacks

Photo Recipes: Bottom Left: Cucumber Sandwiches, Fruit Gondolas. Top Right: Chicken And Squash Taquitos (From Main Dishes), Faux Fried Chicken Tenders. Center: Chickie Dip.

LITE BITES and SUPER SNACKS

Cucumber Apple Chutney

Dream Dates

Fermenator Pickles (Lacto-Fermented)

"Fried" Mozzarella With Marinara Dip

Fruit Gondolas

Greater Tater Skins

Grilled Figs with Hazelnut-Maple Cream

Hazelnut-Maple Yogurt Cream

Hawaiian Ham Sushi

I Poppers

Na'cho Ordinary Nachos

Open Sesame Crackers

Parfait Diem

Pear and Pancetta Bruschetta

Popcorn: Pumpkin Spice

Popcorn: Root Beer

Popcorn: Sweet Treat Caramel Corn

Q-Cumber Sandwiches

Snack Mixes

Veggie Tostada

Very Berry Fruit Salad

Very Apple Salad

Cucumber Apple Chutney

Ingredients:

½ cup diced cucumber (peel optional, seeds removed)

½ cup diced apple (peel optional, 1 medium-sized apple)

¼ cup diced watermelon

Fresh mint

½ teaspoon sea salt

Toss together ingredients and serve!

Apples and berries are anti-oxidant powerhouses. Both are anti-inflammatory/immuno-supportive.

Blueberries, especially, promote digestive health by reducing the inflammation in the digestive system through their tannins. Blueberries have a fairly long shelf life for a fruit, but try to eat them as fresh as possible because they can build mold/yeast on the skin that should be avoided if you are on a yeast-free diet. Blueberries also contain bilberry, which is good for the eyes.

Mint has been used as an antimicrobial and has been found to have a strong killing effect on pinworms. Mint and peppermint can also aid in digestion.

Dream Dates

Ingredients:

4–6 slices bacon (we like Applegate Farms
   Sunday Bacon)
12–18 dried dates or figs
1–2 tablespoons grapeseed oil
1 teaspoon honey to drizzle

Preheat oven to 450°F.

Cut bacon into strips.

Wrap each date in 1 bacon strip (usually 3
dates per slice of bacon) and place onto a
baking sheet.

Brush with grapeseed oil.

Drizzle with a little honey.

Bake for 6 to 8 minutes, or until the bacon
gets browned and a bit crispy.

Delicious and highly addictive!

Dates are very high in fiber and are one of the best sources of potassium, which is an essential mineral for a number of functions, including the maintenance of muscle contractions, a balanced metabolism, and keeping your nervous system functioning healthily.

Just three of these dream dates provide 2 grams of fiber and 11 grams of protein. (Just stick to those three though; this little snack has 15 grams of sugar, albeit natural sugar.)

Fermenator Pickles (Lacto-fermented)

Brine:

2 cups filtered water

1½ tablespoons unrefined salt

Ingredients:

3–5 pickling cucumbers

4 cloves garlic, peeled

½ teaspoon whole peppercorns

½ teaspoon coriander seeds

3–4 sprigs fresh dill

> *Fermented foods are hugely beneficial in the balancing act of good versus bad flora.*
>
> *The second best thing about these pickles is that most vinegar-based pickles are off limits when you are fighting yeast. These are not only fine, they are fine-tastic!*

Make brine by mixing 2 cups filtered water with sea salt until salt is well dissolved.

Wash cucumbers.

Stuff a mason jar with cucumbers, garlic cloves, peppercorns, coriander seeds, and dill.

Pour brine into the jar.

Place lid on the jar.

Ferment at room temperature for 5 to 7 days.

Refrigerate.

"Fried" Mozzarella with Marinara Dip

Ingredients:

1 8-ounce Rice Vegan mozzarella block
½ cup Nature's Path Rice Puffs
½ cup Nature's Path Corn Flakes
1 teaspoon sea salt
1 teaspoon oregano
¼ cup rice flour
¼ cup tapioca flour
3 tablespoons olive oil
1 tablespoon expeller-pressed olive oil
½ cup Muir Glen GFCF Pasta Sauce (like Garden Vegetable)

> *Use a sauce like Muir Glen Garden Vegetable for a great source of extra veggie nutrients!*

Slice block of vegan mozzarella into 8 equal pieces.

Crumb the rice and corn cereal together in a food processor, along with the sea salt and oregano.

Combine the crumb mixture with rice and tapioca flours.

Heat 1 tablespoon of oil in a large skillet over medium heat.

Set up your breading station with 1 plate of the remaining oil and 1 plate or bowl of the cereal crumb mixture.

Dredge each of the "cheese" slices first through the oil, then through the crumbs, and then straight into the skillet.

Cook each piece for 1 to 2 minutes on each side, or until lightly browned. Do not overcook, or you will have a melted pool of crunchy cheese (although sometimes those can be fun too).

Continue with all 8 slices. **Serve** with Muir Glen sauce, either over top or on the side for dipping.

Fruit Gondolas

Ingredients:

2–3 endives

¼ cup pecans

¼ cup walnuts

5–6 dried cherries

2 tablespoons dried blueberries

2 tablespoons honey

½ cup coconut yogurt (vanilla)

Figs are fantastically anti-inflammatory/immuno-supportive! They are high in fiber (3 figs contain 6 grams), promote regularity, and aid in digestion.

Wash endives, pulling the leaves off and setting each aside, ready to fill.

Chop nuts and dried fruit and mix together.

Prepare by filling endive leaves with fruit and nut mixture.

Drizzle honey over the top.

Greater Tater Skins

Ingredients:

4 medium sized potatoes, baked
2–3 slices Applegate Farms Black Forest Ham
1–2 tablespoons Earth Balance
2/3 cup Daiya Cheddar shreds
1 tablespoon chopped fresh chives

> This is a great recipe to add veggies too!
>
> Broccoli, spinach, Swiss chard, or any deep green veggie makes the perfect addition!

Preheat oven to 450°F.

Wash, prick, and **bake** potatoes for 40 to 45 minutes.

Remove potatoes and let cool until comfortable to handle.

Dice ham slices into small cubes.

Slice each potato down the center through the long side of the potato.

Scoop out 1 to 2 tablespoons of potato, leaving the divot face up and ready to fill with toppings. (Note: Save your scoopings for some fantastic hash brown potatoes the next morning.)

Top each half with equal amounts of Earth Balance, Daiya Cheddar, and cubed ham.

Return to oven until cheese melts and edges crisp a bit (5 to 10 minutes).

Garnish with fresh chopped chives.

Serve with Greater Tots Ranch-Ish recipe.

Grilled Figs with Hazelnut-Maple Cream

Ingredients:

8 fresh figs
1 teaspoon almond or walnut oil
Hazelnut-Maple Yogurt Cream
    (recipe below)
Fresh mint leaves

Wash figs and snip off the stems.
Cut each fig in half lengthwise.
Brush the cut sides with oil.
Grill cut-side down over high heat for approximately 3 minutes.
Plate two halves per serving.
Spoon Hazelnut-Maple Cream over top.
Garnish with a fresh mint leaf.

Probiotics to aid in a healthy balance of gut flora.

Acidophilus: for the small intestine.

Bifidus: for the large intestine.

Hazelnut-Maple Cream

Ingredients:

2 tablespoons CoDelicious Coconut Kefir

2 tablespoons hazelnut milk

¼ cup Mimic Crème Healthy top

1 teaspoon organic maple syrup

Pinch of salt

Shake all ingredients together vigorously in a cocktail shaker for 2-3 minutes. (Or use a hand mixer).

Make sure the healthy top is very cold.

Hawaiian Ham Sushi

NUTS

Ingredients:

½ cup cooked brown rice

1 teaspoon apple cider vinegar

1 tablespoon honey or brown rice syrup

Pineapple (time saver: buy fresh from grocer already peeled)

4 slices Applegate Farms Black Forest Ham

1 cucumber, skin and seeds removed and sliced into strips

Mix rice, apple cider vinegar, and honey or brown rice syrup in a bowl and set aside.

Slice pineapple into long ¼-inch-wide strips.

Lay out a slice of ham on a flat prep surface.

Spread a thin layer of rice mixture on the ham
and make a line down the center with a few slices each of cucumber and pineapple.

Roll ham up tightly. You can use a sushi roller or parchment paper for easier rolling.

Slice into ¾ to 1-inch slices and serve.

Excellent for school snacks and/or lunches!

You could also make these with turkey or chicken. I usually make these for lunch with leftover rice from dinner the night before.

Pineapple contains bromelain which is anti-inflammatory/immuno-supportive and can interfere with growth of malignant cells and tumors.

Be sure to choose a lunch meat that is free of nitrites. A favorite brand is Applegate Farms. There are others that are equally delicious. Be sure to use within three days after opening, since there are no preservatives in the meat.

Pepperoni Poppers

Ingredients:

½ recipe focaccia Recipe

Nitrite-free pepperoni

2 tablespoons olive oil

Veggie marinara for dipping (Muir Glen Veggie Pasta Sauce)

Preheat oven to 375°F.

Roll dough out between two sheets of parchment paper.

Cut dough rounds that are the same size as a pepperoni slice, using a round cookie or biscuit cutter (or simply lay down a kitchen bowl and cut around it).

Take one piece of dough and lay one piece of pepperoni on top.

Roll up pepperoni and dough together.

Slice dough roll into sections about 1 to 2 inches wide, and continue until all dough and pepperoni is used.

Transfer pieces to a baking sheet.

Brush each piece with olive oil.

Bake for 12 to 14 minutes, or until the dough is cooked through and golden brown.

Serve with Muir Glen Veggie Pasta Sauce for dipping.

A gluten-free version of a kid-friendly masterpiece. Serving a sensational snack like these with a sidekick that is full of vegetables is a fantastic way to get a vegetable serving into the day!

We always have a supply of this dough in the fridge or the freezer for quick-fixing pizza or breadsticks.

173

Na'cho Ordinary Nachos

Ingredients:

1 bag sweet potato chips (Terra or another brand)

2 tablespoons Greater Tots Ranch-Ish (see recipe)

½ teaspoon chili powder

1 tablespoon fresh chopped cilantro

1 teaspoon apple cider vinegar

½ teaspoon sea salt

1 cup shredded Rice Vegan mozzarella

Meat of your choice: ground turkey, ground pork, bacon, turkey bacon, etc., already cooked.

Sweet potatoes are a starch, but they are considered anti-inflammatory, making them meet our qualification for an immuno-supportive food choice.

Preheat oven to 425°F.

Line a cookie sheet with sweet potato chips, distributing evenly.

Mix the Ranch-Ish with the chili powder and vinegar in a small bowl.

Drizzle over the chips as evenly as possible.

Add the cheese shreds.

Top with the cooked meat of your choice.

Bake just until cheese is melted.

Open Sesame Crackers

Dry Ingredients:

2 cups Kendra's Flour Power
2 tablespoons arrowroot powder
1 teaspoon sea salt
¾ cup sesame seeds
2 tablespoons caraway seeds
1 tablespoon fresh chopped parsley

Wet Ingredients:

2 tablespoons almond oil or other preferred oil

2 tablespoons filtered water

Preheat oven to 350°F.

Mix the dry ingredients together in a large bowl.

Make a well in the center.

Pour in the oil and water.

Mix together until a dough forms.

Divide mixture into two equal sections.

Place a section of dough between two pieces of parchment paper.

Roll dough to □-inch thickness.

Remove top sheet of parchment and carefully turn the dough onto a lightly oiled baking sheet.

Carefully peel the parchment off the dough.
Cut into desired shapes with a pizza roller or knife.

Bake for 12 to 15 minutes, or until crisp and lightly browned.

Repeat with the other section of dough.

Sesame seeds are rich in calcium, so they are a great food to add in to replace the calcium you may be removing from your diet due to being off cow's milk.

Caraway seeds also have anthelmintic oils that can aid in killing some forms of intestinal parasites.

These crackers are almost equal in "good fats" and carbohydrate content, which is a healthier alternative to traditional crackers that are high in carbs.

Five of these crackers provide 44 percent of the RDI of manganese, a trace mineral that is present in spinach, brown rice, garbanzo beans, and others. Manganese is an enzyme activator.

A strong presence of mitochondrial dysfunction is being discovered in children (and adults) on the autism spectrum. Manganese-dependant superoxide dismutase (SOD) is an enzyme that is found inside the mitochondria and needs manganese to activate it's free-radical protecting capabilities.

Parfait Diem

NUTS

Ingredients:

1/3 cup organic mixed berries

1–2 teaspoons finely chopped fresh mint

5–6 drops Vanilla Crème SweetLeaf Stevia drops

6 ounces SoDelicious coconut yogurt (plain) or Amando almond yogurt

2 tablespoons Enjoy Life Perky's Crunchy Flax cereal

Mix together the berries, mint, and Stevia drops in a small bowl.

Scoop yogurt into a separate bowl.

Top yogurt with fruit mixture and then with flax cereal.

A simple and delicious breakfast, snack, or dessert.

Coconut yogurt is a fantastic dairy-free option for a fermented food, providing live bacteria that promote a healthy gut flora (probiotics). The fact that these are available from coconut is fantastic.

Coconut has innumerable benefits to the body. It contains lauric acid, capric acid, and caprylic acid, which have properties that are antimicrobial, antioxidant, antifungal, and antibacterial.

Pear and Pancetta Bruschetta

Ingredients:

Bread:
Schar baguette, sliced into ½-inch rounds

Toppings:
¼ cup diced nitrite-free pancetta
2 tablespoons olive oil
Vegan Parmesan topping

Sauce:
½ cup fresh or frozen pears
½ teaspoon lemon juice
1 teaspoon chopped fresh basil
¼ cup water

Pumpkin seeds make this snack a power food punch!

Pumpkin seeds contain fantastic anti-inflammatory/immuno-supportive properties.

Also, they contain phytosterols that can help prevent prostate disorders, including prostate cancer and L-tryptophan, which can help with depression.

Preheat oven to 425°F.

Slice bread and lay pieces on a baking sheet.

Toss diced pancetta in a frying pan over medium high heat until crispy.

Brush each slice on the top side only with olive oil.

Simmer sauce ingredients in a small saucepan for 5 to 10 minutes, or until it gets syrupy.

Spoon equal amount of pear mixture onto each bread slice.

Sprinkle with Parmesan topping and an inch of pancetta dices.

Bake for 10 to 12 minutes, or until bubbly and toasty.

Popcorn Variations
Pumpkin Spice

Ingredients:

6 cups air-popped popcorn
½ cup pumpkin seeds
3 tablespoons Earth Balance or coconut oil
2 teaspoon pumpkin pie spice mix

Pop the popcorn into a large bowl.

Toss with the pumpkin seeds.

Melt butter or oil and stir in pumpkin pie spice mix until slightly boiling.

Drizzle over popcorn.

Toss to coat.

> *Popcorn is a quick, inexpensive, and simply snack solution. Air pop or pan pop in coconut oil.*
>
> *Remember, though that not all corn is created equal. Find a non-GMO organic corn source for the perfect popping pleasure. (See section of "Stock Your Free Pantry" section.*
>
> *Popcorn can be a great snack to add nuts and seeds to.*

Root Beer Popcorn

Ingredients:

6 cups air-popped popcorn

4 tablespoons Earth Balance or coconut oil

10–12 drops SweetLeaf Stevia in root beer flavor

1 teaspoon sea salt

Pop popcorn into a large bowl.

Melt butter and add in the Stevia drops.

Drizzle butter over popcorn.

Toss to coat, sprinkle with salt, and enjoy.

Sweet Treat Caramel Corn

Ingredients:

6 cups air-popped popcorn
4 tablespoons. Earth Balance or coconut oil
1/3 cup brown rice syrup
1 teaspoon sea salt

Pop the popcorn into a large popcorn bowl.

Melt the butter In brown rice syrup together in a small saucepan.

Drizzle butter over the popcorn.

Toss to coat, sprinkle with salt, and enjoy.

Q-cumber Sandwiches

NUTS

Ingredients:

1–2 cucumbers
½ cup SoDelicious coconut yogurt, plain
½ teaspoon organic all-season salt
3–4 slices Applegate Farms lunch meat
3–4 slices Rice Vegan cheese
Small cookie cutters

Cucumbers are mostly water, so they are highly hydrating to eat! They have a fair amount of Vitamin C and are most known for topical uses for dermatitis and other inflammatory skin ailments.

Keep that skin on for all the beneficial fiber it provides.

Wash cucumbers.

Slice cucumbers into ¼ to ½ inch thick rounds.

Stir together the yogurt and seasoning salt in a small bowl.

Lay slices of lunch meat and cheese on a flat surface.

Cut out cheese and lunch-meat shapes with a small round (or your preferred shape) cookie cutter(s).

Stack cheese, lunch meat, and a spread of yogurt mixture between two slices of cucumber.

Enjoy!

Snack Mixes

Ingredients:

2 cups Health Valley Rice Crunch 'ems cereal

1 cup Nature's Path Corn Flakes cereal

1 cup Glutino Sesame Pretzels (Note: these do have yeast.)

Optional additions: nuts, seeds, coconut flakes

Preheat oven to 300°F.

Toss together with one of the following sauces.

Bake for 45 minutes, stirring every 15 minutes until done.

Pecans and walnuts are a fantastic source of "good fats" as well as fiber.

In fact, the 2005 Dietary Guidelines from the U.S. Department of Agriculture recommend eating four to five servings of nuts each week. (www.happynutritionist.com)

Cherries and blueberries are packed full of antioxidants to fight off free radicals. Anti-inflammatory foods.

Honey Mustard Mix

¼ cup honey

3 tablespoons melted Earth Balance soy free

½ teaspoon ground mustard

Cinnamon-Sugar

3 tablespoons melted Earth Balance soy free

1 teaspoon cinnamon

2 teaspoons organic pure cane sugar

Everyday Snack Mix

(Note: There is not a recommended Worcestershire—Lea and Perrins has high-fructose corn syrup, French's and all of the "natural" or "vegetarian" ones have soy and other added ingredients.)

3 tablespoons melted Earth Balance

1 teaspoon (or more to taste) organic all-purpose seasoning

1 tablespoon Tamari soy sauce

1½ teaspoons raw honey

Veggie Tostada

Ingredients:

Rice tortillas (like Trader Joe's brown rice tortillas)

2 teaspoons avocado oil

Thinly sliced tomato

Thinly sliced zucchini (Or any other vegetable you think you can get away with)

½ teaspoon paprika

½ teaspoon salt

½ teaspoon cumin

½ cup shredded block of rice vegan (mozzarella, Cheddar, or a combination of the two)

Preheat oven to 400°F.

Brush each tortilla with oil and place on a baking sheet.

Bake for 5 to 8 minutes, or until crispy.

Pull the tortillas out of the oven and layer veggies on top.

Season with spices and sprinkle with shredded cheese.

Place the baking sheet back in the oven until the cheese is melted.

Tomatoes are rich in Vitamin C and potassium. Especially when cooked, they are a great source of lycopene, an antioxidant that has anti-inflammatory/immuno-supportive and anti-carcinogenic properties.

Avocado oil is very rich in Vitamin E and is a monounsaturated fatty acid, the "good fat." It is higher in omega-9 fatty acids than olive oil.

Try grating or slicing a variety of veggies—get creative!

Very Berry Fruit Salad

Ingredients:

¼ cup chopped strawberries
¼ cup blackberries
¼ cup chopped fresh pineapple
2 tablespoons chopped fresh mint

Very Apple Salad

Ingredients:

½ cup diced apple (peel optional, 1 medium sized apple)
¼ cup diced honeydew melon
¼ cup diced cucumber (peel optional, seed removed)
¼ cup diced zucchini (peeled)
2 tablespoons pineapple juice
Fresh parsley or mint
Toss ingredients together and serve!

CHAPTER 9

Soups and Stews

Photo Recipes: Top: Beverly's Famous Lentil Soup. Bottom: Spaghetti O Soup.

SOUPS AND STEWS

Azuki Bean Soup

Basic Beef Broth

Basic Standard Turkey Stock

Beverly's Famous Lentil Soup

BROCcoli Soup

Chicken and Rice Soup Avgolemono

Chicken Soup for the Soul

Classic Greek Vegetable Soup

Creamy Aspara-grass Soup

Creamy Broccoli Soup with Bacon Crumbles

Dr. K's Cabbage Soup For the Soul

Garden Ragout Stew

Greek Bean Soup

Onion Soup

Potato Leek and Artichoke Soup

Quick Vegetarian Soup

Rice Noodle Chicken Soup

Spaghetti O Soup

Soup From The Sea

Super Duper Steaky Souper

Tasty Turkey Chili

The Real Veal Stew

Turkey Taco Soup

White Bean Soup

Azuki Bean Soup

SOY

Ingredients:

1 large onion (yellow is strongest)

6–8 quarts water

1 cup azuki beans (washed and drained) (available at most health food stores)

1 strip kombu, 3 inches long and 1 inch wide (available at most health food stores)

4 medium carrots, chopped

6 stalks celery

3–5 cloves garlic, pressed

3–4 tablespoons soy sauce (or Tamari, optional)

1 teaspoon oregano (optional)

Salt to taste

Sauté the onion in olive oil.

Place the onion into a large pot and add the water, azuki beans, kombu, carrots, celery, and garlic.

Bring to a boil.

Cook over low heat for about 1¼ to 2 hours, until the beans are tender.

Add soy sauce (if not allergic).

Simmer 10 to 15 minutes longer.

Add oregano and salt to taste, if desired (only after beans are cooked).

Remove the kombu when serving.

Kombu is seaweed. The purpose of putting the kombu into the beans as they cook is to enhance the flavor of the beans, help soften them as they cook, and add nutrients to the dish that will alkalize them.

Beans are generally acidic due to their high-protein content, so kombu allows you to keep your meal high in protein without worrying that it may cause you to become too acidic.

TIP: Do not season beans with salt until they are at least 80 percent done. The salt can prevent them from softening.

Time Saver: It's not necessary to soak azuki beans. They will be tender without soaking. This soup is a meal in itself.

Basic Beef Broth

Ingredients:

Beef bones to fill a stock pot (use shanks if you prefer)

Water to cover bones

5–8 celery stalks, leaves and all, chopped

1 large onion

2 cloves garlic

Sea salt

Carrots

Combine all ingredients in a larger stock pot.

Boil the mixture for about 2 to 5 hours. (The longer the better.)

Strain, cool, and freeze in ice cube trays.

Pop out of the ice cube trays when frozen solid.

Put into small plastic bags and put back in freezer.

Use in any bean and other recipes to add flavor as well as nutrients.

Broths: one is Kitchen Basics, (www.kitchenbasics.net). Find a source near you on their website. The other brand is Pacific Foods (www.pacificfoods.com). Our local Albertson's grocery store carries both of these brands.

Many store-bought broths are shelf stable. They contain added yeast, MSG, sugars, and other artificial flavor enhancers.

Make it a steady habit once or twice a month to brew up some stocks and broths and freeze for future use.

Bone broths create gelatin that is very healing for the digestive tract. It contains glycerin, which helps to heal the gut, helps with detoxification, and aids in the formation of glutathione.

TIP: To give the broth a darker, richer color, toast the bones in the oven 30 to 45 minutes before boiling.

Basic Standard Turkey Stock

Ingredients:

1 turkey carcass

1–2 yellow onions (skin on), cleaned and cut in half

2 large carrots, scrubbed and cut in half

2 ribs celery (leaves included), cut in half

Parsley stems

2–3 bay leaves

10–12 whole peppercorns

Place all ingredients in a large stock pot and cover with cold water, up to about 1 inch above.

Simmer until turkey is done and vegetables are tender.

Turkey is a very lean protein, a good source of Vitamins B6 and B12, and also rich in zinc, which is very important for a healthy immune system and has been shown to be low in many kids on the autism spectrum. If the methylation pathways are functioning sufficiently, simple food sources are great sources for a healthy diet.

Carrots are rich in Vitamin A and contain carotenoids that can act as antioxidants.

Celery contains luteolin, a bioflavonoid that is anti-inflammatory/immuno-supportive and, according to NaturalNews.com, "Luteolin has high anti-oxidant properties, producing a dose-dependent reduction in oxidative DNA damage that is double the amount produced by Vitamin C."

Beverly's Famous Lentil Soup

Ingredients:

1 medium onion (yellow is best but any will work), chopped

4 quarts water

1 package dried, brown lentils (in the bean and rice section of the grocery store)

3 medium carrots

3 stalks celery, peeled and chopped

4–5 cloves garlic, crushed or sliced

1–2 whole bay leaves

1 teaspoons dried oregano

1 teaspoons dried rosemary or 1 sprig fresh

1 14-ounce can or jar stewed tomatoes (or you may use fresh ripe tomatoes, if available), chopped

½ teaspoon sea salt (or more to taste if you like)

Pepper to taste

Brown the onion in oil in a skillet.

Pour water into a large pot.

Add the lentils and other ingredients, including the onions.

Bring mixture to a boil, then turn down heat to lowest setting.

Simmer for about 1½ to 2 hours.

Stir occasionally to make sure it doesn't stick.

At the table:

Add 1 tablespoon raw, uncooked olive oil and 1 tablespoon wine vinegar (balsamic is tastiest).

Add salt and pepper to taste.

We also like to add some non-wheat bread chunks to the soup, which makes it a very healthy and filling meal.

This hearty soup is a meal in itself. It is an old family recipe, passed down from my grandmother in Greece. It is flexible, in that you can take out ingredients you may be restricted from temporarily. For example, our LAD allergy patients must refrain from onions, garlic, and spices for a short time during LAD month. Almost any combination of these ingredients will taste good together. At our house, my ten-year-old daughter Katerina likes to help peel the vegetables! It is a great recipe for the family to cook together, which makes shorter work for mom. (Remember, if you want, you can add kombu for the benefit of alkalizing the soup.) It tastes even better left over!

Lentils are a legume, and like other legumes they are high in foliate and fiber, but lentils are especially high in molybdenum. Molybdenum is an element that is present in very small amounts in the body. It is involved in many important biological processes, possibly including development of the nervous system, waste processing in the kidneys, and energy production in cells. It has shown promise in animal studies in reducing the harmful effects of certain cancer drugs on the heart and lungs. (Source: www.cancer.org.

Lentils are also high in protein and iron.

Chicken and Rice Soup Avgolemono

Ingredients:

6 cups chicken broth (preferably homemade)
½ cup long-grain rice, washed and drained
Salt and pepper to taste
3 eggs, very well beaten (or egg substitute)
Juice of 3 lemons, strained

Bring the broth to a boil in a large pot and add the rice.

Simmer, partially covered, for 20 minutes, until the rice is tender, then season with salt and pepper.

Beat the eggs and lemon juice together until frothy.

While the soup is still simmering, slowly **drizzle** in a ladleful of soup into the beaten egg and lemon, whisking or beating all the while.

Immediately pour the mixture back into the soup pot, turn off the heat, and stir to combine.

A healthy soup for any day of the week. This soup provides a high amount (and a lean source) of complete proteins, providing your body with its essential amino acid intake.

A one-cup serving provides 9 grams of protein and 15% of your RDI of vitamin C, all for 113 calories.

Eggs add a lean protein source.

TIP~ Make chicken soup by boiling a whole chicken. Then follow the remainder of the recipe.

Chicken Soup for the Soul (Basic Chicken Broth)

Ingredients:
1 large organic chicken
5–8 stalks of celery
1 large onion, whole
2 cloves garlic
Sea salt
Carrots

Boil all ingredients together for about two to three hours.

(The longer you cook this the better! Five hours is fine too.)

Strain, cool, and **freeze** in ice cube trays.

Pop out of the ice cube trays and put into zip-lock bags

in the freezer.

A homemade broth can bode better health boost than store bought brands due to its absence of "fake" ingredients. A free food. Broths have been boasted to have healing powers for centuries.

Bathing these bones with this delicious combination of veggies releases all of the nutrients into the broth and actually helps them easily assimilate into your body.

Just some wholesome nutritional goodness that can be used in a wide array of dishes.

TIP: You may use these in any bean and other recipes to add flavor as well as nutrients.

Classic Greek Vegetable Soup

Ingredients:
1 cup extra virgin olive oil
3 large onions, peeled and chopped
3 large carrots, peeled and cut into ¼-inch slices
2 ribs celery, trimmed and cut into ¼-inch slices
2 large potatoes, peeled and diced
4 large ripe tomatoes, peeled and chopped
1 bunch parsley, finely chopped
8 cups water
Salt to taste
½ pound spinach, washed, trimmed, and shredded
Fresh ground black pepper to taste
Juice of 1 large lemon

Heat half the olive oil in a large soup pot.

Add onions and cook, stirring, over medium heat until wilted, about 8 minutes.

Add carrots and celery and toss to coat with oil. **Sauté** in the pot for 5 minutes, stirring.

Add potatoes, stirring to coat, and add the tomatoes and parsley. Pour in the water.

Season with salt.

Bring soup to a boil, then reduce heat and **simmer** for 30 minutes.

Add spinach and **simmer** for another 20 minutes.

Adjust seasoning, including lemon juice, and **pour** in remaining raw olive oil just before serving.

Ladle into individual bowls. Yield: 6–8 servings.

This classic pot of goodness will fill your bowl to the brim with nutrient-rich vegetables. Many of these vegetables are also antioxidant rich.

One bowl of this superb and hearty soup provides over 100% RDI of both Vitamins A & K.

Vitamin A, according to Dr Mary Megson, a professor of pediatrics at the Medical College of Virginia, may be a key treatment for Children on the Autism spectrum due to related visual distortions. SOURCE: rense.com

In a paper titled "Vitamin K Deficiency as a Cause of Autistic Symptoms", Catherine Tamaro of Mercer Island, Washington proposes that Vitamin K deficiency has a strong link to Autism and that "it appears that one of the important functions of Vitamin K is to regulate the availability and concentration of calcium throughout the nervous system".

Creamy Aspara-grass Soup

Ingredients:
Earth Balance butter
1 small onion
3 cups vegetable broth
2 stalks lemongrass
1 clove garlic, smashed
1 pound asparagus
1 cup hemp milk
1 tablespoon arrowroot powder
¼ teaspoon white pepper

> Asparagus contains inulin, a probiotic, which actually aids in nutrient absorption, lowers risk of allergy, and lowers risk of colon cancer.
>
> It is also an excellent source of vitamin K.

Heat Earth Balance in a stock pot.

Add onion and **sauté** over medium heat until soft.

Pour in vegetable broth, lemongrass, and garlic.

Boil lightly for 20 minutes.

Wash and roughly chop asparagus and add to the pot.

Boil for 7 to 10 minutes to cook asparagus. Remove from heat and set aside.

Heat hemp milk and arrowroot powder in a small saucepan over medium high heat, stirring constantly until milk begins to thicken.

Pour asparagus mixture into a blender. **Pulse** carefully to chop down the larger ingredients.

Incorporate the hemp milk sauce into the blender.

Blend until mixture reaches desired consistency.

Creamy Broccoli Soup with Bacon Crumbles

Ingredients:

1 head broccoli, chopped, including portions of stalk1 onion, diced4 medium potatoes, peeled and diced2 cans chicken stock, gluten-free

Bacon crumbles

1 can coconut milk, unsweetened

Salt and pepper to taste

Combine broccoli, onion, and potatoes in a crockpot or soup pot.

Add chicken stock to barely cover.

Simmer until soft, about 20 minutes.

Process in a blender or food processor until almost smooth.

Return to pot.

Add bacon crumbles.

Add coconut milk and sea salt and pepper to taste.

Broccoli, again, is a super-food extraordinaire, high in calcium and in magnesium with many cancer-fighting connections.

Sulfophrane, found in broccoli, increases enzymes that help rid the body of cancer and help our bodies limit oxidative stress.

TIP: We like Thai Kitchen coconut milk (www.thai-kitchen.com).

Dr. K's Cabbage Soup for the Soul

Ingredients:

6 tablespoons olive oil

3 large onions (one yellow, one red, and one white), chopped

1 head garlic, peeled, each clove cut in half

½ bunch celery, chopped

¼ head red cabbage

¼ head green cabbage

½ cup brown and wild rice

1 teaspoon Celtic sea salt (or to taste)

1 teaspoon fresh grated horseradish (more if you like)

¼ teaspoon cayenne pepper (hotter if you like)

3 tablespoons tomato paste

1 large green pepper, chopped

1 teaspoon oregano

Heat 3 tablespoons olive oil and **sauté** onions until translucent. This makes them sweet.

Add the garlic and sauté. Garlic burns more easily than onion, add the garlic after you start the onions cooking.

Combine onions and garlic and other ingredients in a large 8-quart pot. Cover with water.

Cook until vegetables are done, about 1½ to 2 hours.

After soup is cooked and off the heat, **add** oregano and remaining 3 tablespoons olive oil.

Cabbage has been used and researched as a food remedy for gastro-intestinal disturbances, ulcers, chronic headaches, weight control, in disorders, jaundice, scurvy, arthritis, gout, heart disease, even Alzheimer's. It is actually richer in Vitamin C than an orange. Cabbage is a rich source of fiber, sulphur, and iodine, which helps with proper brain and nervous system function. This is one highly nutritious bowl of delicious!

TIP: This is a "souper soup." It is very healthy from the perspective of electrolyte balance and nutrients.

Garden Ragout Stew

Ingredients:

2 carrots

½ cup fresh or frozen lima beans

1 cup fresh or frozen green bean

1 cup organic cherry tomatoes

1 bunch fresh spinach

4 cups vegetable broth (like Imagine No-Chicken chicken broth)

1 teaspoon Bragg's 24 Sprinkle

Peel and **chop** carrots into ½-inch slices.

Combine all ingredients in a large stock pot and bring to a low boil over medium-high heat.

Reduce heat to medium low and simmer for 30 to 45 minutes.

Nothing like stewing in immune-boosting nutrition. Every veggie in this mix has immune-boosting abilities. Together, 'it's like eating the whole garden.

One bowl provides 100 percent RDI of Vitamin A and 20 percent RDI of Vitamin C, with almost 3 grams of fiber and 5 grams of protein.

Greek Bean Soup

Ingredients:

1 cup extra virgin olive oil

2 large onions, peeled, halved, and sliced

2 medium carrots, peeled and sliced into thin rounds

2 ribs celery, trimmed and sliced thin

2 cloves garlic, peeled and chopped

½ pound great northern or other small white beans, soaked overnight according to package directions

1 cup plum tomatoes, chopped

1 fresh hot pepper (optional)

8 cups water

Salt and pepper to taste

Juice of ½ lemon, strained (or 2–3 tablespoons red wine vinegar)

Onions, carrots, celery, garlic ... all the vegetables in this one-pot wonder offer a wealth of health benefits.

The beans are extremely high in folate, which is critical for healthy brain function, and tryptophan, an essential amino acid the body uses to synthesize proteins. Tryptophan plays an important role as the precursor to serotonin, the brain chemical that regulates our appetite, mood, and even our sleep patterns.

Heat ½ cup olive oil in a large soup pot and sauté onions until wilted.

Add carrots, celery, and garlic and cook until soft. Add beans and toss gently to coat with oil.

Add tomatoes, hot pepper, and water.

Bring to a boil, reduce heat, and **simmer,** uncovered, for 1½ to 2 hours, or until the beans are very tender.

Just before removing from heat, **adjust** seasoning with salt, pepper, and lemon juice or vinegar.

Makes 6 servings.

Onion Soup

Ingredients:

1½–2 pounds onions (yellow, Bermuda, red—or all kinds together)

¼ cup or olive oil

2 tablespoons olive oil

Salt and pepper

¼ teaspoon nutmeg

1 clove garlic, crushed

2 tablespoons flour (rice flour or other non-wheat starch)

2 quarts rich beef broth (non-gluten)

½ cup dry white wine (optional)

3 tablespoons brandy or Madeira (optional)

This soup has a more complex flavor when all three types of onions are used. The brandy or wine can be added to each individual bowl.

Slice onions very thinly and sauté in oil very slowly, about 20 minutes, until softened but not burned.

Season with salt, pepper, and nutmeg, add garlic and stir in flour.

Boil the broth with the wine in a saucepan. Pour over the onions, and simmer gently for 45 minutes.

Heat and add the brandy or Madeira when ready to serve.

Garnish soup with non-wheat toast.

Potato Leek and Artichoke Soup

Ingredients:
6 organic russet potatoes
1 cup leeks, washed and chopped
1 jar artichokes, drained and chopped
8–10 cups water
2½ teaspoons sea salt
3 cups hemp milk
1 teaspoon garlic powder
½ teaspoon white pepper

Wash, peel and **dice** potatoes into 2-inch cubes.

Wash and **chop** leeks and artichokes.

Combine all three into a large pot and cover with water.

Add 2 teaspoons salt and boil over high heat until potatoes are fork tender.

Strain over a wire mesh colander, dumping most of the

water out but reserving a bit at the bottom.

Add in the hemp milk, ½ teaspoon sea salt, garlic powder, and white pepper.

Blend until perfectly creamy using an immersion blender.

Artichokes are a great source of Vitamin C and folate, also magnesium; they contain a flavonoid called Silymarin which is thought to support liver function, is also high in antioxidant

Leeks are anti-inflammatory as well. Studies have shown that

leeks (just as onions and garlic) can improve the immune system, lower bad cholesterol levels, and fight cancer.

Perfect soup for any rainy day!

Top with bacon crumbles or Daiya cheese shreds.

Quick Vegetarian Soup

Ingredients:

2 tablespoons olive oil

1 cup Kitchen Basic roasted vegetable stock

2/3 cup fresh vegetables, sliced thin (carrots, onion, celery, beets, turnips, corn, beans, peppers)

or

2/3 cup frozen mixed vegetables

The more colorful the better! This soup is quick, easy, and immune-friendly.

In medium sauce pan

Heat olive oil and **sauté** mixed vegetables.

Add stock, cover.

Bring to a boil, then reduce heat to a **simmer** and cook 5 to 8 minutes.

Rice Noodle Chicken Soup

Ingredients:
1 package rice noodles
6 cups Chicken Soup for the Soul recipe
1 organic carrot, finely diced or shredded
1 rib celery, finely diced
¼–½ cup kombu or seaweed, diced

Boil rice noodles according to package directions.

Warm 6 cups of Chicken Soup for the Soul in a separate stock pot over medium heat.

Stir in carrots, celery, and Kombu and simmer for 15 to 20 minutes.

Divide noodles into individual bowls.

Pour soup mixture over noodles.

Serve.

Add Chicken Soup for the Soul with organic veggies, rice noodles and this homemade soup will out distance any canned soup in great taste!

It's definitely a free food. The delicious combination of veggies releases all of the nutrients in to the broth and actually helps them to easily assimilate in your body.

Soup from the Sea

FISH

Ingredients:

2/3 cup extra virgin olive oil

3 celery stalks, washed and sliced thin

1 large leek, tough greens and root trimmed, washed thoroughly and sliced thin

3 carrots, peeled and sliced thin

1½ quarts water

½ teaspoon peppercorns

3 pounds large fresh white fish (bass, grouper, snapper, or cod), cleaned and cut in half

3 potatoes, peeled and cut into large chunks

Salt and pepper to taste

Juice of 1 lemon

2 tablespoons extra virgin olive oil to drizzle over cooked fish

2–3 tablespoons capers, rinsed (optional)

This soup is a fantastic source of essential fatty acids; it also packs a punch in the protein department, providing over 25 grams of protein per bowl. Also, it is a rich source of Vitamin A and gives a fair amount of pyridoxine (B6).

Heat ½ cup olive oil in a large soup pot and **sauté** the celery, leeks, and carrots over medium heat, tossing to coat, until softened, about 8 minutes.

Pour in 1½ quarts (6 cups) water and add the peppercorns.

Bring to a boil, lower the heat, and simmer the vegetables for 25 minutes.

Remove vegetables to a platter, using a slotted spoon.

Add fish to the stock and **simmer** for 15 to 20 minutes, until the flesh starts to fall away from the bone.

Strain soup, reserving broth and fish separately.

Add potatoes to the pot together with the remaining vegetables.

Simmer another 10 to 15 minutes, until the potatoes are tender.

Season with salt, pepper, and lemon juice. Just before serving add remaining raw olive oil.

Remove bones from the fish and place the flesh on a platter. Drizzle with olive oil and lemon juice, a few capers, and pepper. Makes 6 servings.

Spaghetti O Soup

Ingredients:
1 cup dry Schar Anellini pasta
½ pound grass-fed ground beef
½ zucchini, finely shredded
1 tablespoon flaxseed meal
1 tablespoon Annie's Naturals Ketchup
4 cups chicken broth
2 cups Eden Organic Pizza and Pasta Sauce

TIP: Make chicken broth ahead of time and freeze it in cup portions.

Preheat oven to 400°F.

Boil pastatough greens and root trimmed,, drain, and set aside.

Mix together the beef, zucchini, flaxseed meal, and ketchup in a mixing bowl.

Roll the beef mixture into mini meatballs, about 1 inch thick.

Place meatballs on a baking sheet.

Bake for 10 to 12 minutes (be sure meatballs are fully cooked)

Heat the chicken broth and pizza sauce in a large saucepan over medium heat.

Add the meatballs and pasta.

Stir gently until all ingredients are well combined.

Serve.

Super Duper Steaky Souper

Ingredients:

2 tablespoons safflower oil

1 pound sirloin or tri-tip beef roast

½ cup arrowroot flour

4 cups beef broth

2–3 red potatoes, washed and diced into 1-inch cubes

1–1½ cups chopped broccoli (or spinach)

½ small onion, chopped

2 cloves garlic, finely chopped

1 teaspoon ground tarragon

1 teaspoon sea salt

½ teaspoon freshly ground pepper

Can't forget that red meat? At least you can pair it with a powerful green like broccoli.

Broccoli is an excellent vegetable source of iron. It's believed to neutralize carcinogens. Sulphophrane, found in broccoli, increases enzymes that help rid the body of cancer. Help our bodies to limit oxidative stress.

Heat safflower oil over high heat in a large stock pot.

Dice beef into 1-inch cubes and **roll** in arrowroot flour to lightly dust.

Throw cubes of flour-dusted beef into the heated oil and brown on all sides; lower heat to medium.

Add beef broth and remaining ingredients and **stir** until well combined.

Bring to a low boil, then lower heat to medium-low and **simmer** for 30 minutes to 2 hours.

Tasty Turkey Chili

Ingredients:

1 pound ground turkey

1 large can organic tomato sauce

1 large can organic stewed tomatoes (with juice)

1 cup diced zucchini

1 can organic kidney beans

1 can organic garbanzo beans

1 cup water

½ cup diced carrot (you can buy frozen)

2 tablespoons chili powder

1 tablespoon paprika

1 teaspoon cumin

½ teaspoon white pepper

1 tablespoon black strap molasses

1 teaspoon garlic salt

2 teaspoon sea salt

Beans: The Lovely Legume! The number-one food on the United States Department of Agriculture's list of 20 high-antioxidant sources of common foods is a bean. In twenty spots, four are taken by a bean variety. Antioxidants, like those found in beans, have been linked to lowering the risk for some types of cancers.

Fill that bowl once, even twice, because this chili is chock full of anti-inflammatory flavor.

Brown turkey in a little bit of oil over medium heat in a large soup pot.

Add remaining ingredients when turkey is cooked through.

Stir well.

Bring mixture to a low boil.

Reduce heat to low and simmer for 20 minutes to 2 hours. The longer it cooks, the better the flavors will incorporate.

Serve as is, top with some organic blue corn chips, or even shred some Rice Vegan Cheddar on top.

The Real Veal Stew

Ingredients:

½ cup olive oil

2½ pounds boneless veal, cut into 1½-inch
  cubes

2 pounds pearl onions, peeled but whole

1½ cups peeled, chopped plum tomatoes

2 cloves garlic, minced

1 large bay leaf

½ teaspoons whole black peppercorns

Salt to taste

3 tablespoons red wine vinegar

Water, if necessary

1 teaspoon sugar (optional)

Veal is a lean source of protein. According to naturalfoodbenefits.com, "Onions are rich in active compounds that successfully inhibit the development of cancerous cells."

Heat olive oil in a large casserole dish.

Brown veal over high heat.

Remove veal with a slotted spoon.

Add onions and **sauté** until wilted.

Add tomatoes, garlic, bay leaf, and peppercorns to the pot.

Return meat to pot.

Season with salt and half of the vinegar.

Lower heat. **Cover** and **simmer** over low heat for 1½ to 2 hours.

Add a little water during cooking if necessary.

Adjust seasoning with salt, sugar, if needed, and additional vinegar, just before removing from heat.

Serve over rice pasta. Makes 6–8 servings.

Turkey Taco Soup

Ingredients:

1 pound ground turkey

1 tablespoon oil

¾ cups celery, chopped

¾ cups frozen carrots

1/3 cups onion, chopped (omit if used within 3 days on rotation)

4 cups turkey broth (find online or make your own

2 bay leaves

Turkey is a very lean protein, a good source of Vitamins B6 and B12, and also rich in zinc.

It is also a good source of the amino acid L-Tryptophan.

Brown ground turkey in oil in a stock pot. Drain off fat.

Add celery, carrots, and onion over medium heat and cook just until soft.

Add broth and bay leaves and cook on medium-low heat for a minimum of 20 minutes. The longer it simmers, the more the flavors will develop. We recommend simmering for at least 30 minutes.

Remove bay leaves before serving.

Serve with rice crackers for added crunch. (Back to Nature brand makes gluten-free crackers now. Read the nutritional panels for the gluten-free product.)

You could also sprinkle in some shredded Rice Vegan cheese.

White Bean Soup

Ingredients:

1 cup extra virgin olive oil

2 large onions, peeled, halved, and sliced

2 medium carrots, peeled and sliced into thin
  rounds

2 ribs celery, trimmed and sliced thin

2 cloves garlic, peeled and chopped

½ pound great northern or other small white
  beans, soaked overnight according to
  package directions

1 cup plum tomatoes, chopped

1 fresh hot pepper (optional)

8 cups water

Salt and pepper to taste

Juice of ½ lemon, strained, or 2–3 tablespoons red wine vinegar

> *Be sure to soak your beans overnight to make them easier to metabolize. If you are still getting a bloated and gassy tummy after using the soaking/sprouting method, add a little kombu to any bean recipe to soften them even further for easy digestion.*

Heat half the olive oil in a large soup pot and sauté onions until wilted.

Add carrots, celery, and garlic and cook until soft.

Add beans and toss gently to coat with oil.

Add tomatoes, hot pepper, and water and bring to a boil. Reduce heat and simmer, uncovered, for 1½ to 2 hours, or until the beans are very tender.

Just before removing from heat, **adjust** seasoning with salt and pepper and lemon juice or vinegar.

CHAPTER 10

Syrups, Salsas, Sauces, and Dips

Photo Recipe: Greater Tots Signature Ranch-Ish

211

Syrups, Sauces, Salsas, and Dips

Alfredo Sauce

Artichoke and White Bean Dip

Basic Chicken Gravy

Beer BBQ Sauce

Black Beauty Bean Dip

Chickie Dip

Cinnamon-Spice Butter

Figgilicious Nut Butter

Greater Tots Signature Ranch-Ish

Greater Tots Signature Ranch-Ish (Soy-Free Version)

Greater Tots Thousand Dollar Dressing

Honeydew Salsa and Sweet Potato Chips

Honey Mustard Cream Sauce

MangoTango Salsa

Nut Butters

Poseidon's Magic Sea Potion

Sesame Nut Butter

Sour Cream Sauce

Sweet Roasted Garlic Salad Dressing and Marinade

Tomato Vinaigrette Dressing

Very Berry Dressing

White Wine and Mustard Marinade

Alfredo Sauce

NUTS

3 tablespoons Earth Balance soy free

2 teaspoons potato starch flour

½ cup MimicCreme unsweetened cream

1 cup non-dairy milk ½ Daiya mozzarella
   shreds

1 teaspoon salt

1 teaspoon chopped fresh parsley

½ teaspoon garlic powder

Fresh cracked pepper to taste

The original recipe for Alfredo sauce is loaded with butter, cheese, and heavy cream. Try this alternative that is completely dairy free!

Heat the butter in a skillet or saucepan over medium heat.

Whisk in potato starch to incorporate lumps.

Add cream and milk, Daiya shreds, and seasonings and herbs.

Stir until cheese is melted.

Serve over gluten-free pasta.

Artichoke and White Bean Dip

Ingredients:

1 can or jar organic artichokes

1 can organic white beans (could also use garbanzo)

1 tablespoon fresh chives

¼ cup almond or hazelnut milk

1 tablespoon sesame oil

1 teaspoon salt

½ teaspoon sweet paprika

½ teaspoon cumin

Artichokes are a great source of antioxidants, Vitamin C, folate, fiber, magnesium, and potassium. They also contain cynarin, a phytochemical that stimulates bile production, which aids in overall digestion, and silymarin, which is thought to support liver function.

Blend ingredients together in a blender or food processor.

Serve warm or cold.

For extra fun, get out your cookie cutters and make some fun corn chips. Simply punch out shapes from a corn tortilla, brush both sides with olive oil, sesame oil, or avocado oil, and bake at 400°F for 6 to 10 minutes or until crisp. (Sprouted corn tortillas will crisp a bit quicker.)

Basic Chicken Gravy

Ingredients:
2 tablespoons Earth Balance
1½ tablespoons potato starch flour
2 cups chicken broth
1 teaspoon Bragg's Sprinkle 24

This is a dairy-free version of the classic chicken gravy—delicious over baked, steamed, or roasted chicken, mashed potatoes, or wild rice.

Heat the butter in a skillet or saucepan over medium heat.

Pour in 1 cup of chicken broth.

Whisk potato starch flour into remaining cup of broth.

Pour the mixture into the saucepan.

Add chicken broth and seasonings.

Simmer, stirring constantly, until gravy thickens.

Beer BBQ Sauce

Ingredients:
1 15-ounce can Muir Glen no salt added
    tomato sauce
1 12-ounce can Zevia root beer
1 tablespoon chili powder
2 teaspoons sweet paprika
½ teaspoon onion powder
½ teaspoon garlic powder
2 tablespoons apricot preserves (non-HFC)
2 teaspoons sea salt

This is a fantastic BBQ sauce recipe for those on an anti-yeast diet—no vinegar and all-natural ingredients only. Use on brisket or to baste a burger!

Keeps really well in the fridge in an airtight container.

Combine all ingredients in a medium saucepan.

Bring to a low boil over medium heat.

Reduce heat to low and **simmer** for 15 to 20 minutes.

Store in a glass mason jar in the refrigerator.

Black Beauty Bean Dip

Ingredients:
1 can organic black beans
2 tablespoons cilantro
2 tablespoons onion
½ teaspoon chili powder
½ teaspoon cumin
½ teaspoon sea salt
½ teaspoon paprika
¼ teaspoon garlic powder
¼ cup Daiya mozzarella shreds

Black Beans: ½ cup serving has 7.4 grams of fiber.

Cumin is a fantastic anti-inflammatory/immuno-supportive spice.

Cilantro lowers triglycerides.

Preheat oven to 400°F.

Blend beans, cilantro, onion, chili powder, cumin, salt, paprika, and garlic powder in a blender or food processor.

Transfer mixture to a baking dish. Top with cheese shreds and bake until cheese is melted.

Serve with a combination of sliced vegetables such as carrots and celery, or with corn tortilla chips.

Chickie Dip

Ingredients:

2 cloves garlic

1 14-ounce can cooked garbanzo beans, drained

½ cup Tahini (Hain or Sunbutter brand)

Juice of 1 small lemon

2 tablespoons olive oil, and more if necessary

Combine garlic and drained garbanzo beans in a food processor or blender.

Add Tahini (sesame butter) and lemon juice.

Add olive oil and process. If mixture is too stiff, add more olive oil to achieve desired consistency.

Serve with carrot or celery sticks, broccoli or cauliflower florets, or rice thins and other gluten-free snack foods.

Traditional hummus dip is super-nutritious! Chickpeas are a great legume and are definitely on the anti-inflammatory food list.

Chickpeas (garbanzo beans) are a rich source of zinc, folate, and protein.

Cinnamon-Spice Butter

Ingredients:

½ cup Earth Balance soy free or Ghee (if no milk allergy)

1½ teaspoons pumpkin pie spice

1 tablespoon brown rice syrup or raw honey

Blend ingredients in a blender or food processor.

Serve with homemade crackers or on rice cakes; even spread on a waffle.

If you do not have a milk allergy, Ghee can be a good substitute. Ghee is a form of clarified butter that originated in South Asia and is commonly used in South Asian Cuisine.

This is a tasty spread for gluten free crackers and even on gluten free pancakes!

Figgilicious Nut Butter

NUTS

Ingredients:
1 cup raw or roasted hazelnuts
1 tablespoon grapeseed oil
3 dried figs
2 tablespoons honey

Blend toasted hazelnuts in a blender or food processor until coarsely chopped, about 1 minute.

Add oil and blend on low speed for 2 to 3 minutes, scraping the sides down occasionally.

When the nuts begin to form into a paste, **blend** on high for 2 to 6 minutes. (Time varies depending upon oil content of nuts.

Add figs and honey.

Blend for another minute, or until the figs are incorporated.

Serve with homemade crackers or on rice cakes; even spread on a waffle.

Hazelnuts are strongly anti-inflammatory/immuno-supportive and a fantastic source of protein, fiber, and Vitamin E.

Figs are also highly anti-inflammatory and very high in fiber.

This Figgilicious dip is delicious on crackers or spread on GFCF toast or even waffles, pancakes, or biscuits.

Greater Tots Signature Ranch-Ish

Ingredients:

½ cup Grapeseed Vegenaise

¼ cup rice milk

¼ teaspoon celery salt

2 tablespoons fresh parsley

2 tablespoons fresh thyme

¼ teaspoon paprika

¼ teaspoon garlic powder

Grapeseed Vegenaise, a "vegan mayonnaise," is dairy-free. This great-tasting mayo is rich in vitamin E, which protects tissues from oxidative damage.

Blend all ingredients together in a blender or food processor.

Keep on hand in airtight container in the refrigerator. You will be using this one quite a bit.

Greater Tots Signature Ranch-Ish (Soy-Free Version)

Ingredients:

½ cup coconut yogurt (plain)

1 tablespoon dairy-free milk or unsweetened MimicCreme

1 tablespoon apple cider vinegar

¼ teaspoon celery seed

1 teaspoon fresh parsley

½ teaspoon fresh thyme

¼ teaspoon paprika

¼ teaspoon garlic salt

Coconut yogurt is a fantastic probiotic alternative to traditional dairy yogurt.

Blend all ingredients together in a blender or food processor, or simply stir with a spoon.

Keep on hand in airtight container in the refrigerator.

We typically use the Grapeseed Vegenaise, but it has soy, so try this combination of yogurt and apple cider vinegar instead.

Greater Tots Thousand Dollar Dressing

Ingredients:

¼ cup finely diced Ferminator Pickles
   (see recipe)
1 cup Vegenaise Organic
1/3 cup Annie's Organic Ketchup
2 teaspoons white truffle oil
1 teaspoon lemon juice

Mix diced pickles together with remaining ingredients.

Store in a mason jar in the refrigerator.

Annie's Ketchup is a great alternative to most store-bought ketchups. It is made with organic ingredients and does not contain high-fructose corn syrup. If you are sticking to a yeast-free diet and avoiding vinegar, try using ¼ cup of Muir Glen tomato paste instead.

Honeydew Salsa and Sweet Potato Chips

Ingredients:
1 cup honeydew melon, cubed
1/3 cup cucumber, peeled, seeds removed
½ cup grapes, white, seedless
¼ cup chopped celery
2 tablespoons parsley
Finely chopped jalapeño to taste

Honeydew melon is very high in Vitamin C and is also a good source of B6 and potassium.

Blend all ingredients in a blender or food processor to desired consistency.

Serve with sweet potato chips, such as Terra Chips Sweet or Mexicana.

Honey Mustard Cream Sauce

Ingredients:

2 cups rice milk

2 tablespoons potato starch flour

2 tablespoons organic mustard

2 tablespoons honey

¼ cup lemon juice

¼ cup finely chopped fresh parsley

1 teaspoon salt, or to taste

¼ teaspoon white pepper

Combine ¼ cup rice milk with the potato starch in a small saucepan over medium-low heat.

Stir constantly until the mixture forms a paste.

Whisk in the remaining milk, mustard, honey,

and lemon juice and cook, stirring constantly, until the mixture is slightly thickened, about 3 to 4 minutes.

Stir in the seasonings.

This is a great sauce to use over fish or chicken.

Mustard seeds have fantastic phytonutrients and enzymes that actually break those glucosinolates down into a separate phytonutrient called isothiocyanates. Isothiocyanates have been studied repeatedly for their anti-cancer effects. (Source: whfoods.com.)

Mustard seeds are also a rich source of selenium and magnesium, both of which have been linked to reduction in the severity of asthma.

MangoTango Salsa

Ingredients:

2 ripe mangoes, skinned and pitted

1/3 cup cucumber, peeled, seeds removed

½ teaspoon fresh jalapeño, no seeds (optional)

2 tablespoons fresh cilantro

½ teaspoon salt

½ teaspoon sweet paprika

Blend all ingredients in a blender or food processor to desired consistency.

Serve with Terra Sweet and Beets or your favorite scooping side.

Mangoes have enzymes that help in digestion. They are a great source of fiber and are rich in beta-carotene which may protect from oxidative stress, and are alkaline forming.

Mango has also been found to interrupt phases of growth during the life cycle of tumor cells.

Nut Butters
Sesame Nut Butter

NUTS

Ingredients:

2 cups sesame seeds (2 cups raw = 1 cup butter)

Whatever quantity of nut butter you want to end up with, you should begin with roughly twice as much bulk. We use a food processor, but most nut butters can also be made in a blender.

Put the nuts or sesame seeds into the food processor or blender. **Process** until soft and creamy.

Almond, Macadamia, and Cashew Nut Butters

Ingredients:

2 cups almond, macadamia or cashews (2 cups raw = 1 cup butter.)

Spread nuts on a baking sheet and **bake** at 250°F.

Bake 45 to 60 minutes.

Process thoroughly into a paste in food processor or blender.

Sesame nut butter tastes very much like peanut butter (many people cannot tell the difference). Sesame seeds can be purchased in bulk at most health food stores for about two to three dollars per pound.

You can also try almond, macadamia nut, and cashew butter.

It is easy enough to find sesame and the other nut butters at the health food store. Instead of making a conventional peanut butter and jelly sandwich, use wheatless bread and use sesame or other nut butter with honey. Brands include Francis Simun Bread and Kettle Nut Butters.

Sesame is high in Vitamin C.

Sesame Nut Butter is a fantastic alternative for those who have a nut allergy.

Poseidon's Magic Sea Potion

Ingredients:

2 avocados

2 tablespoons lemon juice

1 palm-full of Dulse seaweed blend

¼ cup coconut oil, melted

Blend all ingredients together in a food processor or blender.

> Dulse is a sea vegetable. It has a mildly spicy and salty flavor. One serving of this sauce provides more than 100 percent of the RDI of vitamin B6.

Sour Cream Sauce

SOY

Ingredients:
¾ cup Grapeseed Vegenaise
½ cup rice milk
1 tablespoon apple cider vinegar
½ teaspoon garlic powder
Sea salt to taste

Stir ingredients together over medium heat in a saucepan.

Simmer, stirring constantly, until all of the ingredients come together into a sauce.

Serve over chicken enchiladas or grilled chicken.

This is our preferred sour cream sauce recipe, especially since it doesn't use soy sour creams. Vegenaise does contain soy lecithin, but it is a grapeseed oil product, not a soy product. Some people with soy allergies can tolerate soy lecithin, but others cannot.

This is delicious over chicken.

Sweet Roasted Garlic Salad Dressing and Marinade

Ingredients:
1 head garlic
4 tablespoons almond oil
2 tablespoons plum, cherry, or prune juice
1 tablespoon apple cider vinegar
Pinch of salt

Garlic ~has amazing nutritional effects. It can improve the immune system, but also has antibacterial, antifungal, and antiviral capabilities. Garlic actually can inhibit the activity of inflammatory messenger molecules.

Preheat oven to 400°F.

Cut off the top of the garlic head so that the cloves are visible (do not separate the cloves). Peel the excess skin from the outside of the garlic head; it should just flake off.

Drizzle 1 tablespoon oil over the cloves.

Seal the entire head of garlic in foil

Bake for 45 minutes to 1 hour.

Let the garlic cool for about 15 minutes before handling. Then, **squeeze** out the pasty garlic cloves into a blender, discarding the shell(s).

Add the remaining 3 tablespoons almond oil, vinegar, fruit juice, and salt and pepper to taste in the blender.

Blend until smooth.

Keep for 3 to 4 days in the refrigerator in an airtight container.

Tomato Vinaigrette Dressing

Ingredients:
4 tomatoes
¼ cup olive oil
2 garlic cloves
1 tablespoon apple cider vinegar
½ teaspoon sweet paprika
1 tablespoon fresh chopped basil
½ teaspoon sea salt
Honey to taste

Tomatoes are alkaline and are a fantastic source of lycopene, which prevents cancer. Can also raise the SPF of the skin and fights free-radicals.

Preheat oven to 450°F.

Place tomatoes and whole garlic cloves on a baking sheet.

Drizzle with about 1 tablespoon oil. Roast for 25 to 30 minutes.

Toss the roasted tomatoes and garlic along with the remaining ingredients into a food processor or blender. Pulse a few times, then blend on low to medium speed for about 1 minute.

Keep in an airtight container in the refrigerator and serve on salads or use as a marinade to add delicious flavor to meats, poultry, or fish.

Very Berry Dressing

Ingredients:
¼ cup vegetable or olive oil
2 tablespoons raspberry vinegar
2 tablespoons raspberry preserves

Mix ingredients and refrigerate for 15 minutes.

Toss with salad and serve.

Berries are alkalizing fruit choices. Raspberries are loaded with vitamins, antioxidants, and fiber. They are a great source of manganese, an enzyme activator. Manganese-dependant superoxide dismutase (SOD) is an enzyme that is found inside the mitochondria and needs manganese to activate it's free-radical protecting capabilities.

Berries also contain ellagic acid.

White Wine and Mustard Marinade

Ingredients:

2 medium shallots

1 small onion, diced

½ cup white wine

1 cup (8 ounces) chicken stock

2 tablespoons Dijon mustard or Annie's Naturals Yellow Mustard (or use 2 teaspoons mustard powder to avoid milk ingredients)

Chives to taste

Fresh ground pepper to taste

Great for chicken, veal, beef, or any meat

Use 2 teaspoons mustard powder instead of Dijon (or use Annie's Naturals Yellow Mustard**

Mix all ingredients well to make marinade.

Wash meat.

Place meat and marinade in a ziplock bag or airtight container for 1 hour (overnight for more flavor) in refrigerator.

Grill or bake meat, using marinade as a baste.

CHAPTER 11

Salads, Sandwiches, and Such

Photo Recipe: Pork N Pine Pizza Panini and Greek Villager's Salad

Salads, Sandwiches and Such

Cold Apple Chicken Pasta Salad

Cowboy Slaw Y'all

Dijon Green Bean Salad

Eggless Breakfast Tacos

Golden Carrot Salad

Greek Villager's Salad

Green Bean Salad with Pine Nuts and Tomatoes

Ham and Pea Pasta Salad

Pork 'n' Pine Pizza Panini

Pulled Pork Picnic Salad

Quinoa Tabouleh

Roasted Pumpkin Seeds

Smoked Salmon Salad

Very Berry Spinach Salad

We've got the BEET, Apple and Chard Salad

Cold Apple Chicken Pasta Salad

Ingredients:

8–12 ounces chicken breast, baked

4 ounces rice pasta (Lundberg) or fine angel hair (check the Asian aisle for rice noodles)

1 teaspoon avocado oil

½ cup finely chopped celery

½ cup chopped apples (or try shredded parsnips or shredded fennel)

1 tablespoon grapeseed oil

¼ cup walnuts (optional)

For the dressing combine these ingredients:

2–3 tablespoons grapeseed oil

1 tablespoon apple cider vinegar

½ cup coconut yogurt, plain

Sea salt and pepper to taste

This recipe is great made with turkey or even salmon instead of chicken.

Celery contains the bioflavenoid luteolin. It is anti-inflammatory/immuno-supportive. According to NaturalNews.com, "Luteolin has high antioxidant properties. It produces a dose-dependent reduction in oxidative DNA damage that is double the amount produced by vitamin C."

The dressing provides probiotics.

Cook chicken or use leftover chicken. If cooking, simply bake in a glass dish with a lid (add a little oil and 1 or 2 tablespoons of water to the dish before baking).

Boil water in a large pot and cook rice noodles according to package directions, adding the avocado oil and a little salt to the water with the noodles.

Chop and shred vegetables and fruit.

Wisk all ingredients together in a separate bowl.

Drain noodles and put them back in to the large pot.

Add chopped and shredded vegetables and fruit as well as walnuts if using.

Pour dressing over top.

Toss together until ingredients are evenly incorporated.

Transfer to a refrigerator safe dish and chill for at least 2 hours.

Cowboy Slaw Y'all

Ingredients:
1 bag organic broccoli slaw mix
1 can organic pinto beans (or make fresh)
½ cup sunflower seeds
½ cup frozen corn

Dressing:
¼ cup apple cider vinegar
1/3 cup favorite oil
2 tablespoons Vegenaise organic
1 teaspoon chili powder
1 teaspoon paprika
Sea salt to taste

This broccoli slaw salad is packed full of vitamins and nutrients, as well as healthy fats.

One serving provides more than 100 percent RDA of vitamin C, 4.5 grams of fiber, and almost 8 grams of protein. Saddle up!

Combine broccoli slaw mix, pinto beans, sunflower seeds, and corn in a medium bowl.

Prepare dressing by whisking the dressing ingredients together thoroughly.

Pour dressing over salad and **toss** thoroughly to combine.

Serve this delightful, healthy salad!

Dijon Green Bean Salad

SOY

Ingredients:

1 pound green beans

½ cup chopped red onion

¼ cup olive oil

3 tablespoons lemon juice

2 teaspoons grated lemon zest

1 teaspoon Dijon mustard (for milk-free substitute, mix 1 teaspoon mustard, ½ teaspoon Vegenaise)

½ teaspoon dried Italian seasoning

½ teaspoon salt

¼ teaspoon pepper

1 cup cherry tomatoes, halved

Did you know that green beans actually contain carotenoids in amounts that are comparable to carrots? The green pigments are also so abundant as to hide the other hues.

Many kids like green beans too, so they are definitely a family-friendly favorite veggie!

Bring large pot of water to boil over high heat.

Add beans and **cook** until beans are just tender, about 3 to 4 minutes.

Add red onion during last minute of cooking time.

Drain beans and **rinse** with cold water until cooled, then pat dry with paper towels.

Whisk together oil, lemon juice, lemon zest, mustard, Italian seasoning, salt, and pepper in a large bowl.

Add beans and toss to coat.

Stir in tomatoes gently.

Eggless Breakfast Tacos

NUTS

Ingredients:
2 tablespoons avocado oil
2 cups diced pre-baked potatoes
½ cup diced zucchini
½ cup diced tomatoes
½ cup ham or bacon, cut into pieces
6–8 corn tortillas (such as Food for Life Sprouted Corn Tortillas)
1–2 cups chopped spinach leaves
½ cup Daiya Cheddar shreds

Heat oil in a skillet over medium-high heat.

Toss in potatoes, zucchini, tomatoes, and meat.

Cook for 6 to 10 minutes, until potatoes and zucchini are slightly browned.

To serve, place some potato mixture on a tortilla,

sprinkle with spinach leaves and Cheddar shreds,

and fold over like a taco.

Serve with your favorite salsa fresco.

To make this dish vegan, leave out the ham or bacon.

Avocado oil is very rich in Vitamin E and is a monounsaturated fatty acid (the "good fat"). It is higher in omega-9 fatty acids than olive oil.

Spinach contains glutathione, which is a key deficiency that is linked to autism. Spinach is also a good source of CoQ10, which is very significant in mitochondrial energy production. It is abundant with antioxidants, such as alpha lipoic acid, vitamins C, E and K.

Golden Carrot Salad

Ingredients:
2 cups finely grated carrots
¼ cup organic golden raisins
2 tablespoons Grapeseed Vegenaise
2 tablespoons lemon juice
1 tablespoon brown rice syrup

Toss all ingredients together in a mixing bowl.

Refrigerate for at least 1 hour.

Carrots are the richest vegetable in Vitamin A and carotenes, which is directly related to a decreased risk for heart disease. Animal research has shown that diets rich in beta-carotene can reduce the occurrence of emphysema as well as vision/macular degeneration.

Carrots also contain a phytonutrient called falcarinal, which in a study published in the Journal of Agricultural and Food Chemistry was found to be a protective agent against colon cancer.

Golden raisins are a good source of Vitamin B-6 as well as Vitamin C and, of course, fiber. Although they have nutritional value, they should definitely be used in limited amounts due to their high sugar content, especially when fighting yeast. Simply leave them out of this salad if you need to.

Greek Villager's Salad

Ingredients:
3 large firm ripe tomatoes
1 large red onion, peeled, halved, and sliced
    thin
1 medium firm ripe cucumber, peeled, seeded,
    and cut into □-inch rounds
1 cup Kalamata olives
4 tablespoons extra virgin olive oil
1 teaspoon oregano
Salt to taste

This is a delicious and versatile salad, great with any meal.

Wash and dry the tomatoes.

Cut tomatoes in half, core them, and cut each half into chunky wedges.

Toss tomatoes with onion, cucumber, and olives.

Add olive oil, oregano, and salt, and toss to combine.

Sprinkle crumbled feta on top, just before serving.

Serve at room temperature with good, hearty bread.

Makes 4 servings

Green Bean Salad with Pine Nuts and Tomatoes

Ingredients:
1 pound fresh green beans, trimmed
2 large tomatoes, washed and wiped dry
2 cloves garlic, peeled and minced
3 tablespoons pine nuts, lightly toasted
1 small bunch fresh mint, leaves only, shredded
3–4 tablespoons extra virgin olive oil
2 tablespoons red wine vinegar
Salt and pepper to taste

> Green beans are a great provider of those gorgeously green pigments and are abundant in vitamin K and vitamin C. They also actually contain carotenoids in similar content to carrots.

Steam the beans for 10 to 12 minutes, until tender but firm.

Prepare the tomatoes, while the beans are cooking. Using a flat cheese grater, hold the tomatoes one at a time in one hand, with the core facing the palm of your hand, and grate into a bowl.

Strain the tomatoes so that only the pulp and none of the juice remains.

Drain cooked beans in a colander and rinse under cold water.

Toss beans, tomatoes, garlic, pine nuts and mint together.

Drizzle in olive oil and vinegar. Season with salt and pepper.

Toss to combine and let the beans marinate, covered and refrigerated, for 1 hour before serving.

Makes 4 servings

Ham and Pea Pasta Salad

Ingredients:
1 box rice pasta, farfel or rotelle
1 tablespoon Earth Balance
1 teaspoon arrowroot powder
1 cup rice or almond milk
1 teaspoon sea salt
Fresh cracked black pepper to taste
½ teaspoon garlic salt
2 teaspoons organic apple cider vinegar
1 cup frozen peas
4 slices Applegate Farms Black Forest Ham

Coumestral is a polyphenol found in peas that has shown to protect against stomach cancer. This is based upon a daily serving of 2 milligrams of coumestral or higher.

One serving of this pasta (about one-fourth of the recipe) provides you with 2.5 milligrams of coumestral.

Cook pasta according to package directions.

Melt butter in a saucepan over medium-high heat.

Whisk in arrowroot powder, and then add milk. Continue whisking until sauce starts to thicken.

Add salt, pepper, garlic salt, vinegar, peas, and ham and cook for 3 to 5 minutes, until peas are thawed.

Drain pasta and pour into a serving bowl.

Pour ham and pea sauce over the pasta.

Mix to combine.

Garnish with some fresh basil or parsley for beautiful color and an earthy addition.

Pork 'n' Pine Pizza Panini

Ingredients:
2 slices GFCF bread
1–2 tablespoons pizza sauce (like Muir Glen)
1 slice Rice Vegan mozzarella
2 slices Applegate Farms Black Forest Ham
1 slice fresh pineapple
Oil for the grill pan(s)

Lay out 2 slices of bread.

Spread a layer of pizza sauce on each slice.

Layer one slice with cheese, ham, and pineapple.

Place the other bread slice, sauce side down, on top of the pineapple.

Press the sandwich in a lightly oiled Panini press, or use a weighted press and a flat pan.

Grill over medium heat until the bread is crisp and the cheese is melted.

A fun sandwich and it gives you a fruit and a veggie serving.

Pineapple contains bromelain, which is anti-inflammatory / immuno-supportive and can interfere with the growth of malignant cells and tumors.

Pizza sauce gives you a serving of tomatoes.

Pulled Pork Picnic Salad

SOY

Ingredients:
1 pound pork loin
1 box quinoa pasta (elbow)
1 tablespoon oil
½ cup organic frozen peas
½ cup frozen organic non-GMO corn
1/3 cup organic apple cider vinegar
2 tablespoons finely diced onion
2 tablespoons Grapeseed Vegenaise

Prepare the pork roast ahead of time (slow-roast in oven or crockpot), seasoned with salt and ¼ cup apple cider vinegar and enough water or pork stock to keep the roast moist.

Pull apart with a fork when meat is done to get "pulled pork."

Toss together pulled pork, pasta, peas, corn and diced onions.

In a separate bowl stir together the oil, Veganise and apple cider vinegar.

Mix the Veganise mixture into your pasta mixture.

Serve at room temperature or chilled.

Season to taste.

If you can find a good source of non-GMO corn, it is a good source of Vitamin B1, thiamine, and folate. Folate helps lower homocystein, which can be damaging to blood vessels.

Corn also provides pantothenic acid, another B vitamin that is vital for protein and fat metabolism

Anti-inflammatory peas. Pass them please!

Quinoa Tabouleh

Ingredients:
1¾ cups water
1 cup sprouted quinoa
1 tablespoon grapeseed oil
Sea salt to taste
½ cup finely chopped parsley
½ cup diced organic cherry tomatoes
¼ cup diced organic green onion

Dressing:
1 tablespoon coconut yogurt
1 tablespoon grapeseed oil
1 tablespoon organic lemon juice
1 teaspoon salt

Boil water in a stock pot over high heat.

Stir in the sprouted quinoa, oil, and sea salt.

Cover and reduce heat to low.

Cook for 25 to 35 minutes, or until quinoa is cooked and water has been absorbed.

Combine parsley, tomatoes, and green onion in a large bowl.

Stir into the cooked quinoa.

Whisk together the dressing ingredients in a separate bowl.

Add the quinoa and vegetables and transfer to a serving bowl.

Eat warm or refrigerate for a delicious cold salad.

Traditionally, tabouleh is made with bulgur wheat. Enjoy this wheat-free version of a classic Greek recipe.

Quinoa (pronounced keen wa) is the quintessential grain. It is a plant source that provides complete protein. (meaning that it supplies the body with all of the amino acids it needs all in one source). Quinoa is also rich in iron and a good source of saponins, which may have anti-cancer and anti-inflammatory/immuno-supportive properties.

You can buy quinoa already sprouted, or simply soak your quinoa over night or wash them thoroughly to remove the outer layer of saponin.

Quinoa is also rich in the amino acid lysine.

Roasted Pumpkin Seeds

Ingredients:

2 cups raw pumpkin seeds

1 teaspoons salt

1½ tablespoons pure vegetable oil

Preheat oven to 250°F.

Wipe seeds dry with paper towels.

Remove any membranes.

Mix seeds well with salt and oil in a medium bowl.

Spread on an ungreased baking sheet and **roast**, stirring occasionally until browned, about 30 minutes.

Makes 2 cups.

Variations:

Spicy: ½ teaspoon paprika, ¼ teaspoon cumin, ¼ teaspoon cayenne, ☐ teaspoon white pepper

Sweet: mix 2 tablespoons raw honey with oil

Tart: 1 tablespoon apple cider vinegar, ½ teaspoon pickling spices.

Pumpkin seeds are a crunchy treat with great health benefits. Pumpkin seeds are a natural anti-inflammatory. They also have a strong link to decreasing prostate growth in men over fifty (benign prostatic hypertrophy or BPH).

Pumpkin seeds are also among the top sources of phytosterols. According to the web database World's Healthiest Foods, "Phytosterols are compounds found in plants that have a chemical structure very similar to cholesterol, and when present in the diet in sufficient amounts, are believed to reduce blood levels of cholesterol, enhance the immune response, and decrease risk of certain cancers.

Smoked Salmon Salad

FISH **SOY**

Ingredients:

8 ounce skinless, boneless smoked salmon fillet, flaked

3 stalks peeled celery, chopped finely

3 tablespoons chopped parsley or cilantro

4 stalks green onions, peeled and chopped

¼ cup olive oil

3–4 tablespoons lemon juice

Celtic sea salt to taste

Organic olive oil mayonnaise (substitute Vegenaise if you cannot tolerate eggs for a healthier alternative, optional)

Gluten-free casein-free sandwich bread (if making a sandwich)

Salmon is a super fish source for fatty acids like omega-3. Seafood is a lean choice for proteins and amino acids that are important throughout the body. Salmon is widely enjoyed for its texture and flavor by adults and kids alike.

Using a non-wheat, non-gluten containing bread for a Smoked Salmon Salad sandwich will give you more complex carbohydrates.

Combine salmon, celery, parsley or cilantro, onions, olive oil, lemon juice, and salt.

You may want to **add** a little bit of mayonnaise to help bind the mixture. How much oil and mayonnaise you add will, of course, affect the calorie count.

The leftovers taste just as good.

Very Berry Spinach Salad

Ingredients:

1 9-ounce bag fresh spinach

1 pint strawberries, sliced

3 kiwis, peeled and sliced

1 handful chopped macadamia nuts (optional)

Mix all ingredients together in a bowl.

Serve.

Spinach has been a coveted green for as long as we can remember, and for good reason! Those dark green, buttery leaves provide a punch of Vitamins C, A, and K, plus folate, magnesium, iron, calcium, potassium ... the list goes on!

Also found in spinach is an interesting category of nutrients called glycoglycerolipids. These unique lipid molecules can protect the gut lining from damage due to inflammation.

(Source: www.cyberlipid.org/ glycolip/glyl0002.htm; whfoods.com.)

We've got the BEET, Apple, and Chard Salad

Ingredients:
1 large bunch of Swiss chard
1 fresh beet
1 small organic granny smith apple
2 tablespoons avocado oil
1 teaspoon organic sugar
½ cup water
1 tablespoon organic apple cider vinegar
Sea salt and pepper to taste

Wash Swiss chard, beet, and apple.

Cut the beet greens from the beet.

Snap or cut off about 1/3 of the rougher portion of the beet greens and Swiss chard.

Stack leaves and roll into one long roll.

Run knife through roll every ½ inch to get long strips, and set aside.

Core and dice apple. (Peel first, if desired.)

Peel and dice beet into small cubes. (¼–½ inch)

Heat oil over medium-high heat in a large grill pan.

Toss apple, beets, and sugar into heated oil and cook for 4 to 5 minutes, stirring occasionally.

Mix in greens until well incorporated.

Stir in water, vinegar, and salt and pepper.

Reduce heat to medium low.

Cover and simmer for 15 minutes. (May need to add more water.)

Betalains are phytonutrients found in beets. They are antioxidants and anti-inflammatory/immuno-supportive and have been shown to provide support for detoxification. The potency of their health benefits begins to decrease after too much cooking, so try to keep the cooking time to a minimum.

The betanin from beets has been shown to lessen inflammation from tumor enzymes in relation to colon, stomach, nerve, lung, breast, prostate, and testicular cancers. (Source: www.whfoods.com.)

The greens of these beets and the Swiss chard pack a nutritious punch. Swiss chard is a uniquely valuable phytonutrient source. It contains at least thirteen different polyphenol antioxidants. Syringic acid may be a powerful resource for blood sugar control due to its enzyme alpha-glucosidase. The betalain pigments in chard provide support to phase 2 liver detox involving glutathione, triggering glutathione-S-transferase activity needed to rid toxins from the body. Studies have shown very low glutathione in children within the autism spectrum.

(Source: Daniel Murph, DC, FACO, "Autism and Glutathione," www.idealspine.com.)

CHAPTER 12

Main Dishes

Photo Recipe: Lemon Lime Lamb Chops served with Momma's Mashed Potaters

MAIN DISHES

Apricot Meatloaf

Beef and Broccoli Stir-Fry

Beef-Ish Enchiladas

Beverly's Meatloaf

Braised Rabbit

Broiled Salmon With Avocado and Dill

Cabbage Patch Roll-Ups

Chicken and Squash Taquitos

Classic Roasted Leg of Lamb With Potatoes

Crabby Mac 'n' Cheese-Ish

Crabby Patties

Eggplant Parmesan

Festive Pepper Stir-Fry

FeZucchini

Just Plum Glazy Barbeque Pork Roast

Lasagna Magnifique

Lemon-Lime Lamb Chops

One Fish Two Fish

Pam's Rice Spaghetti and Meat Sauce

Peachy Keen Chicken

Pirate's Buried Treasure Meatballs

Pizzaaaaahh!!

Pizza Gobble Burgers

Pork Fried Quinoa

Roasted Beef Tenderloin With Chipotle Au Jus

Salmon and Peas

Savory Roast Beef and Gravy

Shitake Teriyaki

Sock Full of Dirt

Spinach Stuffed Choppers

Stewed Pork Medallions

Zesty Breaded Tilapia With Lemon Tarragon Butter Sauce

Apricot Meatloaf

Ingredients:
1 pound lean ground beef
1 cup peeled and shredded or finely chopped
    eggplant
3–4 dried apricots, finely chopped
1 teaspoon sea salt
½ teaspoon garlic powder (or 2 cloves fresh,
    chopped)
2 tablespoons Annie's Naturals Ketchup
1 tablespoon tapioca flour
½ teaspoon onion powder
1–2 teaspoons grapeseed, sunflower, or saf-
    flower oil

Sauce
6 dried apricots
½ cup boiling water
2 tablespoons Annie's Ketchup
½ teaspoon garlic salt

Dip your knife into water while cutting the apricots to reduce sticking to the knife.

Be sure to wash your hands and surfaces well after handling raw meat to avoid cross-contamination.

Apricots are a highly alkaline food, and they have a very distinct flavor. If you do not like the taste of apricots, try substituting dried peaches or nectarines instead.

Preheat oven to 350°F.

Grease a loaf pan with oil.

Combine all of the ingredients for the meatloaf in a large mixing bowl.

Work together with fingers just until thoroughly combined.

Dump the meat mixture into the prepared loaf pan and press into pan with a spatula.

Place dried apricot in a glass bowl or mug and pour boiling water over them.

Cover and let stand for 10 to 15 minutes to reconstitute.

Pour entire contents of bowl or mug into a food processor.

Add ketchup and garlic salt.

Purée until smooth.

Pour sauce over meatloaf mixture.

Bake for 1 hour to 1 hour and 15 minutes.

Beef and Broccoli Stir-Fry

Ingredients:
1 pound sirloin steak
1 clove garlic
2 cups broccoli
2 stalks green onion
½ cup tamari soy sauce
3 tablespoons apple cider vinegar
1 tablespoon sesame oil
1 tablespoon toasted sesame seeds

Cut raw sirloin steak into thin strips (¼ inch x ¼ inch) and set aside.

Chop or grate garlic, **chop** broccoli into bite-sized pieces, and **chop** green onion. Set aside

Combine the tamari, vinegar, and sun crystals in a small saucepan.

Reduce over medium heat for 5 minutes, stirring occasionally.

Use an organic source of soy due to prominence of GM of soy.

Broccoli is definitely a superfood! It's an excellent vegetable source of iron and is believed to neutralize carcinogens. Sulphophrane, found in broccoli, increases enzymes that help rid the body of cancer. Help our bodies to limit oxidative stress.

Sesame seeds are high in calcium. Also good in vitamin T, which is thrombocyte (or platelet). Great for building blood platelets when the immune system is compromised.

Tamari soy sauce is a wheat-free soy sauce.

Heat oil in a wok or large skillet over high heat.

Add steak and toss for 1 to 2 minutes.

Add vegetables and garlic and toss together with the steak.

Pour reduction sauce over top, giving everything a good stir.

Cook for 30 seconds to 1 minute.

Transfer to a serving dish.

Serve over rice or rice noodles.

For a fun garnish, sprinkle with toasted sesame seeds.

Beef-Ish Enchiladas

Filling:
1 tablespoon avocado oil
1 pound ground turkey
¼ cup chopped onion
1 teaspoon chili powder
Sea salt
½ cup vegetable stock
½ cup shredded Rice Vegan Cheddar
Brown rice tortillas (may need to steam to
   soften)

Sauce:
2 cups spicy black bean soup (Imagine
   organic)
½ cup organic tomato sauce
Cumin to taste
Chili Powder to taste
Salt to taste
White pepper to taste
Garlic salt to taste

Vegan version: Replace ground turkey with chopped zucchini or avocado.

Black Beans ~ ½ cup serving has 7.4 grams of fiber.

Evidence shows that bean, also called lignans, may help to prevent colon, breast and prostate cancer.

Preheat oven to 350°F.

Heat the oil in a large soup pan and brown turkey with onion, chili powder, and salt.

Add vegetable stock, cover, and simmer over low heat for about 10 minutes.

Meanwhile, combine ingredients for the sauce in a saucepan and **simmer** over medium-low heat for about 10 minutes.

Form enchiladas. **Lay** tortilla out on a flat surface.

Place stuffing in the center.

Roll up and place in a baking dish.

Repeat until all of tortillas are filled.

Pour sauce down over rolled tortillas.

Sprinkle with Cheddar shreds or lay down rice vegan Cheddar slices if desired.

Bake for 30 minutes. Enjoy with a side of rice or quinoa!

Beverly's Meatloaf

Ingredients:

1 pound ground lean beef, venison, veal, or turkey

1 cup grated/shredded vegetables, such as cabbage, spinach, zucchini, yellow squash, or carrots

¼ small yellow onion, finely chopped (optional)

1/3 cup finely chopped green pepper (optional)

¾ teaspoon sea salt

¼ teaspoon pepper

¼ cup water

½ cup tomato sauce (optional)

This is an easy way to add other-wise-resisted vegetables into the diet along with enhancing the flavor of the dish. Recipe easily doubles to freeze half-cooked or uncooked for busy schedules.

TIP: Vegetables can also be added to homemade hamburgers.

Preheat oven to 350°F.

Mix the meat, vegetables, salt, and pepper together with a wooden spoon until thoroughly mixed.

Shape the mixture into a loaf.

Place in a large casserole dish.

Add water to the bottom of the dish.

Cover with foil.

Bake for 45 minutes.

Uncover and bake another 20 to 30 minutes to brown.

Add tomato sauce in the last 15 minutes of baking.

Braised Rabbit

Ingredients:
2–2½ pounds rabbit
¾ cup water
¼–½ teaspoon sea salt
¼ teaspoon pepper
1½ teaspoons chopped dried rosemary or
   sweet basil (if using fresh, increase to 1
   tablespoon)

Rabbit is an extremely lean source of animal protein. Just 3 ounces provides 28 grams of protein.

Preheat oven to 350°F.

Clean rabbit and cut into pieces of desired serving size.

Place rabbit pieces in a single layer in a 9x13-inch baking dish.

Pour water into the bottom of the dish.

Sprinkle with seasonings and herbs.

Cover with lid or foil.

Bake for 1 hour.

Uncover and bake an additional 30 minutes to 1 hour, until browned and water is evaporated.

Broiled Salmon with Avocado and Dill

FISH

Ingredients:

4 salmon fillets (6–7 ounces each)

¼ cup olive oil

4 teaspoons fresh lime juice

2 medium ripe avocados, seeded, peeled, and diced

1 2/3-ounce package fresh dill, snipped, stems removed

Salt and pepper to taste

Preheat broiler.

Rub salmon fillets with 3 teaspoons olive oil.

Drizzle 2 teaspoons lime juice over salmon.

Let stand while preparing sauce.

Combine avocado, remaining olive oil, dill, and remaining lime juice with salt and pepper in medium mixing bowl.

Arrange salmon skin-side down on a broiling pan.

Season with salt and pepper.

Broil without turning until just opaque, about 9 minutes per inch of thickness.

Transfer to serving plates and spoon avocado over salmon.

Salmon is a great source of "good fats," those essential fatty acids that the human body needs to manufacture and repair cell membranes. This allows the cells to obtain optimum nutrition and rid the body of harmful waste products.

Also rich in good fats in this dish are avocados. The monosaturated fats are burned more quickly than the saturated fats found in meat and dairy. One avocado provides 4 grams of protein.

TIP: If desired, salmon can be grilled rather than broiled.

Cabbage Patch Roll-Ups

Ingredients:
8–12 cabbage leaves
2 tablespoons olive oil
1 pound ground turkey
¼ cup chopped onions
1 clove garlic, finely chopped (or grated)
1 can organic stewed tomatoes
2 medium-sized red potatoes, finely diced or grated
½ cup finely chopped kale
1 teaspoon sea salt
1 teaspoon paprika
1 cup beef stock
Red pepper flakes to taste, if desired
1 cup Muir Glen Garden Vegetable pasta sauce

Preheat oven to 350°F.

Blanche cabbage leaves in boiling water, cover, and boil for 3 minutes.

Drain well in a colander, then cover with a napkin or tea towel and set aside.

Heat the oil in a large skillet over medium-high heat and sauté ground turkey, onions, and garlic. **Drain** excess fat.

Add stewed tomatoes, potatoes, kale, salt, and paprika.

Cook, stirring constantly, for 2 to 3 minutes.

Pour in the beef stock, cover, and reduce heat to medium low.

Cook for 10 to 15 minutes.

Place one cabbage leaf on a flat surface. **Scoop** ¼–½ cup of the meat mixture onto the leaf.

Roll leaf up and place, seam down, into a casserole dish.

Continue with the remaining cabbage leaves and meat mixture.

Spoon a large spoonful of pasta sauce over each cabbage roll.

Cover and bake for 30 to 35 minutes.

Cabbage is a detoxifier. Rich in vitamin C, it is a definite immune-booster.

There are a number of varieties, but the redder the cabbage, the higher the nutritional value.

Sinigrin is one of the cabbage glucosinolates that has received special attention in cancer prevention research. The sinigrin in cabbage can be converted into allyl-isothiocyanate, or AITC. This isothiocyanate compound has shown unique preventive properties with respect to bladder cancer, colon cancer, and prostate cancer.

(Source: www. whfoods. com.)

This meal is packed full of vegetable servings!

Chicken and Squash Taquitos

Ingredients:
6 oz. Ground Chicken
1 cup butternut squash
2 tablespoons. cilantro
¼ teaspoon sea salt
¼ teaspoon cinnamon
¼ teaspoon paprika
¼ teaspoon cumin
¼ teaspoon onion powder
6 non-GMO corn tortillas (or use rice tortillas)
2 tablespoons. avocado oil

Preheat oven to 400°F.

These are a great freezer-friendly and kid-friendly entrée!

Cumin has anti-inflammatory properties.

Butternut squash is a sweet vegetable that is easy to sneak into a kids meal without any of those scrunched-up faces.

Or make them enchiladas by rolling, topping with Sour Cream Sauce (see recipe) and rice vegan mozzarella, and bake at 350°F for 30 minutes.

In a large skillet over medium-high heat:

 Brown ground chicken until cooked through.

Add the chicken and all remaining ingredients except for tortillas and oil in a food processor and pulse to a coarse mixture.

Separate chicken mixture evenly into each tortilla and roll up into small tubes or taquitos.

Place taquitos on a cookie sheet and brush the outside of each with the avocado oil.

Bake for 8 to 12 minutes or until taquitos are crispy.

Serve with Greater Tots Ranch-Ish Dip or Black Beauty Bean Dip.

Classic Roasted Leg of Lamb with Potatoes

Ingredients:
1 leg of lamb, about 4 pounds, fat trimmed
4–6 cloves garlic, peeled and crushed
1 teaspoon black peppercorns
¼ cup fresh chopped parsley
2 tablespoons oregano, or more to taste
Salt to taste
½ cup olive oil
3 pounds small red potatoes, washed thoroughly, peeled, and halved
1/3 cup fresh lemon juice, or more to taste
1 cup dry white wine (optional)

Rich in selenium, lamb is a very popular protein in Greek dishes.

Studies have shown links between deficiencies in selenium and asthma attacks.

Preheat oven to 350°F.

Make shallow incisions all over the leg of lamb using a sharp knife.

Grind garlic, peppercorns, parsley, and oregano together in a spice mill or with a mortar and pestle.

Force a little of the spice mixture into each of the incisions.

Season the lamb with salt, pepper, and a little more of the crushed herbs, and **rub** with 2 tablespoons olive oil.

Place lamb in a large, shallow baking dish.

Place the potatoes in the baking dish all around the lamb.

Pour in the remaining olive oil and lemon juice. Season with salt, pepper and a little more garlic and oregano.

Cover with foil and **roast** for 2 hours, basting occasionally and adding a little water or dry white wine to the pan if necessary to keep the meat moist.

Remove the foil 20 to 25 minutes before removing meat from oven.

Continue roasting until lamb is crisp and brown.

Makes 6–8 servings.

Crabby Mac 'n' Cheese-Ish

FISH

Crab is a lean protein choice and a good source of omega three fatty-acids. It is also known to be lower in mercury levels than other seafood option.

Ingredients
1 pound crab meat, cooked
1 box quinoa pasta (macaroni or bowtie)

Cheese Sauce:
2 tablespoons butter or ghee
1 tablespoon potato starch flour
¼ teaspoon turmeric
1 teaspoon sea salt
¼ teaspoon white pepper
1 cup MimicCreme Unsweetened
1/3 cup rice milk
1 cup Daiya Cheddar shreds
½ cup Daiya mozzarella shreds
2 tablespoons rice vegan plain cream cheese
2 teaspoons apple cider vinegar
White truffle oil for drizzling

Preheat oven to 375°F.

Cook pasta according to package directions, drain and set aside.

Heat butter over medium heat in a large saucepan.

Whisk in potato starch until lumps are gone.

Add the cream, milk, salt and pepper, turmeric, ¾ cup Cheddar shreds, and the mozzarella shreds.

Simmer, stirring constantly, until the cheese is melted.

Stir in the cream cheese and apple cider vinegar.

Add the cooked pasta to the cheese sauce and stir to coat all of the noodles.

Pour into a greased 9 x 13 baking dish and cover with remaining ¾ cup Cheddar shreds.

Bake for 20 to 25 minutes. Enjoy!

Drizzle with truffle oil before serving.

Crabby Patties

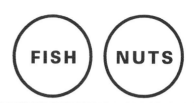

FISH **NUTS**

Ingredients:
1 pound crab meat
2 tablespoons ground flax meal
1½ teaspoons egg-replacer powder
1/3 cup coconut yogurt
2 tablespoons water
1/3 cup shredded zucchini
2 slices nitrite-free bacon, cooked and
    crumbled
½ teaspoon sea salt
¾ cup pistachios
¼ cup grapeseed oil

A delicious version of crab cakes that are made egg-free. The flax meal serves as a binder and also carries good nutritional value.

Make-Ahead Tip: Prepare and shape crab cakes. Cover and chill up to 8 hours before cooking, or freeze for up to 3 months.

Thaw crab, if frozen and drain.

Combine flax, egg replacer, yogurt, water, zucchini, bacon, and salt in a mixing bowl.

Stir in crab, and mix well.

Shape into 4 patties about 1 inch thick.

Place pistachios in a food processor and grind into small crumbs.

Coat crab cakes in pistachio crumbs.

Heat oil in a large skillet and add crab cakes.

Cook over medium to medium-high heat for about 4 minutes on each side or until golden and cooked through. **Add** additional oil if necessary.

Eggplant Parmesan

Ingredients:
1 large eggplant
½ cup rice milk
1 cup blanched almond flour
½ cup brown rice flour
2 tablespoons tapioca flour
1 tablespoon sesame seeds
1 teaspoon sea salt
¼ cup + 2 tablespoons oil (sesame or sunflower or safflower)
2 cups Muir Glen Vegetable Pasta Sauce

Preheat oven to 400°F.

> *Eggplant is a great non-inflammatory veggie selection. It is the perfect veggie for a meatless meal! Be sure to leave the skin on these deep purple plants, as the skin contains a phytonutrient called nansunin, a fantastic antioxidant.*
>
> *According to research, nansunin has been particularly protective for the lipids of brain cell membranes.*

Cut eggplant into ½-inch rounds, discarding the top and bottom pieces.

Combine almond or hemp milk and ¼ cups oil in a shallow dish.

Combine almond flour, tapioca flour, sesame seed meal, and salt in a separate dish.

Dip each eggplant round into the milk mixture and then into the flour mixture, pressing into the crumbs to coat completely. Transfer to a greased baking sheet.

Repeat with the remaining eggplant pieces.

Brush each piece generously with oil.

Bake for 10 minutes, flip, and then bake for another 6 to 8 minutes.

Serve with Muir Glen Pasta Sauce.

FAUX THE LOVE OF FRYING

Here are some simple substitutes to the wheat-based breaded fried chicken, pork chops, fish, etc. We call it faux frying because these recipes are baked in the oven.

Getting Sticky with It: stick your crumbs to your protein of choice using the following options:

Milk—almond, soy, hazelnut, coconut, etc.

Oils—any of the nut oils are great; avocado, sunflower, or safflower oil, are great for high-heat coking.

Fruit—jelly or jam (find organic with no high-fructose corn syrup) can be a great addition of flavor. For example, you could use an apricot jelly to bread some coconut shrimp or some apple butter to bread a pork chop.

I Thee Bread: Get creative with your breading. Try some of the following options:

Brown rice flour

Organic cereals, like Nature's Path Puffed Rice or Cornflakes

GFCF bread, toasted and crumbed (some are sold as crumbs)

Coconut—look for organic unsweetened

Almond flour

Tapioca flour

Quinoa flour

Cornmeal

Oat flour (certified GF)

Ground up GF lemon cookies

Think outside the box and get creative! Your family will thank you for a change of flavors.

Festive Pepper Stir-Fry

Ingredients:
4 tablespoons olive oil
½ yellow bell pepper, chopped
½ red bell pepper, chopped
2 tablespoons sesame seeds
1 9-ounce bag fresh spinach
½ teaspoon sesame oil
Pinch salt and pepper

Heat olive oil in a deep sauté pan.
Add chopped peppers and sesame seeds.
Stir 5 times.
Add fresh spinach, a handful at a time.
Stir until hot.
Toss with sesame oil.
Add salt and pepper to taste.
Makes 4 servings.

Peppers are excellent sources of Vitamin C and beta-carotene. They are also an alkaline food source.

Studies have shown that red bell peppers have a higher nutrient count than that of green bell peppers.

FeZucchini

Ingredients:
1 pound rice fettuccine or rice spaghetti
½ stick butter *(not margarine)* or ¼ cup olive oil
2–4 cloves garlic, crushed
1 pound zucchini, chopped small
¾ cup Daiya cheese
1 teaspoon dried basil
¼ cup olive oil

Cook pasta according to package directions.

While pasta is cooking, **heat** butter in a large skillet and add garlic and zucchini.

Cook over medium heat until tender, about 1 to 2 minutes, stirring occasionally.

Drain pasta and pour into an oven-safe serving dish

Add zucchini sauce, cheese or cheese substitute, basil, and olive oil.

Toss well, and keep warm in oven until ready to serve.

Serve warm.

Zucchini is a very versatile veggie and is well liked by many kids. It can be found in a multitude of cuisines around the world. It is a solid choice for a vegetable, as it has a mild flavor and an appealing texture. It is rich in foliate, high in vitamin C and A. Zucchini is also a decent source of dietary fiber.

Recommended Brand~ there are many good rice pastas on the market. Our favorite is Pastariso brand. We prefer it because it has less of a tendency to stick together when it cooks. It is available in most health food stores and even in some supermarkets

TIP: You can also do this recipe with rice spiral pasta. It is very tasty to both children and adults.

*If you are deleting milk from your diet, leave out the cheese.

Just Plum Glazy Barbeque Pork Roast

Ingredients:
6 plums, divided (about 2 pounds)
¼ cup packed light brown sugar
1 teaspoon ground ginger
½ teaspoon salt
¼ teaspoon garlic powder
¼ teaspoon ground all-spice
☐ teaspoon cayenne pepper
1 5-pound bone-in pork loin roast
1 tablespoon oil, preferably avocado oil
1 shallot, minced
1/3 cup port wine or grape juice or fruit juice
½ cup plum preserves

Glaze:
Heat oil in pot over medium to high heat.
Add shallots and cook until just tender. About 2 minutes.
Add port and cook 1 minute.
Stir in preserves, reserved chopped plums, and remaining spice mixture.
Bring to boil. Reduce heat to medium-low; stirring occasionally, until reduced to 1 cup, 30 minutes.
Reserve 2 Tbs. glaze.

Plums have a high count of dietary fiber, plums are good for the digestive system.

Plums are rich in minerals like phosphorus, copper, manganese, magnesium and potassium.

Plums can help to neutralize the oxygen radical called superoxide anion radical, as well as oxidative damage to fats. This can be protective for a large portion of our brain cells,, or the fats that make up our cell membranes.

Prepare a barbeque grill for indirect heat cooking.

Peel, pit and **finely chop** 2 plums, and set aside. **Quarter** remaining plums, and set aside.

Combine the brown sugar, ginger, salt, garlic powder, all-spice, and cayenne pepper in a small mixing bowl.   **Rub** roast with 2 tablespoons of the spice mixture. **Grill** roast over direct heat, turning once, until browned, 2 minutes per side. **Transfer** to indirect heat. Cover. **Cook** bone-side down, until meat thermometer inserted into thickest part of roast away from bone registers 155°F, about 1 hour and 50 minutes.

Brush with glaze several times during last 15 to 20 minutes of cooking time.

Let roast stand 10 minutes before carving.

While roast is standing: Place quartered plums over direct heat, skin side up and grill, turning once, 1 minute per side.

Lasagna Magnifique

Ingredients:

1 package DeBoles lasagna ready bake
   noodles

2 zucchinis, washed and shredded

½ cup Galaxy Foods Vegan grated Parmesan

Ready-bake rice lasagna noodles make this traditionally gluten-filled pasta entrée a super simple conversion to the "Free food" kitchen.

Red Sauce:

1 pound ground beef, pork, or turkey

½ small onion (about 2 tablespoons finely chopped)Muir Glen Garlic Roasted Garlic

2 teaspoons fresh chopped basil

White Sauce:

½ cup Grapeseed Vegenaise

1 cup rice milk

½ teaspoon sea salt

½ teaspoon garlic powder

2 teaspoons potato starch flour dissolved in 2 tablespoons of water plus 1 tablespoon
   apple cider vinegar

Preheat oven to 375°F.

Build lasagna by starting with a layer of red sauce. Then a layer of noodles. Next, a layer of white sauce. Now, sprinkle on a layer of zucchini shreds and top with the red sauce and then noodles. Continue layers of noodle,
white sauces, zucchini, and red sauce, ending with red sauce on top.

Sprinkle Vegan Parmesan on top of lasagna.

Cover and bake for 40 minutes.

Remove cover and continue cooking for 15 to20 minutes.

You can always add cheese into the layers, like Daiya mozzarella shreds, but this is equally yummy without the extra calories and starches!

271

Lemon-Lime Lamb Chops

Ingredients:
1 rack of lamb or 6–8 lamb loin chops
Sea salt and freshly ground pepper to taste
3 cloves garlic, pressed
1 teaspoon dried oregano or parsley
Juice of 1 small lemons
Juice and zest of 1 small lime
¼ cup olive oil
Parsley for garnish

Preheat the barbecue (or other) grill on high.

Season the lamb generously with salt and pepper and rub garlic all over the lamb.

Combine the oregano or parsley, lemon juice, lime juice, lime zest, and olive oil in a small bowl.

Cook lamb on a grill to desired doneness and remove from the grill. (We like medium rare.)

Brush with the lemon juice mixture.

Serve on a platter. **Garnish** with parsley.

Lamb is one of the few meats the agriculture industry has not toyed with very much. Generally, they do not tamper with these livestock by feeding them antibiotics or by irradiation. In some areas, however, it may be hard to find lamb on a regular basis.

Since quality and texture is not significantly affected by freezing, if you find lamb, buy it and freeze it. In some rural areas, neighbors may raise lamb and may be willing to sell it to you.

Lamb is considered a "rare" food because it is not a staple of the American diet. However, at the Kotsanis house lamb is anything but rare. Because we are of Greek ancestry, we eat it about two to three times a week.

One Fish Two Fish

FISH

Ingredients:

1 egg

¼ cup hemp or almond milk

1½ cups almond flour

1/3 cup tapioca flour

1 teaspoon sea salt

1–2 pounds cod fillets, fresh or frozen and wild-caught, whole or cut into "sticks"

2 tablespoons safflower oil

Preheat oven to **375°F.**

Two servings of omega-3-rich fish per week can lower triglycerides, and eating more fish in your diet is associated with greater protection against heart attacks.

Almond flour used to crust this fish actually gives each serving an extra 8 grams of protein.

Serve with a side of steamed broccoli.

Set up a breading station with a bowl of egg wash (whisk egg and milk together) and a plate of well-mixed almond flour, tapioca flour, and salt.

Dip each cod filet first in the egg wash and then into the breading mix. Press into the flour until fully covered and transfer to an oiled baking sheet. Repeat until all fillets are coated with flour.

Brush fillets generously with oil.

Bake for 10 to 12 minutes, until fish is white and flaky and breading is golden.

Pam's Rice Spaghetti and Meat Sauce

Ingredients:

1 pound rice spaghetti

2 gallons filtered water (for boiling the spaghetti)

¼ cup olive oil

1 large onion (yellow is best but any will work), chopped

2 pounds ground lamb, venison, or buffalo (or any combination)

3–5 cloves garlic, crushed

1 whole green and/or red bell pepper, chopped

1 14½-ounce can stewed tomatoes

1 14½-ounce can tomato sauce

1 teaspoon dried basil (or fresh if you have it)

¾ teaspoon sea salt (or to taste)

½ teaspoon chili powder

1 whole bay leaf

Giving up gluten does not mean you have to give up pasta! Use rice pasta instead and you can still enjoy home-cooked meals as delicious as this one, done up with a lean lamb instead of a fattier ground beef version.

Serve with a fresh green salad for a perfect meal!

Rice spaghetti tastes almost like wheat spaghetti and is readily available in most metropolitan areas.

If you do not have a gluten restriction, you may also use spelt spaghetti. Any spaghetti substitute is workable. We have also tried quinoa spaghetti.

This dish tastes even better left over!

Heat olive oil in a large skillet and brown onions and garlic.

Add bell pepper and sauté.

Add meat to onion, garlic and bell pepper mixture and brown.

Add tomatoes, sauce, and seasonings.

Simmer for 1 or more hours on low heat.

Cook spaghetti in 2 gallons water according to package directions. Drain.

Serve spaghetti with sauce over top.

Peachy Keen Chicken

Ingredients:
1 large (about 8 ounces) peach, chopped
1 large (about 8 ounces) tomato, chopped
¾ cup chopped red onion
2 tablespoons chopped fresh mint
1 jalapeño pepper, seeded, ribs removed, minced
2 tablespoons lime juice
1 teaspoon grated lime zest
¼ teaspoon garlic powder
1¼ teaspoon salt
6 boneless skinless chicken breast halves (about 2 pounds, 4 ounces)
4 teaspoons Chinese five-spice powder

Peaches and nectarines are good sources of lycopene and lutein.

Lutein comes from the marigold flower and gives the red, orange, and yellow colors to fruits and vegetables. These phytochemicals are especially beneficial in the prevention of heart disease, macular degeneration, and cancer.

(Source: www.everynutrient.com)

Prepare grill for direct-heat cooking.

Combine peach, tomato, onion, mint, jalapeño, lime juice, lime zest, garlic powder, and ¼ teaspoon salt in a bowl to make salsa.

Sprinkle chicken with remaining 1 teaspoon salt and five-spice powder.

Grill chicken, turning once, until no longer pink in center, about 6 to 7 minutes per side.

Transfer to a serving platter.

Serve with salsa.

Pirate's Buried Treasure Meatballs

Ingredients:
½ cup finely diced eggplant
¼ cup chopped onion
½ cup garbanzo beans
1½ tablespoons flax seed meal
2 teaspoons fresh basil
1 teaspoon sweet paprika
1 teaspoon sea salt
½ teaspoon dry mustard
1 clove garlic
4 dried figs
¼ cup golden raisins
4 tablespoons Muir Glen tomato sauce
1/3 cup water
1 pound ground beef, 85 percent lean

Preheat oven to 400°F.

These really are full of treasures—immuno-supportive island riches.

Two cups of garbanzo beans provide a day's worth of fiber content.

Flax meal is a great source of omega-3 fatty acids and especially great for those who have an allergy to fish.

Figs and eggplant are fantastic and immuno-supportive, too!

Arrrr'ntcha gonna eat some more of these meatballs, Matey?

Combine all ingredients except for beef in a food processor

Pulse until thoroughly combined, but still having a chunky texture.

Place beef in a medium bowl and add eggplant mixture. Work in with fingers just until combined.

Roll into 2-inch balls.

Place meatballs in the cups of a mini muffin tin. (Meatballs should not touch the bottom of the muffin cup.)

Bake for 20 to 25 minutes.

Serve over pasta with a Muir Glen Pasta Sauce (be careful to look for casein in the ingredients; some contain cheese) or with a side of mashed potatoes. This is comfort food at its finest.

PIZZAAAAAHH!!

Ingredients:

Pizza Crusts: Focaccia bread (yeast-free—great for breadsticks too!)

2 cup GF all-purpose flour blend

1 tablespoon egg-replacer powder

1 teaspoon guar gum

1½ teaspoons baking soda

1 teaspoon baking powder

1 teaspoon onion powder

1 teaspoon garlic powder

1 teaspoon agar flakes

½ teaspoon sea salt

1 cup almond or rice milk

¼ cup carbonated water

2 tablespoons oil, plus more coating pan and on top of bread

½ teaspoon apple cider vinegar

> *At our house, a simple pizza dough works like magic for getting extra veggies on the plate!*
>
> *This is a favorite dough recipe because it is yeast-free and completely versatile.*

Nitrite-Free Toppings: Fiorucci is a favorite brand for Italian cold cuts like pepperoni, prosciutto, and salami. Find it at Sprouts, Whole Foods, and Henry's (www.fiorucci-foods.com).

NOW YOU CAN GO PIZZA CRAZY!

Pork and Pine Pizza	Ground Pork and Pineapple
Peppy Pepper	Pepperoni and Pepperoncini
Olive It, Olive It, Olive It	Black and Green Olives
White Pizza Florentine	Alfredo, Spinach, Garlic and Mozzarella
California Bacon Burger	Hamburger Meat, Bacon, Avocado
Pear Salad Pizza (delicious!) ~	Pear, Arugula, Goat Cheese

For a thicker crust or for breadsticks, oil a baking dish or iron skillet. Press dough into oiled dish, drizzle oil on top or place desired toppings, and bake for 25 to 30 minutes at 375°F.

For cheesy breadsticks, add rice vegan shredded cheese.

For a thinner crust, roll the dough out between two sheets of parchment paper.

The dough keeps well in the fridge; just grab a ball of dough when you need to make a pizza.

Pizza Gobble Burgers

DAIRY

Ingredients:
1½ pounds ground turkey
1/3 cup grated Parmesan cheese
6 tablespoons pizza sauce from a jar
1½ teaspoons dried minced onion
½ teaspoon dried oregano
½ teaspoon salt
¼ teaspoon garlic powder
¼ teaspoon crushed red pepper flakes
4 4-ounce slices mozzarella cheese
4 hamburger buns (like Ener-G tapioca rolls)
4 leaves romaine lettuce
4 slices tomato

Turkey is a much leaner protein choice than the traditional ground round burgers.

Pile on the veggies—dark green lettuce, tomatoes, and ketchup.

Prepare grill for direct-heat cooking.

Combine turkey meat with Parmesan, 2 tablespoons pizza sauce, onion, oregano, salt, garlic powder, and red pepper flakes in a large bowl. Mix with fingers to incorporate all ingredients.

Divide mixture into 4 equal pieces.

Shape into patties.

Grill, turning once, until no longer pink in centers, about 5 to 6 minutes per side.

Place 1 cheese slice on top of each burger. Grill until melted, about 1 minute.

Serve each burger on a bun with lettuce, tomato, and 1 tablespoon pizza sauce on top.

Pork Fried Quinoa

SOY

Ingredients:
2 cups quinoa
2 pork chops (approximately 6 ounces each)
1 tablespoon grapeseed oil
½ cup diced carrots
¾ cup soy beans (non-GMO)
1½ tablespoons Tamari soy sauce

Heat 1 cup quinoa with 1¾ cups water in a large saucepan. Bring to a boil.

Reduce to simmer, cover, and cook for approximately 18 minutes or until liquid is absorbed.

While quinoa is cooking:

Grill, fry, or **broil** pork chops in about 1 teaspoon of grapeseed oil until fully cooked (center should read 160°F on a food thermometer).

Set out on counter to cool, then slice into thin strips.

Heat the remaining oil over high heat in a wok or large skillet.

Add quinoa, carrots, soybeans, pork, and Tamari sauce.

Toss pan continuously for about 30 seconds.

Transfer to a serving bowl.

Quinoa (pronounced keen wa) is the quintessential grain. It is a plant source that provides complete protein, meaning that it supplies the body with all the amino acids it needs all in one source. Quinoa is also rich in iron and a good source of saponins, which may have anti-cancer and anti-inflammatory/immunosupportive properties.

You can find sprouted quinoa at Whole Foods.

TIP: This is a fantastic recipe to add some extra veggies into, like peas, broccoli, or even water chestnuts.

Roasted Beef Tenderloin With Chipotle Au Jus

NUTS

Ingredients:
2 cloves garlic, chopped
1 onion, diced
1 carrot, diced
1 stalk celery, diced
½ tablespoon dried oregano
½ tablespoon dried thyme
1 bay leaf
1 cup red wine
1 tablespoon tomato paste
32 ounces beef broth
¼ teaspoon chipotle pepper
2 tablespoons extra virgin olive oil
5 pounds beef tenderloin
Salt and pepper to taste

Preheat oven to 350.

Combine garlic, onion, carrot, celery herbs, bay leaf, and red wine in a saucepan and bring to a boil.

Cook until about ½ cup of liquid remains.

Add tomato paste, broth, and chipotle pepper.

Cook for about 10 to 15 minutes over medium heat.

Strain through a fine sieve. Keep warm until ready to use.

Heat oil in a very large, ovenproof sauté or roasting pan until smoking hot.

Season beef with salt and pepper, then **sear** beef on all sides, about 6 minutes.

Roast in oven until the internal temperature reaches 135°F. About 20 to 25 minutes.

Remove from oven and let rest about 5 minutes.

Slice beef thinly and serve with warm au jus on the side.

"Green" this meal up with grilled Romaine leaves or sautéed spinach drizzled with olive oil.

If you are cooking for kiddos, know that when cooking with wine, the alcohol evaporates. The flavor actually concentrates and the nutrients remain.

Parents cooking for kids on the autism spectrum should pay close attention to reactions in their children when ingesting phenols (as there are in wine from grapes). Some children have a hard time processing phenols and are highly sensitive. The highest levels of phenols are found in malbec red wines.

Salmon and Peas

FISH

Ingredients:

1 14-ounce can coconut milk

½ cup chickpea flour

½ cup water

2 14¾-ounces packages (or cans) skinless, boneless smoked salmon (see note at right)

1 16-ounce package frozen peas

Warm the coconut milk in a saucepan, stirring constantly.

Combine the chickpea flour with water in a small sealed container and shake vigorously until smooth.

Add to coconut milk.

Continue to stir until the mixture thickens.

Add salmon and peas and heat throughout.

Serve over rice pasta, rice, or gluten-free toast.

This recipe is ideal for adding electrolytes and/or free-form amino acids.

Opt for vacuum-packed wild caught salmon over canned salmon. We highly recommend the Vital Choice brand. (www.vitalchoice.com). We prefer the smoked salmon that is vacuum-packed in plastic pouches rather than cans.

Vital Choice claims to follow sustainable fishing practices in Alaska. This fish should also have a much lower metal content than Atlantic salmon.

In addition, since this fish is not farm-raised, the color is naturally reddish rather than dyed by food coloring as is most Atlantic salmon. The Alaskan salmon that are caught in the wild feed in their natural habitat on plankton and other sea animals. They then have a naturally high content of the fatty acids your body needs for good health.

You can use rice flour instead of chickpea flour if you prefer.

Savory Roast Beef and Gravy

Ingredients:
Beef:

3 pounds eye round, sirloin, or rump roast

11/3 tablespoons Worcestershire sauce

1 cup (8 ounces) beef stock

2 teaspoons paprika

2 teaspoons granulated onion (or substitute3 teaspoons finely chopped fresh onion)

1 teaspoon marjoram

1 teaspoon salt

1 teaspoon pepper

> *Sirloin is a lean protein choice. This dish is delicious with a mountain of fresh steamed broccoli or spinach.*

Beef:

Preheat oven to 350°F.

Mix paprika, onion, marjoram, salt, and pepper in a bowl.

Place beef in a covered roasting pan.

Rub beef with Worcestershire sauce.

Pour beef stock around (not on) meat.

Sprinkle spice blend over entire roast.

Cook for 2½ hours.

Ingredients:
Gravy:

2 tablespoons cornstarch

2 tablespoons flour

2 tablespoons water

Gravy:

Mix cornstarch, flour, and water into a paste.

Pour drippings from roast into a small pan over medium heat.

Pour paste mixture gradually into drippings and whisk until gravy is of desired consistency.

Shitake Teriyaki

SOY

Ingredients:

1 cup organic Tamari soy sauce

½ cup organic apple cider vinegar

½ cup fresh chopped pineapple

2 tablespoons molasses

1 clove garlic, minced

1 teaspoon grated fresh ginger

2 tablespoons toasted sesame oil

6–8 ounces shitake mushrooms, wiped and sliced

¼ cup chopped scallions

12 ounces kelp noodles

Combine soy sauce, vinegar, pineapple, molasses, garlic, ginger, sesame oil, mushrooms, and scallions in a saucepan over medium heat.

Stir until shitakes are cooked through, about 10 to 12 minutes.

Serve over kelp noodles.

Shitake Mushrooms ~ a great non-animal source of iron, used in traditional Chinese medicine, they are an excellent source of B vitamins. Shitake as a medicinal supplement is amazing for the immune system. The effects are not as significant in the less concentrated form, but are an excellent addition to a diet that is balancing to the immune system as a whole.

(If you are fighting yeast, you may want to limit funguses in your diet)

Pineapple~ Bromelain – anti-inflammatory/immuno-supportive and can interfere with growth of malignant cells and tumors.

Kelp noodles~ Kelp is a type of seaweed and is rich in numerous minerals and nutrients. It is known to aid in digestion, metabolism, and help with thyroid function. High in folic acid. Also high in calcium and magnesium, the magnesium can act as an anti-inflammatory/immuno-supportive.

Sock Full of Dirt

Ingredients:
4 medium poblano peppers
1 pound ground chicken or turkey
¼ cup diced onion
1 tomato, diced
½ cup grated potato (or use organic frozen hash browns)
½ cup grated zucchini (about 1 medium zucchini)
¼ cup sunflower seeds
½ teaspoon chili powder
½ teaspoon paprika
Sea salt and pepper to taste
½ cup water

Preheat oven to 350°F and lightly oil a baking dish.

Brown meat and drain excess fat in a large skillet.

Add onion, diced tomato, chili powder, paprika, and salt and pepper.

Stir to combine.

Add water, cover, and **simmer** for 10 to 15 minutes over medium-low heat.

Wash poblanos. Carefully cut around the stem with a paring knife and remove the stem and seeds from each pepper. Rinse the pepper out to be sure the seeds are gone (unless you don't mind a little spice—poblanos are mild peppers). Take the "socks" over to the skillet.

Add sunflower seeds and potatoes to the skillet and **stir** to combine.

Spoon meat mixture into the opening of each pepper.

Lay peppers in prepared baking dish.

Bake for 30 to 35 minutes.

We know, it doesn't sound very appetizing, but names like this get our little ones so excited!

With a mild "hotness" factor, poblano peppers are a great stuffing agent, and this dish has some fantastic hidden nutritional gems like the sunflower seeds and zucchini.

Like most peppers, poblanos are high in vitamin C.

You may want to try sneaking a veggie into this dish, like finely diced eggplant or grated Brussels sprouts.

Spinach Stuffed Choppers

NUTS

Ingredients:
2 tablespoons olive oil
4 pork chops (preferably 1 inch thick or more)
1 tablespoon Earth Balance
1½ teaspoons potato starch flour
1 cup non-dairy milk
2 cloves garlic, finely chopped
½ teaspoon sea salt
1 teaspoon lemon juice
3 cups fresh spinach
1 cup chicken stock
½ cup artichokes

Spinach contains glutathione, which is a key deficiency linked to autism. It is a source of CoQ10 and is very significant in mitochondrial energy production! Antioxidants alpha lipoic acid; Vitamins C, E, and K; magnesium; and zinc also are a plant-source of omega-3 fatty acids.

Preheat oven to 375°F.

Heat 2 tablespoons olive oil in a Dutch oven or oven-safe skillet over medium-high heat. **Brown** pork chops on each side, approximately 3 minutes per side. Set aside.

Slice down the center of each chop as if butterflying it.

Add 1 tablespoon Earth Balance to the same skillet along with the pork drippings.

Whisk potato starch into 1 cup non-dairy milk. Add the milk, garlic, salt and lemon juice to the skillet and stir.

Add cream, garlic, salt, and lemon juice and **stir** to combine.

Add spinach and cook, stirring, until spinach cooks down.

Fold in artichokes.

Stuff each pork chop with spinach stuffing mixture.

Add pork chops back into the Dutch oven.

Pour in chicken stock, cover, and finish cooking for 30 minutes, or until pork chops are cooked through.

Stewed Pork Medallions

Ingredients:
½ cup olive oil
2 large leeks, trimmed, tough upper greens removed
1 small celeriac, peeled and diced (if available)
3–4 large stalks celery, trimmed and coarsely chopped
2 pounds boneless pork, cut into medallions
2 cups dry white wine or chicken stock
Salt and white pepper to taste
2 eggs or egg substitute (reconstituted)
Juice of 1 lemon, strained

Leeks, like garlic and onion, belong to the allium family of vegetables. Research suggests that alliums are beneficial when added daily to your diet. Like garlic and onion, leeks can help with many health problems associated with oxidative stress.

For a vegan variety of this savory stew, replace the pork medallions with large peeled and chopped carrots. Use the white wine and not the chicken stock (or use a vegetable stock) and omit the eggs.

Heat olive oil in a large casserole dish or Dutch oven.

Sauté the leeks, celeriac, and celery until wilted.

Remove with a slotted spoon.

Add pork to the pot and brown.

Place leeks, celeriac, and celery back in.

Pour in wine and enough water to cover.

Bring to a boil. Reduce heat.

Season with salt and white pepper.

Simmer for about 1½ hours, or until pork is very tender. Add more water during cooking if necessary.

Beat eggs until frothy.

Add lemon and **beat** to combine.

Gradually stream a ladleful of the pan liquids from the pork into the egg-lemon mixture, **beating** constantly.

Pour the egg-lemon mixture back into the pot.

Stir to combine and remove immediately from heat.

Serve hot.

Zesty Breaded Tilapia With Lemon Tarragon Butter Sauce

Ingredients:
½ cup almonds
1 lemon cookie (like Nana's Lemon Dream Cookies)
½ teaspoon salt
¼ teaspoon thyme
4 tilapia fillets
1 lemon
1–2 tablespoons grapeseed oil

Tilapia is a lean fish that contains essential fatty-acids

Limonene, found in lemon, is anti-cancerous and rich in Vitamins C and A, folate, and calcium. It is also alkaline.

Preheat oven to 400°F.

Finely grind almonds, lemon cookie, salt, and thyme in a coffee grinder or food processor.

Pour out onto a shallow dish for breading.

Generously brush oil on both sides of each tilapia fillet.

Dip directly into breading until fillets are completely coated.

Place on a baking sheet.

Bake for 12 to 15 minutes or until fish is cooked through and crust is golden and crunchy.

Sauce Ingredients:
¼ cup Earth Balance butter
1 teaspoon potato starch
2 tablespoons fresh lemon juice
1 teaspoon lemon zest
½ teaspoon salt
1 teaspoon fresh chopped tarragon

Melt butter in a saucepan over medium heat.

Whisk in potato starch until lumps are incorporated.

Add lemon juice, zest, salt, and tarragon.

Simmer until sauce thickens, about 1 to 2 minutes.

Serve with your favorite rice, pouring sauce over the fish and serving with a lemon wedge for garnish.

CHAPTER 13

Savory Sides

Photo Recipe: Mac 'n' Cheese-Ish

Savory Sides

Adzuki Bean Basic Recipe

Alex's Rice

Asparagus Vinaigrette

Basil Pesto Sauce

Brussels Sprouts Gratin

Cool Ranch Rice

Cooked Wild Greens (Horta)

Grecian Style Green Beans (or Okra)

Greek Lima Beans, Artichokes, and Peas

Honeyed Carrots

Hot Bacon and Apple Broccoli

Katerina's Wild Rice

Lemon Basil Couscous

Lemon-Oregano Greek Potatoes

Mac 'n' Cheese-Ish

Maple Sweet Potatoes With Bacon

Maple Yam and Apple Bake

Momma's Mashed Potaters

Pesto Pasta Toss

Pickled Potato Wedges

Risotto

Risotto Variations

Southun Smuthern' Corn on the Cob

ToMAYto ToMAHto Roasted Ensalata

Wild Blend Sauté

Adzuki Bean Basic Recipe

Ingredients:

1 cup adzuki beans, washed and drained

1 strip kombu, about 4 inches long and 1 inch wide

4½ cups water

1 teaspoon natural soy sauce (if not allergic to soy)

Place beans, kombu, and water in a 4-quart cooking pot.

Cook on medium 1½ hours on top of the stove, until beans are tender.

Add soy sauce.

Simmer for 19 to 15 more minutes.

Do not season beans with salt unless they are at least 80 percent done. The salt can prevent them from softening.

The purpose of putting kombu into the beans as they cook is to enhance the flavor of the beans. Kombu helps soften the beans as they cook and adds nutrients to the dish that will alkalize them.

Beans are generally acidic due to their high protein content. Kombu keeps this meal high in protein without making it too acidic.

Shopping Tip: Find adzuki beans (also spelled azuki), kombu, and natural soy sauce at the health food store.

Serving Tip: Serve with a garnish of raw scallions. Great for lunch or dinner. Tastes even better left over!

Alex's Rice

Ingredients:

2 cups gluten-free chicken stock

1 cup brown rice, not sucrose-covered

½ cup broccoli florets

½ carrot, grated

½ pound silken tofu, thoroughly mashed

Bring stock to boil in a large saucepan.

Add rice, broccoli, and carrots. Return to boil.

Stir and reduce heat to low.

Cook for 30 to 40 minutes, until rice tastes done.

Stir in tofu.

> This rice can be a side or a perfect vegetarian/vegan meal choice. The tofu adds about 12 grams of protein to this dish.

Asparagus Vinaigrette

Ingredients:

½ pound asparagus

Italian dressing or French vinaigrette

Rice vegan Parmesan sprinkles (optional, contains soy)

Blanch asparagus in a saucepan until almost tender, about 3 to 4 minutes.

Drain and rinse with cold water to halt the cooking process.

Pour Italian dressing over the asparagus.

Marinate for 4 hours or overnight.

Before serving, **sprinkle** with Parmesan cheese.

Asparagus contains inulin, a "prebiotic" that actually aids in nutrient absorption, lowers risk of allergy, and lowers risk of colon cancer.

It is also an excellent source of vitamin K.

Basil Pesto Sauce

Ingredients:

2 cups fresh basil leaves

4–5 cloves garlic

1 teaspoon lemon juice

1 teaspoon sea salt

¼ cup Rice Vegan grated Parmesan topping
   (optional, contains soy)

½ cups organic olive oil (or more if needed)

Blend the basil, garlic, lemon juice, sea salt, and Parmesan in a food processor or blender.

Slowly **incorporate** the oil and blend to desired consistency.

This sauce is a lean, green machine of alkaline sauciness!

Basil is a great anti-inflammatory food choice that is rich in Vitamin K and Vitamin A and is a good source of fiber.

Basil contains an oil component called eugenol. It shares the same enzyme-blocking function as aspirin, ibuprofen, and acetaminophen.

Brussels Sprouts Gratin

Ingredients:

1 pound Brussels sprouts, stems and outer leaves removed

2 tablespoons chopped sun-dried tomatoes

2 tablespoons almond, sunflower, or safflower oil

½ cup shredded Rice Vegan mozzarella

½ cup almond milk or hemp milk, unsweetened

½ teaspoon garlic powder

½ teaspoon onion powder

2 tablespoons almond flour

Preheat oven to 375°F.

Place Brussels sprouts in a large stock pot and add enough water to cover them. Bring to a boil.

Boil for 8 minutes.

Drain and coarsely chop Brussels sprouts.

Transfer to a baking dish.

Distribute chopped sun-dried tomatoes evenly over the Brussels sprouts.

Drizzle with oil, and sprinkle cheese shreds on top of that.

Combine the milk, garlic and onion powders, and salt and pepper to taste in a small bowl.

Pour over Brussels sprouts.

Sprinkle almond flour evenly on top.

Cover and bake for 20 to 25 minutes.

Brussels sprouts are well known for their glucosinolate content, important in helping protect against cancer and inflammation. They are immune-supportive food choice, and this recipe is a great way to get kids to try them. Yummy!

A recent study has shown improved stability of DNA inside of our white blood cells after daily consumption of 1¼ cups of Brussels sprouts. Interestingly, it's the ability of certain compounds in Brussels sprouts to block the activity of sulfotransferase enzymes that researchers believe to be responsible for these DNA-protective benefits.

(Source: www.whfood.com)

Cool Ranch Rice

Ingredients:
2 cups water
1 cup brown rice
1 teaspoon salt
2 tablespoon Vegenaise
¼ teaspoon celery salt
¼ teaspoon all-purpose seasoning
1 teaspoon apple cider vinegar

Boil water in a saucepan over high heat.

Stir in rice, salt, Vegenaise, celery salt, seasoning, and vinegar. Bring back to a boil, stirring constantly.

Reduce heat, cover, and simmer for 50 to 60 minutes.

Serve.

Brown rice is a fantastic source of magnesium, iron, selenium, manganese, and vitamins B1, B2, B3, and B6. It is also a great source of fiber.

Brown rice is a healthier choice than white rice, since white rice is basically stripped of all of its nutrients. As an added bonus, brown rice takes fewer resources to process, so it is actually better for the environment too!

Cooked Wild Greens (Horta)

Ingredients:

2½ pounds dandelion greens, chard, beet greens, collard greens, or escarole

½ cup Krinos extra virgin olive oil

2–4 tablespoons Krinos red wine vinegar (or lemon juice)

Salt to taste

Wash and **trim** the greens.

Fill a large pot halfway with water and add salt.

Bring to a boil and **add** greens.

Simmer, partially covered, for 15 to 20 minutes, until greens are tender.

Drain and cool.

Transfer to a serving bowl and **toss** with olive oil, vinegar or lemon juice, and salt to taste. Serve at room temperature.

The greens may be stored without dressing in a covered plastic container in the refrigerator for several days and dressed just before serving.

Greens Greens Greens!

Greens have fantastic nutritional value and are fantastically alkaline.

Each green has a unique benefit to your body and those benefits are abundant. Eat the colors of the rainbow! In addition, greens have bright and vibrant pigments that provide vibrant healthful benefits!

Grecian Style Green Beans (or Okra)

Ingredients:

¼ cup olive oil

1 large onion, diced (we prefer yellow)

4 cloves garlic, minced

2 9-ounce packages frozen green beans or okra (or 1½ to 2 pounds fresh)

2/3 teaspoon oregano

Sea salt and pepper to taste

1 14-ounce can stewed tomatoes

1 small can tomato sauce

Optional: If you feel adventuresome or just like wine, try adding about ¼ to ½ cup of red wine to this for a richer flavor.

TIP: If you use okra instead of beans, sprinkle the okra lightly with wine vinegar after washing. Let the vinegar soak in for about 5 minutes before placing okra in the cooking pot.

Heat the olive oil in a large skillet or wok. **Brown** onion and garlic.

Add green beans, seasonings, and tomatoes, breaking up larger chunks of tomatoes.

Add tomato sauce and bring to a boil.

Cook over low to moderate heat for 45 minutes, or until green beans or okra are cooked.

Green beans have great anti-oxidant content, Vitamin C , beta-carotene, and manganese. They are a common and easy-to-love anti-inflammatory/immuno-supportive food.

This recipe comes from the church cookbook of Beverly's old parish, St. John the Baptist Greek Orthodox Church in Des Plaines, Illinois. We have enjoyed the recipe and the cookbook for more than twenty years in our family.

This recipe can be adapted not only to okra but also to zucchini and probably other green vegetables. Or why not mix?

For extra protein, try adding tofu, which adds nutritional value but takes on the flavor of the other ingredients. This could turn the dish into a main course meal.

TIP: When you use fresh vegetables, cooking time can vary depending on how tender the vegetables are.

Greek Lima Beans, Artichokes and Peas

Ingredients:

¼ cup olive oil

1 bunch green onions, sliced crosswise and chopped

2 teaspoons dried dill (or 3 tablespoons fresh chopped)

3–4 tablespoons chopped fresh parsley

1 teaspoon sea salt

2 2-pound packages frozen Fordhook lima beans

1 1-pound package frozen peas

2 9-ounce packages frozen or marinated artichokes (be sure to read label)

2 14½-ounce cans stewed tomatoes, chopped

Fresh ground pepper to taste

Combine all ingredients and cook in one of two ways:

(1) ON THE STOVETOP:

Use an 8-quart pot.

Cook over low to medium heat for about 1½ to 2 hours.

Stir often to avoid sticking to the pot. Check periodically to make sure there is enough liquid to cook the beans. If needed, add a little bit of water.

(2) BAKED IN THE OVEN:

Use a 9 X 13-inch casserole dish or pan.

Cover but *do not seal* with aluminum foil.

Bake at 325°F for 2½ to 3 hours. Make sure you check for salt before baking.

Uncover for the last 60 minutes to allow any excess moisture to cook out.

Lima beans are a good source of protein and essential amino acids, and green peas are antioxidant rich and anti-inflammatory.

Artichokes pack a fiber punch and are a great source of Vitamin C. This is a fresh, flavorful, and functional combination!

One serving of this salad provides 100 percent RDA of Vitamin C, 50 percent RDI of Vitamin A, and 20 grams of fiber, and is through the roof in manganese!

TIP: If you use marinated artichokes, drain them well. This dish also tastes good the day after. You can cut this recipe in half or make it with any one of the veggies omitted—it still tastes great. Leftovers can be sent to school or work for lunch and can even be eaten at room temperature. (We actually think it tastes better this way.)

Honeyed Carrots

Ingredients:
3 tablespoons Earth Balance soy free
2 cups sliced carrots (3–4)
2 tablespoons raw honey
½ teaspoon salt
1 tablespoon lemon juice or apple cider
   vinegar
1 cup water

Melt butter in a medium skillet or saucepan over medium heat.

Add sliced carrots, honey, salt, lemon juice, and water.

Cover and **cook** for 8 to 10 minutes, or until the carrots are tender crisp.

Check occasionally to be sure you don't need to add more water to the pan.

Garnish with fresh herbs.

Animal research has shown that diets rich in beta-carotene, which is abundant in carrots, can reduce the occurrence of emphysema. Beta-carotene also helps protect against macular degeneration.

Other research, done on humans, suggests that consuming foods that are high in carotenoids can actually make insulin more effective in our bodies, improving blood-glucose control (important for diabetes).

Hot Bacon and Apple Broccoli

Ingredients:
3 cups broccoli
1 package Applegate Farms Sunday Bacon
½ granny smith apple, finely chopped
¼ cup apple cider vinegar
1 tablespoon brown rice syrup
½ teaspoon sea salt

Broccoli is definitely a super-food!

It is an excellent vegetable source of iron and is believed to neutralize carcinogens.

Sulphophrane, found in broccoli, increases enzymes that help rid the body of cancer. Help our bodies to limit oxidative stress.

Wash the broccoli, cut off stems, and break into bite-sized pieces.

Steam broccoli in a stock pot or vegetable steamer.

Heat a large skillet over medium high heat and carefully lay in bacon.

Cook bacon until crisp and set aside on a paper towel to cool.

Drain the all of the bacon grease except for about 1 tablespoon.

Return skillet to stove, reducing the heat to medium low.

Add apples and cook for a minute or two. Add vinegar, brown rice syrup, and salt and stir just to combine.

Place steamed broccoli in a serving dish. Pour the hot bacon dressing over top.

Crumble cooked bacon and sprinkle over top of broccoli. Serve.

Katerina's Wild Rice

Ingredients:
2 cups blended wild and brown rice (like Lundberg Wild Blend)
4 cups chicken or vegetable broth (gluten-free)
2 tablespoons butter (Earth Balance soy free)

Variations: Be creative!

Veggies-Peas, Carrots, Celery

Mushrooms

Onions

Toasted almonds or pine nuts

Grilled chicken

Tofu

Combine rice and chicken broth in a large pot.

Bring to a boil. Then simmer for 45 minutes on the lowest heat.

Add butter, mix, and let sit for 10 minutes before serving.

Wild rice is wildly higher than other grains in protein, minerals, B vitamins, folic acid, and healthy carbohydrates.

One-half cup of wild rice provides more than 3 grams of protein!

The Lundberg Wild Blend rice is very good. Your local grocer may carry one or more of them.

The Kotsanis family loves this rice!

You can also add toasted almonds or pine nuts. We toast nuts in butter on top of the stove. You can also toast them in the oven on a baking sheet with no oil.

Use your imagination, and try this as a basic recipe to which you can add grilled chicken, tofu, or veggies to make this a main dish.

Lemon Basil Couscous

Ingredients:
2 cups (16 ounces) Kitchen Basics chicken stock
1 cinnamon stick
2 tablespoons basil, chopped
2 tablespoons fresh lemon juice
1 teaspoon lemon zest
2 teaspoons olive oil
1 cup Lundberg Brown Rice Couscous

Combine stock, cinnamon, basil, lemon juice, lemon zest, and oil in a medium saucepan. Bring to a quick **boil,** and then remove from heat.

Stir in the couscous, cover, and allow to stand for 5 minutes.

Remove cinnamon stick and serve.

It is important to note that regular couscous is made from semolina flour, and is not gluten-free. However, there are gluten-free versions, like Lundberg Farms' Brown Rice Couscous, that are the perfect gluten-free option.

The lemon and basil give this starch dish a higher alkalinity and a bright flavor!

Lemon-Oregano Greek Potatoes

Ingredients:

2½–3 pounds potatoes, sliced 6 mm thick with food processor (about ¼ inch thick)

Juice of 3 small lemons

½ cup olive oil

2 teaspoons dried oregano

¾ teaspoon sea salt, or to taste

½ cup chopped green onions (optional)

Pepper to taste (optional)

¾ cup Parmesan cheese, grated (Rice Vegan Parmesan topping contains soy and may be an option if avoiding dairy)

Preheat oven to 350°F.

Slice enough potatoes to fill a 9 x 13-inch glass baking dish or pan. Potatoes can be sliced lengthwise or crosswise.

Mix in herbs and add cheese, if desired.

Do not seal with foil, but lay a piece of foil over the pan to avoid burning.

Bake for 1½ to 2 hours.

Lemon juice makes this such a refreshing flavor composition, and it is a fantastic alkalizing addition to this starchy dish.

This dish can be made using the following types of potatoes: russet, Idaho, new (red), or Yukon Gold. If you are not on a dairy-restricted diet, you can add cheese, such as Parmesan or Romano. A favorite variation is to use 6 to 8 tablespoons fresh parsley instead of the oregano. But if you are on an antifungal diet, then oregano is the better way to go.

Tastes great even without the cheese!

Note: If you slice the potatoes thicker, it may take a little longer to cook.

Mac 'n' Cheese

Ingredients:

1 box rice macaroni noodles

1 tablespoon plus 1 teaspoon grapeseed oil

1½ cups Rice Vegan Cheddar Shreds (or other nondairy cheese)

½ cup nondairy milk (unsweetened)

1 teaspoon salt

¼ teaspoon turmeric (optional, some kids are sensitive to the flavor and don't like it)

Sea salt and pepper to taste

Add more turmeric if you like the flavor. The curcumin in turmeric has fantastic anti-inflammatory properties, especially for chronic skin conditions.

Cook macaroni in water with salt and 1 teaspoon oil added, according to package directions.

Drain and return to pan.

Keep heat at low to medium low and add 1 tablespoon oil, nondairy cheese, and nondairy milk.

Stir constantly until cheese is melted.

Stir in turmeric. Add salt and pepper to taste, if desired.

Serve.

Maple Sweet Potatoes with Bacon

Ingredients
1 sweet potato

2 slices of bacon

1 tablespoon Earth Balance soy free or grape-seed oil

2 teaspoons organic maple syrup

Sweet potatoes are very high in vitamin A and also a good source of vitamin C.

Preheat oven to 400°F.

Wash sweet potato and poke with a fork or knife a few times.

Place bacon on a baking sheet or broiling pan.

Bake for 45 minutes, placing the bacon in the oven to cook after 30 minutes.

Let cool before handling.

Take the skin off sweet potato or simply cut in half and scoop out the soft potato into a small bowl.

Mash sweet potato to desired consistency.

Place half of mashed sweet potato on a plate. Top with ½ tablespoon Earth Balance, 1 teaspoon syrup, and 1 slice of bacon crumbled. Repeat with other half of potato.

Serve.

Maple Yam and Apple Bake

Ingredients:
2 organic yams or sweet potatoes
2 organic honey crisp (or granny smith) apples
Grapeseed oil
¼ cup organic lemon juice
¼ cup butter, melted
¼ cup maple syrup
½ cup chopped pecans (optional)

Preheat oven to 400°F.

Wash, peel, and chop potatoes and apples into 1-inch cubes.

Grease a 9 x 13-inch baking dish with grapeseed oil.

Mix the yams, apples, lemon juice, butter, syrup, and pecans (if desired) in a large mixing bowl. Toss to combine.

Pour into prepared baking dish and bake for 45 minutes to 1 hour, until soft and caramelized.

Apples contain fiber and yams are rich in Vitamin C and potassium, both of which play a role in a healthy immune system.

Yams are a complex carbohydrate and pack a lot of fiber content, so their sugars are released slowly. They also contain manganese, which helps with carbohydrate metabolism.

It is funny how the simplest of dishes can put the biggest smiles around your dinner table.

Momma's Mashed Potaters

Ingredients

6 organic red or white potatoes (skin can stay on reds)

1 stalk celery

½ cup leeks

1 cup cauliflower

2 teaspoons sea salt

½ cup free-range organic chicken stock

½ cup coconut milk

¼ cup Earth's Balance

Wash and peel (if desired) potatoes.

Wash celery, leeks, and cauliflower. (For leeks, chop the dark green tops off, then cut down the length of the leek stalk, exposing all of the layers. Wash really well as dirt can get into those layers fairly easily.)

Roughly chop all of the vegetables.

Steam in a stock pot or a vegetable steamer until fork tender.

Transfer to a food processor or blender and add the salt, stock, milk, and butter.

Blend until desired consistency is reached.

Potatoes are an excellent source of fiber, Vitamin C, and B vitamins such as biotin and folate.

The British Journal of Cancer says I3C (indole-3-carinal sulforaphane) helps the liver produce cancer-fighting enzymes.

Celery contains poly-acetylenes, which help fight bacteria and fungi and are anti-inflammatory.

Pesto Pasta Toss

Ingredients:

1 16-ounce package rice pasta

1 7-ounce package basil pesto sauce

1 7-ounce jar roasted red peppers, drained and finely chopped

Cook pasta in a large saucepan according to package directions.

Drain.

Toss basil pesto sauce and red peppers with hot pasta.

Serve.

A gorgeously green pasta dish!

Basil is in the same botanical family as mint. In some cultures, basil is used medicinally (topically) for inflamed joints and even colic and is used in teas for a wide variety of ailments.

TIP: Make ahead. This pasta can be enjoyed cold. Prepare as directed. Cover. Refrigerate until serving.

Pickled Potato Wedges

Ingredients:
4-6 large organic Yukon Gold potatoes
¼ cup avocado oil
1½ teaspoons Frontier Pickling Spices

Preheat oven to 425°F.

Wash potatoes, leaving skin on.

Slice potatoes in half lengthwise, then slice into large wedges.

Mix avocado oil and pickling spices in a separate bowl or cup.

Lay potato wedges out in a single layer on a parchment-lined or lightly oiled baking sheet.

Brush each wedge liberally with oil mixture.

Bake for 22 to 25 minutes.

Serve with Thousand Dollar Dressing as a dip.

Avocado oil is very rich in vitamin E and a monounsaturated fatty acid, the "good fat." it is higher in omega-9 fatty acids than olive oil.

These are a healthier version of traditional French fries, since they are not deep-fried. However, always remember to stick to your 80/20 chart of inflammatory vs. anti-inflammatory foods.

Any starchy foods should be limited, but at least when you are eating them they can be fun.

Risotto

Ingredients:
1 cup arborio rice (risotto)
1 medium onion, diced
4 tablespoons olive oil
4 to 5 cups chicken broth
Sea salt and pepper to taste

Heat olive oil in a large saucepan over medium-high heat.

Add onion and sauté until onions begin to get translucent—don't over-brown.

Add dry risotto and sauté for 2 to 3 minutes, stirring frequently.

Reduce heat to medium.

Stir in about 1 cup broth.

Continue adding broth a little at a time while simmering and stirring frequently (don't let the risotto get too dry, and don't make it swim). The idea is to add just enough broth to keep the pot simmering, allowing the risotto to slowly absorb it.

If making a variation: Add extra ingredients after you've added about half of the broth. Try adding other vegetables and broth. Experiment and enjoy!

Continue to cook until sauce becomes creamy and risotto is al dente (soft, but not mushy). If you like softer pasta, add more broth and cook a bit longer.

Add salt and pepper to taste, and serve.

Sprinkle with real or rice/soy "Parmesan" cheese.

Risotto is short-grain rice and a very versatile alternative to traditional gluten pastas. Like rice and gluten-free pastas, risotto is a fantastic vessel to which a plethora of nutrient-rich vegetables can be added.

This is one flavorful variety of this delicious dish.

Storage Tip: Cooked risotto freezes well. You may need to add some water when you reheat.

Risotto Variations

"MacRice and Cheese"

Substitute risotto for macaroni and try it with dairy-free cheese for a variation on Mac and Cheese.

Zucchini Risotto

Slice two medium zucchini lengthwise into quarters, then slice each quarter into ¼-inch slices (you should end up with a pile of "pie-slice-shaped" zucchini pieces.

Add zucchini halfway through cooking.

A simple and delicious dish perfect for any summer dinner!

Mushroom Risotto

Add a package of sliced mushrooms half-way through cooking.

Try adding in some of your favorite colorful vegetables to increase the nutrient value to the dish.

Mark a main dish of it by adding chicken, fish, shrimp, and other nutrient rich vegetables.

Use your imagination!

Tips and Tricks: If you or your kids miss macaroni and cheese or get tired of eating plain rice try making risotto instead. This rice dish is creamy and can be flavored in a variety ways.

When making a variation, add extra ingredients after you've added about half of the broth. Try adding other vegetables, organic vegetable or beef broth, shrimp, or crab. Experiment and enjoy!

ToMAYto ToMAHto Roasted Ensalata

Ingredients:
1 large red heirloom tomato
1 large orange heirloom tomato
1 large yellow heirloom tomato
2 tablespoons avocado oil
1 teaspoon sea salt
Fresh cracked pepper to taste
6–8 fresh basil leaves, slices

Tomatoes are rich in vitamin C and potassium. Especially when cooked, they are a great source of inflammatory/immuno-supportive and anti-carcinogenic properties.

Avocado oil is very rich in vitamin E and is a monounsaturated fatty acid, the "good fat." It is higher in omega-9 fatty acids than olive oil.

Preheat oven to 450°F.

Wash tomatoes and remove stem and core.

Slice each tomato into ¼-inch rounds.

Lay tomatoes in a large roasting pan, overlapping each row slightly. You can organize the colors into striped rows, or simply mix them for a beautiful display.

Drizzle oil down evenly over top.

Sprinkle with salt, pepper, and basil.

Roast for 10 to 12 minutes.

Wild Blend Sauté

Ingredients:

2 cups blended wild and brown rice

4 cups gluten-free chicken stock

4 tablespoons butter or olive oil

1 cup chopped celery

2 cups sliced mushrooms

1 large red onion, chopped

2 cloves garlic, minced

4–6 tablespoons teriyaki

Combine rice and chicken stock in a pot.

Bring to a boil, and then simmer for 45 minutes on the lowest heat.

Heat the butter or olive oil in a large saucepan and **sauté** the vegetables and garlic over medium heat for 5 to 7 minutes.

Add teriyaki and simmer until liquid is absorbed.

Stir in rice and serve.

With wild rice and brown rice, this saucy side dish boasts a larger amount of protein and folic acid as compared to white rice or brown rice alone.

Did you know that wild rice is actually not a rice at all, but a grass?

Be careful when selecting your teriyaki sauce, as most have gluten in them. San-J manufactures a gluten-free option (which contains soy).

If you cannot find these rice already blended, just buy brown and wild rice and mix them, although the flavor won't be as tasty and complex.

Any kind of brown rice variety will usually take a little longer to cook than white rice.

Southun Smuthern' Corn on the Cob

Ingredients:

4 ears sweet corn (organic and non-GMO if possible)

¼ cup Earth Balance soy free

1 cup diced organic zucchini

1 organic green tomato, diced (use red if you can't find green)

½ cup chopped organic okra (frozen)

1 cup coconut milk (vanilla, unsweetened)

¼ cup Grapeseed Vegenaise

½ teaspoon sea salt

¼ teaspoon organic sweet paprika

6–8 slices nitrite-free turkey bacon, cooked and crumbled (optional; try Applegate Farms brand)

This is a fun, southern-style dress-up of an old favorite—corn on the cob. Try to find a non-GMO corn if possible. Or obtain heirloom seeds online from a handful of sources and grow your own!

To make this dish vegetarian, simply sprinkle with your favorite fresh herbs and enjoy.

Allergic to corn? Simply substitute a piece of lean meat like baked chicken, turkey, or fish for the corn.

Boil about 8 cups of water in a large stock pot with a lid.

Shuck corn, remove silk threads, and drop in the water as soon as it is boiling.

Cover and cook for 8 to 10 minutes.

Melt butter or oil in a skillet over medium heat, and **sauté** zucchini, tomato, and okra for about 5 minutes, just until tender.

Add coconut milk, Vegenaise, and spices.

Stir until well combined.

Serve: place one ear of corn in a shallow soup bowl, then drizzle a few large spoonfuls of cream and vegetable mixture down over the corn. Top with crumbled bacon for a side dish gone mainstream!

Warm Buttered Apples

Ingredients:

2 tablespoons Earth Balance

2 organic granny smith apples

2 organic honey crisp apples

1 tablespoon organic lemon juice

¼ cup honey

½ teaspoon potato starch mixed with ¾ cup warm water

1 teaspoon vanilla extract

Peel and **chop** apples into ½-inch slices or cubes.

Heat butter in a saucepan over medium heat and add apples, butter, lemon juice, and honey.

Bring to a low boil.

Combine potato starch and water in a separate bowl until lumps are incorporated.

Add starch mixture to the apples.

Reduce heat to medium low and simmer for 20 to 25 minutes, stirring occasionally.

When apples are done to preferred softness, **serve** alone or as a topping.

Apples provide vitamin C, which is essential to a balanced immune system. It is a water-soluble antioxidant and a key component in collagen synthesis.

Low on the glycemic index, it is a great source of dietary fiber.

The lemon juice provides an alkaline property to this recipe.

This is the perfect topping for pancakes or waffles!

CHAPTER 14

Sweet Indulgences

Photo Recipe: Caramel Oats Brulée

Sweet Indulgences

Awesome Almond Birthday Cupcakes

Basic White Cake Without Eggs

Beverly's Fluffy Frosting

Carob Cake

Caramel Oats Brulée

Chocolate Chocolate Chip Cupcakes

Chocolate PEAcan Squares

CinnaDOODLE Cookies

Coco-Nut-Butter Balls

Coconut Fluff Frosting

Cream Cheese Fluff Frosting

Easter Envy Carrot Cupcakes

Gingerbread Cookies

I ☐ CCCs (Chocolate Chip Cookies)

Just Plain Delicious Cookies

Just Plain Delicious Cookies—Variations

Lemon Chia Cake

Lime in Da Coconut Dream Bars

Lil' Pink Princess Cupcakes

Maple Fluff Frosting

Matcha Made in Heaven Macaroons

Molasses Cookies

Oh My Gosh! Fluffy Ganache Frosting

Super Whooper Whoopie Cookies

Toaster Tartlets

Toasted Almond Chocolate Chipper

Awesome Almond Birthday Cupcakes

NUTS

Dry Ingredients:
2½ cups Bob's Red Mill Almond Flour
1½ teaspoons egg-replacer powder
½ teaspoon baking soda
¼ teaspoon sea salt
1 cup organic raw cane sugar

Wet Ingredients:
¼ cup brown rice syrup
¼ cup grapeseed oil
2 tablespoons water
1 tablespoon vanilla extract
2 teaspoons apple cider vinegar

Cupcakes can be nutritious!

These almond flour cupcakes provide great protein content and have great fiber content as well. What better way to get kids some healthy nutritional elements than in a cupcake. Sweet!

Preheat oven to 350°F.

Sift dry ingredients into a large mixing bowl.

Mix wet ingredients together in a separate bowl.

Incorporate wet ingredients into dry ingredients.

Mix until thoroughly blended and smooth.

Pour into a cupcake pan, with paper liners in the cups (or spray with cooking spray).

Bake for 20 to 25 minutes, or until a toothpick inserted into the center comes out clean.

Cool cupcakes completely.

Ice with any of the powder-sugar free icing recipes!

Basic White Cake Without Eggs

Dry Ingredients:
1 cup white or brown rice flour
½ cup potato starch
¼ cup tapioca flour
½ teaspoon xanthan gum
2¼ teaspoons baking powder
¼ teaspoon sea salt

Wet Ingredients:
2/3 cup honey
½ cup grapeseed oil or safflower oil
2 teaspoons gluten-free vanilla extract
½ cup soft silken tofu (or substitute with coconut yogurt)
1 lemon peel, grated
½ cup boiling water

This cake was created for people who are sensitive to eggs.

It can be baked in several versions:

Loaf cake

Pineapple upside-down cake

Layer cake

Cupcakes

Preheat oven to 325°F

Lightly coat a 9 x 5-inch loaf pan or two 5 x 2½-inch cake pans with cooking spray.

Sift together dry ingredients.

Combine honey, oil, vanilla, tofu, and lemon peel in food processor.

Process on high until completely smooth and glossy.

Add boiling water and process on high until completely mixed.

Add dry ingredients and process until smooth.

Spoon batter into pan(s).

Bake 30 to 40 minutes for two small pans and 1 hour for larger pan. *Cake will not brown.*

Remove from oven and cool for 10 minutes before removing from pan(s).

Cool completely before cutting.

Beverly's Fluffy Frosting

(EGGS)

Ingredients:
1 cup pure maple syrup
2 large egg whites (room temperature)
☐ teaspoon sea salt
1 teaspoon gluten-free vanilla extract

Pour maple syrup in a heavy, narrow saucepan.

Attach a candy thermometer to edge of saucepan.

Cook syrup over low heat until it registers 239°F, stirring occasionally.

While syrup is cooking:

Beat egg whites and sea salt until stiff peaks form in a large bowl.

When the syrup reaches 239°F, begin to

Drip it very slowly into the egg whites.

Continue beating until icing begins to thicken.

It is ready when it falls off a spatula in a thin, threadlike fashion.

Stir in vanilla.

Ice the cooled cake immediately with a spatula.

Use wide, sweeping movements around sides and top of cake.

Add other decorations as desired.

A fluffy whipped delight made with real maple syrup instead of loads of powdered sugar.

For the best nutritional value, use organic grade B maple syrup, because it is collected at the end of the season, yielding the best nutrient composition. The organic version does not go through the refining processes and therefore is more natural.

TIPS: Fluffy and irresistible, this frosting is so elegant it can be used for special occasions. This recipe requires a candy thermometer, so be sure you have one. Also, you must work quickly once the frosting is ready, so have your cake cooled and ready. For safety's sake, use only fresh eggs and refrigerate the frosted cake. Persons strongly allergic to egg whites should avoid this frosting.

Caramel Oats Brulée

Ingredients:
1 cup filtered water
¾ cups gluten-free rolled oats
½ cup non-dairy milk of choice
¼ teaspoon sea salt
4 teaspoons brown rice syrup
4–6 teaspoons rapadura or turbinado sugar

Find gluten-free rolled oats in your local health food store.

You will need a kitchen torch for this recipe to heat the tops of the brulées, which are prepared in four baking ramekins.

Boil water in a small saucepan.

Stir in oats, non-dairy milk, and salt.

Reduce heat to medium low and simmer, stirring occasionally, for 20 to 25 minutes, or until the oatmeal reaches desired consistency.

Drizzle 1 teaspoon brown rice syrup in each ramekin.

Top with oatmeal and flatten tops with a spatula.

Sprinkle with sugar to cover completely.

Torch the sugar until it forms a crystallized top, like traditional crème brulée.

Carob Cake

DIARY

Dry Ingredients:
½ cup brown rice flour

½ cup potato starch

¼ cup tapioca flour

½ cup carob powder

½ teaspoon xanthum gum

2¼ teaspoons baking powder (aluminum-free)

½ teaspoon salt

¾ cup dried cane juice or maple sugar, or 2/3 cup honey with ¼ teaspoon baking soda

Wet Ingredients:
¼ cup butter or other oil substitute

¼ cup prune purée or applesauce or 1 jar prune baby food (2.5 ounces)

2/3 cup boiling water

¼ cup silken tofu

2 teaspoons gluten-free vanilla extract

Both the prune purée and the tofu add protein power to this dessert, as well as a fiber count and vitamin C!

Tip: This is a very versatile dessert. Serve it plain, with a dusting of powdered sugar (or 1 cup organic raw cane sugar), or your favorite frosting.

Leftovers freeze well, or use them to crumble into crusts for pies or cheesecakes.

Preheat oven to 350°F.

Coat a 9-inch round or square pan with cooking spray.

Combine flours, carob powder, xanthan gum, baking powder, and salt in a mixing bowl.

Cream together the sugar, oil (or ghee) and vanilla (at room temperature), prunes (or applesauce) and, tofu in a food processor until smooth.

Add boiling water. **Process** on high until completely blended.

Add flour mixture and **process** until smooth.

Spoon batter into prepared 9-inch round or square pan.

Bake for 20 to 30 minutes, or until top is firm and toothpick inserted into center comes out clean.

Remove from oven.

Cool for 5 minutes before removing from pan.

Chocolate Chocolate Chip Cupcakes

Dry Ingredients:
1 cup Bob's Red Mill Chocolate Brownie Mix
1 cup Bob's Gluten-Free All-Purpose Flour
2 teaspoons baking powder
¼ teaspoon sea salt
1½ teaspoons egg-replacer powder
¼ cup Enjoy Life chocolate chips

> *A sweet treat, all free of gluten ad casein. These are a perfect treat to take along to a birthday party or a school event. Who can resist a double dose of chocolate?*

Wet Ingredients:
1 teaspoon apple cider vinegar
1¼ cups water
2 teaspoons vanilla extract
½ cup shredded zucchini

Preheat oven to 350°F. Grease muffin pans or use paper liners.

Mix dry ingredients in a large mixing bowl.

Combine vinegar, water and vanilla extract in a separate bowl or large measuring cup

Pour vinegar mixture into dry ingredients and stir to combine.

Fold in zucchini and chocolate chips.

Fill muffin cups 2/3 full. Bake for 18 to 22 minutes, or until a toothpick inserted into the center comes out clean.

Chocolate PEAcan Squares

Ingredients: Crust:

1¼ cups blanched almond flour 2 tablespoons tapioca flour

1 tablespoon pea protein powder

¼ teaspoon GF baking soda

¼ cup SoDelicious Coconut Yogurt (plain)

2 tablespoons almond oil

2 tablespoons honey

¼ cup water

Filling:

1½ cups water

1½ tablespoons agar flakes

½ teaspoon salt

1/3 cup honey

1 tablespoon vanilla extract

4 ounces Baker's 100% chocolate, coarsely chopped

1 tablespoon pea protein powder

3 cups whole pecans

> Pea protein powder is a great non-dairy protein source.
>
> Add this to a sweet treat dish like PEAcan Squares and you will never even know you're getting a protein-rich treat.

For the Crust:

Preheat oven to 350°F.

Whisk together the dry ingredients in a large mixing bowl.

Stir in wet ingredients until fully combined.

Press into an oiled 11 x 7-inch baking dish.

Bake for 10 minutes.

Top It Off! With whipped vanilla almond milk for a perfect dish!

For the Filling:

Bring water to a boil in a medium saucepan over high heat.

Stir in the agar flakes

Cook, stirring frequently, until the agar flakes are completely dissolved (approximately 10 minutes). It will start to thicken, as when dissolving gelatin.

Reduce heat.

Stir in sea salt, honey, vanilla extract, and bakers chocolate pieces and pea protein power.

Simmer until combined, about 3 minutes.

Turn off heat and let stand to cool for approximately 15 minutes.

Stir in pecans.

Pour the mixture into the baked crust.

Refrigerate to set, at least one hour.

CinnaDOODLE Cookies

Wet Ingredients:
7 tablespoons Earth Balance, room temperature
½ cup brown rice syrup
1 tablespoon vanilla extract
¼ cup rice milk

Dry Ingredients:
2½ cups Kendra's Flour Power
2 tablespoons tapioca flour
1½ teaspoons egg-replacer powder
½ teaspoon sea salt
1 teaspoon baking soda
Ground cinnamon, to sprinkle on top

Cinnamon has been widely used medicinally as an anti-microbial and as an anti-fungal.

Preheat oven to 350°F.

Cream together wet ingredients using an electric mixer.

Sift dry ingredients together into a separate bowl.

Incorporate the dry ingredients gradually into the wet ingredients until well mixed.

Spoon heaping tablespoons of dough onto a parchment-lined or lightly greased baking sheet, leaving 2 inches between each.

Shape dough into macaroon cookie shapes using fingers or the back of a spoon.

Sprinkle with cinnamon.

Bake for 8 to 10 minutes. (Do not over bake.)

Cool on pan for 5 minutes then transfer to a cooling rack.

Coco-Nut-Butter Balls

NUTS

Ingredients:

½ cup tahini (you can use any kind of nut butter)

1/3 cup brown rice syrup

2 tablespoons cocoa powder

1 cup organic raw cane sugar

½ cup chopped walnuts

½ cup unsweetened organic shredded coconut

Combine nut butter, brown rice syrup, cocoa powder, and organic raw cane sugar.

Add walnuts and coconut, and stir to combine.

Roll dough in 1-ounce portions (about 1 to 1½ tablespoons) into balls.

Dust with powdered sugar.

Tahini contains vitamins B1, B2, B3, B5, and B15. B vitamins play an essential part in the running of the body. They promote healthy cell growth and division, including that of red blood cells, which will help prevent anemia. They also support and increase the rate of metabolism, enhance immune and nervous system function, and help maintain healthy skin and muscle tone. Recent studies have also shown that Vitamin B can help protect against one of the most deadly forms of cancer, pancreatic cancer, but only when consumed in food.

(Source: www.naturalnews. com/026409_tahini_calcium_ cancer.html#ixzz1KGlGyyYL)

Coconuts have antibacterial and antiviral properties, but eating the "meat" of the coconut is very rich in dietary fiber and protein.

Walnuts are high in vitamin E and a great source of EFA's. These natural foods help regulate blood lipids and glucose to lower the risk of heart disease and help prevent diabetes.

Coconut Fluff Frosting

Ingredients:
1 box MimicCreme Healthy Top
   (extremely cold)
½ teaspoon vanilla
1 tablespoon coconut milk
1/3 cup unsweetened organic coconut

Whip Healthy Top.

Whip in vanilla and coconut milk.

Fold in unsweetened coconut shreds.

Refrigerate until very cold.

Serve.

A fluffy whipped delight made with real maple syrup, instead of loads of powdered sugar.

These frostings are all made with MimicCreme's Healthy Top whipped cream alternative. It is a shelf-stable dairy-free whipped cream made from cashews and almonds. This obviously does not work for those who have sensitivity to tree nuts.

This has been a fantastic substitute in our testing and preparation kitchens. So much healthier than the traditional nutrient-void processed powdered-sugar frostings.

Cream Cheese Fluff Frosting

NUTS

Ingredients:
1 box MimicCreme Healthy Top
1 container Rice Vegan cream cheese
½ teaspoon Vanilla

Whip Healthy Top in a large mixing bowl.

Add cream cheese.

Stir in vanilla.

Refrigerate until very cold.

Whip 2 to 3 minutes on high.

Serve.

A fluffy whipped delight made with Rice Vegan cream cheese, instead of loads of powdered sugar.

This frosting is made with MimicCrème's Healthy Top Whipped Cream alternative. It is a shelf-stable dairy-free whipped cream made from cashews and almonds.

This has been a fantastic substitute in our testing and preparation kitchens.

Easter Envy Carrot Cupcakes

NUTS

Dry Ingredients:
2¼ cups Kendra's Flour Power
2 tablespoons tapioca flour
2 teaspoons baking powder
½ teaspoon baking soda
2 tablespoons egg-replacer powder
1 teaspoon cinnamon

Wet Ingredients:
1 cup oil
¾ cup brown rice syrup
1 teaspoon apple cider vinegar
½ cup carbonated water

Miscellaneous:
2 cups finely shredded carrots
½ cup finely chopped pineapple
½ cup raisins

Preheat oven to 350°F.

Whisk dry ingredients together in a large mixing bowl.

Stir wet ingredients together in a separate bowl.

Incorporate wet ingredients into dry ingredients.

Fold in carrots, pineapple, and raisins.

Fill oiled muffin cups two-thirds full.

Bake for 20 to 25 minutes, or until a toothpick inserted into the center comes out clean.

Ice with Coconut Fluff Frosting.

Animal research has shown that diets rich in beta-carotene can reduce the occurrence of emphysema. Beta-carotene also helps protect against macular degeneration. Other research, done on humans, suggests that consuming foods that are high in carotenoids can actually make insulin more effective in our bodies, improving blood-glucose control (important for diabetes).

Pineapple contains an enzyme called bromelain. Bromelain in pineapple has the special ability to help our body balance and neutralize fluids so that it's neither too alkaline nor too acidic. It also stimulates hormonal secretions in the pancreas that aid digestion and decreases inflammation and swelling.

Gingerbread Cookies

NUTS

Ingredients:
8 tablespoons Earth Balance (1 stick)
1/3 cup brown sugar
½ cup blackstrap molasses
2 tablespoons water
3 cups Bob's Red Mill All-purpose Flour
1 teaspoon ground cinnamon
1 teaspoon baking soda
1 teaspoon ground ginger
½ teaspoon ground cloves

Preheat oven to 325°F.

Cream together butter, brown sugar, molasses, and water in a large mixing bowl with an electric mixer.

Combine flour, cinnamon, baking soda, ginger, and cloves in a separate bowl.

Slowly incorporate the dry ingredients into the wet ingredients.

Chill in refrigerator for 15 minutes (or up to 3 days).

Roll chilled dough out on a flat surface (use Bob's GF all-purpose flour to keep it from sticking).

Cut out shapes with cookie cutters.

Cook for 9 to 11 minutes.

Sprinkle with powdered sugar, or decorate with icing as desired.

These are a terrific allergy-friendly treat—wheat-free, milk-free, egg-free, nut-free, and stress-free!

It is fairly well-known that ginger is used as a relief for nausea. Ginger also contains very potent anti-inflammatory compounds called gingerols.

Gingerols may inhibit the growth of human colorectal cancer cells.

(Sources: www.whfood.com, www.pubmed.com)

I ♥ CCCs (Chocolate Chip Cookies)

Ingredients:
1 cup brown rice syrup
1 tablespoon blackstrap molasses
1/3 cup Earth Balance
2–3 tablespoons water
2 teaspoons vanilla extract
1 cup plus 3 tablespoons Bob's Red Mill all-purpose flour
1 teaspoon baking powder
1 teaspoon baking soda
½ teaspoon salt
1½ teaspoons egg-replacer powder
½–¾ cups chocolate chips (Enjoy Life)
¼ teaspoon xanthan gum

Preheat oven to 350°F.

This recipe works well for our household because of our allergy to cane sugar.

Try using Lundberg Farms' brown rice syrup in place of the sugar. It is a bit lower on the glycemic index and has a delicious caramel-like flavor.

It is important to note that any sweetener, even brown rice syrup, can exacerbate yeast overgrowth issues when present.

Enjoy informed eating of these deliciously classic cookies surely, but sparingly!

Cream together the brown rice syrup, molasses, and butter in a mixing bowl.

Add water and vanilla extract. Stir to combine.

Stir together flour, baking powder, baking soda, salt, and egg-replacer in a separate bowl.

Slowly incorporate dry ingredients into wet.

Fold in chocolate chips.

Form cookies on greased or nonstick cookie sheet. For best results, press cookies into the exact shape you want them to bake into.

Bake for 9 to 11 minutes.

Just Plain Delicious Cookies

Ingredients:
¼ cup butter or oil spread
2 tablespoons honey
½ cup brown rice syrup
1 ½ teaspoons gluten-free vanilla extract
¾ cup brown rice flour
½ cup white rice flour
3 tablespoons potato starch
2 tablespoons tapioca flour
½ teaspoons xanthan gum
½ teaspoons sea salt
1 teaspoons baking powder
1 large egg white
2 tablespoons water (or more)

Preheat oven to 325°F.

Enjoy!

Tip: The egg white can be omitted and will produce a crisp cookie.

For great tasting variations of Just Plain Delicious Cookies, see our Creative Variations on the next page.

Enjoy, much more!

Let's do vegan sprinkles! Colored with natural ingredients!

Combine butter (room temperature), honey, brown rice syrup, and vanilla in a mixing bowl.

Add flours, xanthan gum, salt, baking powder, and egg white.

Blend until mixture forms large clumps. *(If using a mixer, blend wet ingredients until fluffy, then add dry ingredients and blend well.)*

Add water if needed, 1 tablespoon at a time.

Divide dough into 2 parts and shape each into a ball.

Cover and refrigerate for 1 hour.

Sprinkle rice flour onto sheets of wax paper or plastic wrap.

Roll dough to ¼-inch thickness between the sheets. Keep remaining dough chilled until ready to use.

Spray baking sheet with cooking spray.

Cut into desired shapes and place 1 inch apart on baking sheet.

Bake for 10 to 12 minutes or until edges are set.

Turn pans halfway through baking for even heat distribution.

Remove from oven and cool 2 minutes before transferring to a wire rack to cool.

Just Plain Delicious Cookies: Creative Variations!

Preheat oven to 325°F.
Bake for 10 to 12 minutes or until edges are set.

Variations:
Anise–Pine Nut Cookies:
Add 1 teaspoon gluten-free anise flavoring
   and ½ cup toasted finely chopped pine nuts.

> *Experiment with different variations!*
>
> *Look for gluten-free flavorings at your health food store.*

Pecan Cookies:

Add ½ teaspoon finely chopped pecans, 1 teaspoon each gluten-free pecan extract and butter extract (optional) and ☐ teaspoon baking soda.

Bake as directed.

Spice Cookies:

Add ¼ teaspoon freshly ground nutmeg, ½ teaspoon ground cinnamon, and ☐ teaspoon ground cloves.

Bake as directed.

Lemon Poppy Seed Cookies:

Add 2 tablespoons poppy seeds and 2 tablespoons grated lemon peel.

Bake as directed.

Lemon Chia Cake

Dry Ingredients:
2¼ cups Kendra's Flour Power
2½ teaspoons baking soda
2 tablespoons egg-replacer powder
2 tablespoons chia seeds

Wet Ingredients:
1 cup brown rice syrup
1 cup pear purée (or use organic baby food)
¼ cup fresh lemon juice
½ cup carbonated water
¼ teaspoon guar gum
1 teaspoon lemon extract
Zest of 2 lemons
1–2 teaspoons organic lemon juice

Preheat oven to 350°F.

Whisk together all of the dry ingredients in a large mixing bowl.

Add wet ingredients (including the fruit).

Stir until fully incorporated. Easy!

Transfer batter to an oiled loaf pan and bake for 35 to 45 minutes, or until a toothpick inserted into the center comes out clean.

Another easy-to-prepare baked treat!

Though they are acidic before digestion, lemons are actually alkaline-forming in the body. They are rich in vitamin C, B6, potassium, and folate. Lemons contain a fantastic phytochemical called limonene, which actually increases the level of enzymes that detoxify carcinogens, giving it cancer-fighting effects.

Fresh lemon juice is a great immune-supportive food choice.

Chia Seeds are a miraculous food. They can actually absorb up to 12 times their weight in less than 10 minutes. Chia seeds are extremely high in antioxidants. They're like an intestinal broom, dislodging intestinal waste as they move through.

Lil' Pink Princess Cupcakes

Dry Ingredients:
2¼ cups all-purpose flour
1 cup organic raw cane sugar
½ teaspoon sea salt
4 teaspoons baking powder
1 teaspoon agar powder
2 tablespoons egg-replacer powder
½ teaspoon xanthan gum

Wet Ingredients:
1 cup pear purée
1 teaspoon vanilla
1 cup grapeseed oil
½ cup coconut milk
½ cup water

Miscellaneous:

1½ cups organic strawberries, puréed (fresh or frozen)

1 cup unsweetened coconut flakes (ground or chopped)

Preheat oven to 325°F.

Mix together dry ingredients in a large bowl.

Stir in wet ingredients.

Fold in strawberries and coconut.

Bake for 25 to 30 minutes.

Ice with Coconut Cream Cheese Fluff.

Vitamin C, folate, anthocyanin, quercetin, and kaempferol are all important flavonoids in strawberries, which serve as powerful antioxidants and anticarcinogenics. Together, they form an excellent team to fight cancer and tumor. A daily intake of strawberries is seen to have remarkably brought down the growth of cancerous cells.

(Source: www.organic-facts.net)

Ice with Coconut Cream Cheese Fluff for the perfect compliment—fit for a princess!

Lime in Da Coconut Dream Bars

Crust:
3 tablespoons coconut oil
1 cup graham cracker crumbs (Kinnikinnik)
½ cup unsweetened coconut flakes, chopped
    or ground
1 tablespoon tapioca flour

Cream:
½ box of MimicCreme Healthy Top, whipped
1 tub rice cream cheese (Galaxy Foods)
Zest of 1 lime
1 teaspoon pure lime extract
1/4 cup organic raw cane sugar

Topping :
1/3 cup coconut flakes
½ cup walnuts

Coconut has innumerable benefits to the body—lauric acid, capric acid, and caprylic acid—and is antimicrobial, antioxidant, antifungal, and antibacterial.

Lime is also alkalizing.

Preheat oven to 325°F.

Melt coconut oil in a small saucepan.

Stir together with the graham cracker crumbs, coconut flakes, and tapioca flour until well combined.

Press the crumb mixture into a Pyrex 3-quart oblong glass baking dish.

Bake for 8 minutes.

Remove from oven and let cool.

Whip the MimicCreme.

Whip in the rice cream cheese, lime zest, lime extract, and organic raw cane sugar.

Spread whipped mixture into the cooled crust.

Top with coconut flakes and walnuts. (You may want to toast the coconut and walnuts for a different flavor and crunch.)

Freeze for at least 1 hour before serving.

Maple Fluff Frosting

Ingredients:
1 box MimicCreme Healthy Top (very cold)
2 tablespoons organic pure maple syrup
¼ teaspoon vanilla

Whip Healthy Top in a large mixing bowl.

Add maple syrup.

Stir in vanilla.

Refrigerate until very cold.

Whip 2 to 3 minutes on high.

Serve.

See our other frostings including Coconut Fluff and Cream Cheese Fluff Frosting listed in alphabetical order in this section.

Mimic Crème Healthy Top Whipped Cream alternative is a shelf-stable dairy-free whipped cream made from cashews and almonds.

This obviously does not work for those who have sensitivity to tree nuts.

This has been a terrific substitute with our kid testing panels. It is a great alternative to the traditional powdered sugar and nutrient-void frostings.

Matcha Made in Heaven Macaroons

Ingredients:
2 tablespoons psyllium husk, mealed
1 cup water
1 cup organic raw cane sugar
¼ cup coconut flour
2 tablespoons brown rice flour
1 tablespoon arrowroot powder
1 tablespoon green tea powder (Matcha powder)
½ teaspoon baking powder
2 cups finely grated organic unsweetened coconut flakes

Preheat oven to 350°F.

Grind psyllium husk in a food processor or coffee grinder.

Transfer to a bowl and add in the water, stirring to combine.

Add remaining ingredients except for the coconut flakes and stir until fully incorporated.

Fold in coconut flakes.

Knead dough.

Form macaroons with fingers and place on a parchment-lined baking sheet.

Bake for 20 minutes, until bottom of macaroons are a golden brown.

Remove from oven and let cool on a wire rack.

Store in an airtight container.

Green tea powder (Matcha Powder) is a rich source of antioxidants called catechins. One of the catechins, EGCG (epicgallocatechin gallate) is the catechin with the broadest and most potent cancer-fighting properties. Sixty percent of the catechin content of Matcha tea is EGCG.

Matcha is renowned for numerous health benefits. It is also rich in fiber and chlorophyll. It is sugar-free, making it an ideal drink for diabetics and others wishing to reduce their sugar intake. The health benefits of Matcha exceed those of other green teas because Matcha drinkers ingest the whole leaf, not just the brewed water. One glass of Matcha is the equivalent of ten glasses of green tea in terms of nutritional value and antioxidant content.

(Source: www.matcha-source.com)

Molasses Cookies

Ingredients:
¾ cup grapeseed oil
½ cup organic sugar
½ cup sugar substitute (Stevia in the Raw)
¼ cup blackstrap molasses or brown rice syrup
1☐ cup brown rice flour
1☐ cup white rice flour
2 teaspoons baking soda
¼ teaspoons sea salt
½ teaspoons cloves
1 teaspoons cinnamon
1 teaspoons ginger

Preheat oven to 375°F.

Mix grapeseed oil, organic sugar, Stevia, and molasses in a

large mixing bowl.

Sift together brown rice flour, white rice flour, baking soda,

sea salt, cloves, cinnamon, and ginger in a separate bowl.

Add the dry ingredients to the oil mixture. Mix until dough comes together.

Roll dough into balls the size of large walnuts.

Place on lightly greased baking sheets.

Bake for 10 to 12 minutes.

These are a much lower glycemic option. Fantastic for appeasing that sweet tooth if you are diabetic or limiting sugars due to yeast or sensitivities.

If you are cutting out sugar completely, you may omit all the sugar and substitute it with Stevia in the Raw. (Find it at your local grocery or health food store.)

Since these cookies do have some sugar in them, it is best to eat sparingly on special occasions. The remainder will freeze well.

Oh My Gosh! Fluffy Ganache Frosting

Ingredients:
1 7-ounce 100% chocolate bar (dairy free)
½ teaspoon vanilla
½ cup MimicCreme Healthy Top whipped
  cream

Melt chocolate in a double boiler.

Stir in vanilla.

Slowly incorporate chocolate into Healthy Top cream.

Refrigerate until very cold.

Whip for 2 to 3 minutes on high.

Serve.

A delightful fluffy whipped Frosting! Better yet, it's chocolate!

This recipe calls for MimicCrème's Healthy Top Whipped Cream alternative. It is a shelf-stable, dairy-free whipped cream made from cashews and almonds.

This clearly does not work for those who have sensitivity to tree nuts.

Make this a staple in your "Free Pantry". Kids love it and it can be used with many deserts.

Super Whooper Whoopie Cookies

Ingredients:

1/3 cup Earth Balance, softened
1 cup organic raw cane sugar
6 tablespoons blackstrap molasses
1/3 cup organic applesauce
¼ cup water
1 teaspoon vanilla extract
½ cup Bob's Red Mill GF All-Purpose Flour
¼ teaspoon sea salt
½ teaspoon xanthan gum
1 teaspoon baking soda
1 teaspoon baking powder
1½ teaspoons egg-replacer powder
¼ cup Justin's Chocolate Hazelnut Butter
1 cup Perky's flax cereal
1 cup unsweetened organic coconut flakes
1 cup gluten-free oats

Oats and flax make this take on a childhood favorite an extra-special nutritional treasure.

Like any sweet treat, these should be treated as such ... a "treat." One of these cookie sandwiches has a little over 15 grams of sugar, but the flax cereal and oats give these cookies a nice punch of fiber content.

MimicCreme Healthy Top, whipped

Preheat oven to 350°F.

Mix Earth Balance, cane sugar, molasses and nut butter in the bowl of a stand mixer.

Add applesauce, water and vanilla extract, and mix to combine.

Combine flour, salt, xanthan gum, baking soda, baking powder, and egg-replacer powder in a separate bowl.

Slowly incorporate into butter mixture.

Fold in cereal, coconut flakes, and oats.

With a large spoon, **drop** 1½-inch clumps of dough onto a greased cookie sheet. Press each clump down with the back of a spoon to about ½-inch thickness.

Bake for 9 to 11 minutes.

Whip Mimic-crème according to directions on box.

When cookies have cooled completely, sandwich a spoonful of whipped Mimic-crème between two cookies. Continue making all cookie sandwiches.

Place in freezer for at least 30 minutes before serving.

Toaster Tartlets

Dry Ingredients:
¾ cup all-purpose flour
¼ cup blanched almond flour
1 tablespoon tapioca flour
¼ teaspoon xanthan gum
Wet Ingredients:
1 tablespoon honey
6 tablespoons cold Earth Balance butter
½ teaspoon sea salt
2–3 tablespoons cold water

Preheat oven to 375°F.

Stir together dry ingredients in a mixing bowl.
Cut in butter.
Add honey.

Icing Recipe: (optional)
¼ cup organic powdered sugar
1–2 teaspoons liquid (water, milk, juice)

Add cold water a tiny bit at a time until dough forms into a ball.
Roll dough out between two sheets of parchment paper.
Cut dough into 3 x 5-inch rectangles.
Place about 1½ teaspoons filling in the center of each rectangle.
Fold dough over and seal edges.
Transfer to lightly greased or parchment-lined baking sheet.
Bake for 8 to 12 minutes, or until golden brown.

These are a gluten-free version of a Pop Tart—add alkaline fruits or healthy nut butters for a "real"-food version of this kid favorite.

Keeps well in fridge for future uses, not sure how long—it never lasts long at our house! You can also bake them, freeze them, and keep them on hand in the freezer. To reheat, simply stick in the toaster oven.

Suggested fillings:

Figgie-licious: 2 figs, reconstituted with ¼ cup hot water and blended. Very alkaline!!

Elderberry Jelly: ½ cup Biotta Elderberry juice, 3–4 dried prunes, 1 tablespoon tapioca flour, 1 tablespoon honey. Heat over medium heat, stirring constantly, until sauce starts to thicken. Blend in food processor or blender (this is a great one for flu season).

Justin's Chocolate Hazelnut Butter

Cinnamon Sugar: ¼ cup brown rice syrup mixed with 2 teaspoons cinnamon.

Toasted Almond Chocolate Chipper

NUTS

Dry ingredients:
2½ cups ground almond flour
1½ teaspoons egg-replacer powder
½ teaspoon sea salt
½ teaspoon baking soda

Wet Ingredients:
½ cup safflower oil
½ cup brown rice syrup
1 tablespoon vanilla extract
2–3 tablespoons water

Miscellaneous:
¼ cup Enjoy Life Brand chocolate chips

Are you noticing a pattern here? Yes, it's almond flour again. Nut flours are nutritionally rich when compared to other flours because of their low carbohydrate, low sugar, and high protein content.

King Arthur Flour makes a toasted almond flour, although they are not a dedicated gluten-free facility.

Preheat oven to 350°F.

Spread almond flour in a thin layer on a lipped baking sheet.

Toast for 5 to 7 minutes in oven.

Whisk together dry ingredients.

Stir wet ingredients together in a separate bowl.

Incorporate wet ingredients into dry ingredients, stirring until well mixed.

Fold in chocolate chips.

Spoon dough in heaping tablespoons onto a greased baking sheet, spacing 2 inches apart.

Press down dough with the palm of your hand or the back of a spatula or spoon.

Bake for 8 to 10 minutes, then transfer to a wire rack to cool.

CHAPTER 15

Delightful Drinks!

Photo Recipes: Front: Strawberry Garden Smoothie, Back: Loco Coco Milk Shake

Delightful drinks!

Almond Milk or Hazelnut Milk

Basic Protein Shake

Christmas Break Shake

Elder-Cherry Fizz

Hempy Hummm Shake

Hempy Milk

Hot Coco

Lemon Chia-ller

Loco Coco Milk Shake

Orange Ya Gonna Smoothie

Passion Fruit Sorbet

Root Beer Fizzy

Root Beer Flurry

Strawberry Garden Smoothie

Almond Milk or Hazelnut Milk

NUTS

Ingredients:

1 cup raw almonds or hazelnuts (soak first if desired;

 simply discard water and continue with recipe)

5 cups water

1 tablespoon raw honey, maple syrup, , or Stevia equivalent

1 teaspoon lemon juice

½ teaspoon salt

Combine all ingredients in a blender.

Blend on medium to high speed. Until a milky consistence forms. (Add more water if desired.)

Pour mixture into a fine mesh bag or cheesecloth over a container.

Squeeze liquid through the bag. Serve chilled as is or use in dairy-free recipes.

There's no doubt that nut milks are a nutritious substitution to cow's milk, but what you may not realize is just how easy it is to make your own at home!

Many shelf-stable non-dairy milks can have added flavoring ingredients and preservatives, even added sugars that are not necessary. Some use thickening agents like xanthum gum.

Simply make you own and sweeten with regular or flavored Stevia drops, maple syrup, or even a vanilla bean.

Basic Protein Shake

NUTS

Ingredients:
1 tablespoon coconut oil
1 scoop of "All One Kids"
1 scoop Milo "Brown Rice"
1 teaspoon Salba, ground in a coffee grinder
Stevia to taste
Liquid (water, almond milk, or hemp milk)
1 capful Fulvic Mineral Complex

Mix together 1 tablespoon coconut oil, All One Kids, Brown Rice, and Salba in a blender.

Add Stevia to taste.

Add liquid and Fulvic Mineral Complex. Blend to combine.

For extra flavor add any of the following:

- Vanilla
- Cinnamon
- ½ banana
- 6 strawberries
- Blueberries
- Any other seasonal fruit (avoid any allergic fruit)

Salba is a seed that provides essential nutrients, including essential fatty acids (omega-3) and an abundance of both soluble and insoluble dietary fiber. In addition, it is an exceptionally rich source of vitamins and minerals.

All of these ingredients can be found at Healthy Approach and Whole Foods Markets.

Christmas Break Shake

Ingredients:

8 ounces unsweetened vanilla almond milk

4–5 ice cubes

6–8 drops SweetLeaf Stevia in peppermint flavor

4–5 drops SweetLeaf Stevia in vanilla crème SoyaToo!

Rice Whipped Cream to top

Cinnamon

A great treat for the holiday. Sugar free and equally as delicious!

Blend milk, ice, and sweeteners in a blender.

Pour into a glass.

Top with rice whipped cream and a sprinkle of cinnamon.

Elder-Cherry Fizz

Ingredients:

¼ cup Biotta elderberry juice

¼ cup cherry juice

1–2 cups carbonated water

Mix together elderberry and cherry juices.

Distribute into four ice-filled glasses.

Pour in carbonated water to fill glass.

Stir to mix.

Other Variations:

Use this "elder-cherry" mixture with 2 cups of hemp or almond milk, mix, and freeze for a delicious ice cream alternative.

Put the elder-cherry juice into popsicle molds for a yummy frozen treat.

Cherries contain anti-inflammatory phytochemicals. The tart varieties are richer in health value. The anthocyanins have reduced cancer growth in mice.

Elderberries are also anti-inflammatory, are very rich in Vitamin C, and are a home remedy for flu symptoms.

This is a fantastic concoction to boost your immune system.

Hempy Yumm Shake

Ingredients:

2–4 tablespoons hemp protein powder (like Nutiva Organic)

8 ounces hemp milk, unsweetened

¼ teaspoon vanilla extract

Stevia to taste (or try vanilla cream Stevia drops)

4–5 ice cubes

Blend all ingredients in a blender or food processor.

Serve.

Hemp is getting a lot of hype for very good reasons.

Hemp is a very allergy-friendly source for protein, omega-3, omega-6 fatty acids and fiber.

It is a complete protein source—and a great one at that. The proteins consist of about 66 percent edestin, which resembles globulin found in human blood plasma and has been used medically in this capacity. Albumin, a powerful scavenger of free radicals in the body, makes up 33 percent of the protein.

Hempy Milk

Ingredients:
¼ cup organic hemp seeds (like Nutiva)
4 cups filtered water
1 teaspoon maple syrup
Munchies (optional)

Blend all ingredients in a blender or Vitamix until completely mixed.

Store in a glass container in the refrigerator.

If mixture separates, simply give it a stir or run it back through the blender.

The seeds of the plant cannabis sativa are commonly referred to as hemp. Hemp seed contains all the essential amino acids and essential fatty acids necessary to maintain healthy human life. No other single plant source has the essential amino acids in such an easily digestible form, nor has the essential fatty acids in as perfect a ratio to meet human nutritional needs.

Further, the protein content of the hemp seed is apparently very digestible. Many people noted that hemp seed protein did not cause bloating or gas, like some whey or other protein shakes did.

Moreover, unlike soy, which has high amounts of phytic acid (that anti-nutrient that prevents us from absorbing minerals), hemp seed does not contain phytic acid. At the very least, this makes hemp seed a step up from soy.

(Source: Hemp Line Journal, July–August 1992, pp. 14–15, Vol. 1)

Hot Coco

Ingredients:

8 ounces coconut milk

2 tablespoons gluten-free 100% cocoa powder

6–10 drops SweetLeaf Stevia drops, vanilla crème flavor

½ teaspoon pure vanilla extract

Heat coconut milk in a saucepan until hot, but not boiling.

Spoon cocoa and Stevia drops into a mug.

Spoon in approximately 1 tablespoon milk and stir until smooth.

Add remaining milk and vanilla.

Stir well and enjoy.

This sugar-free version of a traditional chocolaty favorite drink that warms the tummy, can indulge your sweet tooth any day of the week!

Paired with coconut milk, this "coco" drink actually has health benefits!

Stevia, the only alternative sweetener we recommend, can be found in a variety of scrumptious and familiar flavors at www.amazon.com and www.vitacost.com.

Lemon Chia-ller

Ingredients:
2 teaspoons chia seeds
10 ounces filtered water
Juice of 1 lemon
Raw honey or Stevia to taste

Combine all ingredients in a glass.

Stir and serve.

Chia seeds are most commonly known as the "hair" on Chia Pets, but they are actually highly nutritious little seeds! They absorb more than twelve times their weight in liquid.

That means you need to drink this one down fast, or you will need a spoon for the gelatin that it becomes.

Loco Coco Milk Shake

Ingredients:

8 ounces chocolate milk (hazelnut or almond), unsweetened

4–8 Stevia drops in chocolate flavor

4–5 ice cubes

SoyaToo! rice whipped cream

Sprinkelz Chocolatey Vegan Sprinkles

Blend chocolate milk, Stevia drops, and ice cubes in a blender.

Pour into a glass.

Top with rice whip and a sprinkle of sprinkles.

Using the unsweetened versions of the non-dairy milks saves big on sugar contents! Just sweeten with natural flavors or flavored Stevia drops.

A fun treat!

Orange Ya Gonna Smoothie

Ingredients:

½ cup cultured coconut milk (SoDelicious brand)

½ cup fresh-squeezed orange juice

4–5 ice cubes

1 teaspoon orange zest

Blend all ingredients in a blender to desired consistency.

Garnish with an orange wedge.

Serve.

Oranges: An obvious choice for Vitamin C, the vital vitamin for a healthy immune system.

One unique flavanone in oranges is herperidin. Herperidin has been shown to lower blood pressure and cholesterol in animal studies, and has strong anti-inflammatory properties. (Source: www.whfoods.org)

Coconut yogurt contains probiotics with ten active and live cultures.

Passion Fruit Sorbet

Ingredients:

1 tablespoon arrowroot powder
1 bottle Biotta exotic juice blend
¼ cup honey
¼ cup water
1 tablespoon fresh lime juice
1 tablespoon fresh orange zest

Bring all ingredients to a boil in a medium saucepan over medium-high heat.

Simmer for 1 to 2 minutes.

Remove from heat and let cool to room temperature.

Pour mixture into a glass dish with a lid and freeze.

Scrape around the container every 30 minutes or so, until mixture is frozen through.

Passion fruit is rich in vitamin A and a fantastic source of Vitamin C and iron.

Mangoes, the "king of Asiatic fruits," are an anti-inflammatory fruit. The famous Unani physician Hakeen Hashmi teaches that mangoes strengthen and invigorate the nerve tissues in the muscles, heart, brain, and other parts of the body.

(Source: www.disabled-world.com/artman/publish/mangoe

Guava is higher in vitamin C than citrus. Rich in phytochemicals. Also has quercitin, which has an anti-diarrheal effect.

Root Beer Fizzy and Flurry

Root Beer Fizzy
Ingredients:

8 ounces carbonated water

6–10 drops SweetLeaf Stevia drops, root beer flavor

Stir together and enjoy for a guilt-free pleasure!

These root beer options are a treat. They are gluten-free and do not contain the dairy that can sometimes be present in the caramel coloring in most root beer drinks.

Root Beer Flurry
Ingredients:

6 ounces hazelnut milk (or use rice milk for a nut-free version)

2 ounces carbonated water

10–12 drops SweetLeaf Stevia drops, root beer flavor

4–5 ice cubes

Blend all ingredients together in a blender.

Pour into a glass and serve.

Strawberry Garden Smoothie

Ingredients:

2 tablespoons fresh strawberries, chopped or mashed

2 tablespoons pineapple juice

2 tablespoons carrot juice (Biotta, available at Whole Foods, Sprouts, and Central Market)

2 tablespoons celery juice (Biotta)

Mix all ingredients together and

Serve over ice.

Vitamin C, folate, and anthocyanins quercitin and kaempferol are all important flavonoids in strawberries. They serve as powerful antioxidants and anticarcinogenics. Together, they are known to fight cancer. A daily intake is reported to have remarkably brought down the growth of cancerous cells (www.organicfacts.net).

Pineapple juice contains bromelain and is anti-inflammatory. It can interfere with the growth of malignant cells.

Carrots are the richest vegetable in Vitamin A, carotene. It is directly related to a decreased risk for heart disease. Animal research has shown that diets rich in beta-carotene can reduce the occurrence of emphysema and vision/macular degeneration.

A pH neutralizer, the phytochemical coumarins, present in celery juice, prevents the formation and development of colon and stomach cancers. The polyacetylene in celery is an amazing relief for inflammation like rheumatoid arthritis, osteoarthritis, gout, asthma, and bronchitis.

TIP: If you aren't going to use all of the juice within 2 weeks of opening, simply freeze into ice cube trays, then pop out and put into a ziplock bag in freezer.

CHAPTER 16

Measurements, Equivalents, and Food Substitutions

MEASUREMENTS AND EQUIVALENTS

The information below shows measuring equivalents for teaspoons, tablespoons, cups, pints, fluid ounces, and more. This section also includes the conversions for metric and U.S. measurements.

Measurement Conversions Source: United States Dept. of Agriculture (USDA).

A dash	Less than □ teaspoon
A pinch	□ teaspoon
1 tablespoon	3 teaspoons
1 fluid ounce (fl oz)	2 tablespoons
1/16 cup	1 tablespoon
□ cup	2 tablespoons
1/6 cup	2 tablespoons + 2 teaspoons
¼ cup	4 tablespoons
1/3 cup	5 tablespoons + 1 teaspoon
3/8 cup	6 tablespoons
½ cup	8 tablespoons
2/3 cup	10 tablespoons + 2 teaspoons
¾ cup	12 tablespoons
1 cup	48 teaspoons
1 cup	16 tablespoons
1 cup	8 fluid ounces (fl oz)
1 pint (pt)	2 cups
1 quart (qt)	2 pints
1 quart (qt)	4 cups
1 gallon (gal)	4 quarts
1 gallon (gal)	16 cups
1 pound (lb)	16 ounces (oz), dry weight
1 milliliter (ml)	1 cubic centimeter (cc)
1 inch (in.)	2.54 centimeters (cm)

Measurements, Equivalents, and Food Substitutions
U.S. TO METRIC CONVERSIONS

Capacity		Weight	
¹/5 teaspoon	1 milliliter	1 ounce	28 grams
1 teaspoon	5 ml	1 pound	454 grams
1 tablespoon	15 ml		
1 fluid oz	30 ml		
¹/5 cup	47 ml		
1 cup	237 ml		
2 cups (1 pint)	473 ml		
4 cups (1 quart)	.95 liter		
4 quarts (1 gal)	3.8 liters		

Read more: Cooking Measurement Equivalents—www.Infoplease.com.

METRIC CONVERSION FACTORS

Multiply	By	To Get
Fluid ounces	29.57	Grams
Ounces (dry)	28.35	Grams
Grams	0.0353	Ounces
Grams	0.0022	Pounds
Kilograms	2.21	Pounds
Pounds	453.6	Grams
Pounds	0.4536	Kilograms
Quarts	0.946	Liters
Quarts (dry)	67.2	Cubic Inches
Quarts (liquid)	57.7	Cubic Inches
Liters	1.0567	Quarts
Gallons	3,785	Cubic Centimeters
Gallons	3.785	Liters

FOOD SUBSTITUTIONS

For Missing Ingredients

If you're ever short on one ingredient or another, there are always a few quick and easy substitutions that you can use. Just consult the table below.

In Place of	Use
1 cup buttermilk	1 tablespoon lemon juice or vinegar plus milk to equal 1 cup (stir; let stand 5 minutes)
1 tablespoon cornstarch	2 tablespoons all purpose flour or 2 teaspoons of arrowroot
1 whole egg	2 egg yolks plus 1 teaspoon cold water
1 small clove garlic	☐ teaspoon garlic powder
1 cup tomato sauce	½ cup tomato paste plus ½ cup cold water
1 teaspoon vinegar	2 teaspoons lemon juice
1 cup whole milk	1 cup skim milk plus 2 tablespoons melted butter
1 teaspoon baking powder	¼ teaspoon baking soda plus ½ teaspoon cream of tartar
1 cup ketchup	1 cup tomato sauce plus ½ cup sugar and 2 tablespoons vinegar (for use in cooking)
1 cup powdered sugar	1 cup granulated sugar plus 1 teaspoon cornstarch
½ cup brown sugar	½ cup granulated sugar plus 2 tablespoons molasses
1 cup tomato juice	½ cup of tomato sauce plus ½ cup water

FOOD SUBSTITUTIONS

For Common Foods

If you wish to increase your immune system competency, you can do so by making the following substitutions for these common types of foods. For foods not listed here, follow the basic guidelines of common sense. Read labels! Do not buy foods that contain MSG (monosodium glutamate) papain, sulfites, nitrates, refined sugars, food dyes, or other artificial additives. If you can't pronounce it or identify it, don't buy it. These substitute items can be found in either your local grocery or health food store. The long-term value to your family's health is worth the extra attention. (Refer to the book *Special Diet Solutions* for more detail on the substitute options and how to use these new ingredients.)

Reduce or Omit	Use Instead	Proportion Changes or Comments
Bacon, Sausage, Lunch Meat	Select nitrate-free deli meats and turkey sausage. The only natural brand of deli meats we are aware of is Boars Head, which is available at most grocery stores. Avoid pork products.	
Breakfast Cereal	Buy cereals at the health food store. Example: rice puffs sweetened with honey.	Many cereals that look like the popular brands advertised on TV are now available. Read the labels to make sure you can have all the ingredients.
Canned Vegetables	It's always best to use fresh. Canned vegetables have been processed to the point where they do not have many nutrients left. If fresh is not available, use frozen or dried.	Another reason to avoid canned vegetables is because of the aluminum, which can leach out into the food. When consumed, aluminum can remain in your body. Many autistic and learning-challenged individuals already have excess amounts of heavy metals to deal with.

Measurements, Equivalents, and Food Substitutions

Reduce or Omit	Use Instead	Proportion Changes or Comments
Cheeses	Use silken tofu in recipes instead. In general, if you have a milk allergy or a casein sensitivity, you should not have real cheese. You may want to experiment with goat cheese if you have no casein allergy.	If you can have cheese, read the labels. Most cheeses contain colors. Look for the words "100% natural." There are tofu cheeses on the market that can be used in sandwiches. They do not perform the same as real cheese in recipes that call for melting (like lasagna). These "cheeses" burn easily.
Chocolate	Carob powder or chips.	Carob-flavored drinks are available in health food stores. **3 tablespoons carob + 2 tablespoons milk = 1 square of chocolate**
Coffee	Roasted grain substitutes or herbal tea.	
Dried Fruits	Use only unsulphured dried fruits.	Sulfur dioxide can cause headaches, respiratory, and gastrointestinal problems.
Fruit Drinks	Make sure that the fruit juice has no added color or high-fructose corn syrup.	Juices should be labeled as 100% natural.
Ice Cream	The best product to substitute is called Rice Dream. It is made from rice milk and comes in a variety of flavors. Most health food stores carry it, and even some conventional grocers have it. Tofutti is a tofu-based ice cream.	
Margarine	Butter, flax oil, olive oil, canola oil	

Reduce or Omit	Use Instead	Proportion Changes or Comments
Milk Products	Rice milk, almond milk, soy milk, and coconut milk.	The thinner the liquid, the less you'll need. If the liquid is similar in density to regular milk, then use it in the same proportion. There is a difference between a cow's milk allergy and a casein allergy. If you have a casein allergy, you may want to stay away from other animal milks as well. You will be better off with rice, almond, soy, and coconut milk. You can buy nut milks or make your own.
Pancake Syrup	Use only pure maple syrup. Or try using honey, molasses, and applesauce or fresh fruits on waffles and pancakes.	
Peanut Butter	You can make your own nut butter, if you wish. For example, sesame nut butter tastes like peanut butter. Almond and cashew nut butter are also very good.	Nuts and nut butters should be avoided if possible. If you are going to make your own nut butter, make sure you toast the nuts in a 250-degree oven for about 15 minutes before using them. This helps kill any molds.
Red Meats	Choose naturally raised meats, free of growth hormone, antibiotics, steroids, and stimulants.	Some larger grocery chains carry natural meats, such as Laura's natural beef brand. Ask for it by name.
Refined Salt	Always use sea salt.	Sea salt also contains important trace minerals that are vital to health.
Shortening	Unrefined oils, olive, canola, flax, sunflower oil, sesame oil.	When storing oils, always store in a cool place with no light. Light and heat break the carbon bonds and spoil the oil.

Measurements, Equivalents, and Food Substitutions

Reduce or Omit	Use Instead	Proportion Changes or Comments
Soft Drinks	You can make a soda-like drink from fruit juice and club soda. Other substitutes are fruit juices, sparkling water, and herbal teas.	Try mixing bottled organic lemonade with 1:1 Celestial Seasonings mint magic tea and red zinger tea. This is a yummy, citrus treat you can prepare and refrigerate in the summer. Everybody loves this. We call this Beverly's tea, since this was her recipe. (For 1 quart of lemonade use 2 bags mint and 2 bags zinger.) You may add some water to dilute if you want to stretch your tea supply.
Sugar	Honey, rice syrup, molasses, pure maple syrup, Stevia. DO NOT USE EQUAL OR NUTRASWEET.	One-fourth to one-half the amount.
White Bread	Breads can be purchased at the health food store to substitute for wheat bread. Or make your own. To bake your own bread see recipes in this book.	Francis Simun Bakery in Dallas offers an array of breads and bagels made from non-wheat flours. They are very tasty and can be shipped all over the U.S. Call 214-741-4242. You can put your name on an automatic order system and get bread delivered right to your doorstep weekly, biweekly, or whenever.
White Flour	Arrowroot, bean flour, rice flour, potato starch, tapioca, kudzu.	Kudzu (available in health food stores) is a starchy root plant that yields a white starch that can be used to thicken sauces. It can be used just like flour or cornstarch.
Yeast	Vitamin C crystals can perform the function of yeast.	It is always best to use a tested bread recipe.

NONDAIRY HIGH CALCIUM FOODS

One cup of cow's milk provides around 300 mg of calcium. The following foods may be used to replace cow's milk for those who do not tolerate milk.

250 mg = 1 cup cooked spinach	
300 mg = 1 cup cooked collard greens	
280 mg = 1 cup cooked mustard greens	
450 mg = 1 cup cooked turnip greens	
330 mg = 1 cup cooked bok choy	
450 mg = 1 cup cooked soy beans	
340 mg = 1 cup cooked garbanzo beans	
410 mg = 3 teaspoons blackstrap molasses	
250 mg = 3.5 ounces salmon with bones	
500 mg = 4 ounces sardines with bones	
375 mg = ½ cup almonds	
280 mg = 1 cup walnuts	
260 mg = 1 cup hulled sunflower seeds	
310 mg = ½ cup dried banana chips	
426 mg = 3½ ounces sesame butter	
270 mg = 3½ ounces almond butter	
195 mg = 3½ ounces filbert butter	

RECOMMENDED DAILY ALLOWANCE FOR CALCIUM

AGE	Calcium Needed in mg
Infants:	
0–6 months	400 mg
6 months–1 year	600 mg

Children: 1–10 years	800 mg

Males:	
11–24	1200 mg–1500 mg
25–51+	800 mg

Females:	
11–24	1200 mg–1500 mg
25–51+	800 mg

Pregnant or Lactating Women	1200 mg–1500 mg

GLUTEN CONTENT OF VARIOUS ALTERNATIVE FLOURS

If you are new to using non-wheat flours, do not attempt to simply substitute any of the following flours for wheat in your own recipes (except spelt). Start with recipes designed for these grains until you get a feel for how they work in a recipe. Please keep in mind that our recipes do not constitute an entire dietary plan for essential nutrients. They are simply designed to help you cook/bake for your specific diet. This information should not take the place of advice from your doctor. Many thanks to the nonprofit website Recipes for Natural Health, at www.recipenet.org, which was the source of this information and is sponsored by www.rainbowfoods.net. We suggest you visit both of these websites for additional recipes and tips on substitutions and healthy eating.

Amaranth	
Origin	South/Central Americas; Mexican Aztecs, 15th century.
Flavor	Robust; nut-like.
Gluten Content	Gluten-free. Contains glycogen.
Nutrients	High protein, (12–17%); "Complete" protein; contains lysine, calcium, iron, potassium, phosphorus, magnesium, vitamin C, beta carotene.
Baking Tips/Info	Best used as complementary flour rather than primary flour; will add flavor when added to rice flour; great for muffins, baking powder, breads, pancakes, waffles, and cookies.
	Texture: smooth crisp crust; fine crumb not recommended.
	Not recommended for yeast breads.
Barley	
Origins	Various ancient civilizations.
Flavor	Sweet; nutty.
Gluten Content	Contains Gluten.
Nutrients	High protein; contains niacin, folic acid, thiamin, calcium, phosphorus magnesium.
Baking Tips/Info	Must be combined with high gluten flours or baked goods will turn out too moist.
	Enhances yeast cell growth and adds a sweet flavor to baked goods.
Brown Rice	
Origins	Asia.
Flavor	Mild.
Gluten Content	Gluten-free.
Nutrients	B vitamins and Vitamin E.

Baking Tips/Info	Pie and pizza crusts; batter breads, crackers, cookies, cakes, pancakes, waffles.
	Yeast breads made from 100% brown rice flour (i.e.: totally gluten-free) require xanthan gum (a vegetable gum) to help bread rise.
Buckwheat	
Origins	Russia.
Flavor	Robust; slightly sweet.
Gluten Content	Gluten-free; wheat free (in spite of name).
Nutrients	Bioflavonoid rutin, protein, folic acid, vitamin B6, calcium, iron.
Baking Tips/Info	Can be used in combination with blander flours.
	Use in pancakes, waffles, blintzes, pastas.
	Not recommended for gravies or sauces.
	Texture: moist, fine crumb.
Corn: Flour and Cornmeal	
Origins	North and Central Americas; Mexico.
Flavor	Slightly sweet.
Gluten Content	Low gluten to gluten-free.
Nutrients	Protein, lysine, vitamin A, folic acid, potassium, calcium, phosphorus, manganese.
	Blue corn has 21% more protein; 2 x potassium, manganese; 50% more iron than yellow corn.
Baking Tips/Info	Eggs and chemical leaveners required when baking with the flour due to low gluten.
	Atole: finely ground flour from roasted blue corn.
	Used for puddings, tortillas, and other flat breads and as a thickening agent.
	Cornmeal: Great in pancakes, muffins, corn bread, polenta, tortillas, and as a thickening agent.
Garbanzo/Chick Pea	
Origins	Mediterranean; Middle East; Central Asia.
Flavor	Sweet; rich.
Gluten Content	Gluten-free.
Nutrients	High in protein, calcium, and potassium. Also contains: iron, vitamin C, and vitamin A.
Baking Tips/Info	When substituting, use 2 tablespoons per cup of wheat flour.
	Use in crépes, dosas (East Indian flat breads).

Hemp	
Origins	Originated in the Mediterranean, Middle East, and Central Asia; has been used all over the world for thousands of years.
Flavor	Nutlike.
Gluten Content	Gluten-free.
Nutrients	Excellent source of essential fatty acids: omega-6 (58%); omega-3 (20%); super omega-6 GLA (.6%).High-quality protein (24%); "complete" protein.
Baking Tips/Info	Hemp flour needs to be combined with other flours due to the high oil content of hemp.
Kamut (Unhybridized strain of wheat)	
Origins	Ancient Egypt. Now grown in Montana.
Flavor	Rich, buttery flavor.
Gluten Content	High gluten; not recommended for those following a gluten-free diet; however, those on a wheat-free diet may tolerate Kamut, as it digests easier than common wheat.
Nutrients	40% more protein and 65% more amino acids than common wheat. Pantothenic acid, calcium, magnesium, phosphorus, potassium, zinc.
Baking Tips/Info	Good substitute for wheat in baking, though final product will be heavier and denser.
Millet	
Origins	Asia and Africa.
Flavor	Mild.
Gluten Content	Gluten-free.
Nutrients	Protein, calcium, iron, magnesium, potassium, phosphorus.
Baking Tips/Info	Used in puddings, breads, cakes, and cookies. For a stronger flavor, use in combination with other flours.
Oats	
Flavor	Slightly sweet.
Gluten Content	Low gluten.
Nutrients	Up to 15% protein, calcium, iron, potassium, vitamin A, thiamin, pantothenic acid.
Baking Tips/Info	Can be added to cookies, pie crusts, muffins, and breads. Oats contain a natural antioxidant that helps baked goods maintain freshness.

Measurements, Equivalents, and Food Substitutions

Oat Bran	
Flavor	Sweet.
Gluten Content	Low gluten.
Nutrients	Good source of soluble fiber.
Baking Tips/Info	Can be added to many baked goods to increase fiber content.

Quinoa	
Origins	South America.
Flavor	Delicate; nutty.
Gluten Content	Gluten-free, but contains glycogen.
Nutrients	High in protein, is a "complete" protein; also contain calcium, iron, phosphorus, vitamin E, and lysine.
Baking Tips/Info	May be used as sole flour in pancakes, crêpes, muffins, crackers, and cookies. Produces a cake-like crumb. Blend 50-50 with another flour when making cakes. Combine with a gluten flour for bread baking. Grains must be thoroughly rubbed and rinsed under water to remove a sticky bitter-tasting coating called saponin. Saponin is a natural bird and insect repellant and may irritate digestion or allergies in people.

Rye	
Origins	Northern Europe.
Flavor	Strong and heavy.
Gluten Content	Low gluten.
Nutrients	12% protein; calcium, magnesium, lysine, potassium.
Baking Tips/Info	Tastes best when combined with flour that has a milder, sweeter flavor. Used in breads such as pumpernickel and black breads; and pancakes. Produces a moist, dense crumb.

Soy	
Origins	China.
Flavor	Mild.
Gluten Content	Gluten-free.
Nutrients	High in protein, contains calcium and magnesium.

Baking Tips/Info	Add soy flour to batters and breading for fried foods to help inhibit fat absorption.
	Use up to 25% in combination with other flours in cakes, and even less in breads, otherwise they will rise too fast.
Spelt	
Origins	Southern Europe.
Flavor	Rich and sweet.
Gluten Content	Moderate gluten content.
Nutrients	Protein; B vitamins, iron, potassium.
Baking Tips/Info	Good substitute for wheat in most recipes. (Use 25% less liquid when substituting for wheat.)
	Gluten is sensitive—do not over knead.

Teff Flour	
Origins	Ethiopia.
Flavor	Sweet and malty.
Gluten Content	Gluten-free.
Nutrients	High in protein, calcium, and iron.
Baking Tips/Info	Great for quick breads, pancakes and waffles.
	For yeast breads: use 5 parts wheat flour (or other high gluten flour) to 1 part Teff flour.
	Substitute up to 20% in recipes.

Addendum

A. Shopping, Food Sources, Books, APPS and Websites

This is a treasure trove of resources and food sources our patients, customers, moms, dads, clinical staff, and friends have recommended. You will find these useful for many special-needs diets and to support your goal of achieving optimum health. We hope you find them helpful.

We encourage you to go to our website www.foodforthoughtbook.com if you find other sources you would like to share.

Cookbooks and Nutrition	Autism and Allergy Resources, Websites, and Books
• Special Diets and Nutrition	• Autism Resources and Websites
• Juicing and Raw Foods	• Books About Autism, Special Education, and Allergies
Food Sources	**Integrative Cancer Therapy Resources**
• Food Buying Consortiums	• Books
• Food Ingredients by Company and Website	• Articles and Studies
• By Company Website with Product Description	**Resource List—US Federal Government 2010**
• Networking Directories	

COOKBOOKS AND NUTRITION

Books that we recommend adding to your arsenal of knowledge are listed in this section. You will find they cover special diets and nutritional research. They are listed with a brief summary of the purpose and contents. We have divided this listing into two sections—one for special diets and the other for juicing and raw foods.

Special Diets and nutrition	
American Dietetic Association Complete Food and Nutrition Guide By Roberta Larson Duyff, MS, RD, FADA, C www.eatright.org FCA	Includes the most up-to-date dietary guidelines for Americans.
The China Study By T. Colin Campbell, Ph.D. and Thomas M. Campbell II www.thechinastudy.com	The most comprehensive study of nutrition ever conducted.
Cooking Free www.savorypalate.com	200 flavorful recipes for people with food allergies and multiple food sensitivities.
Cooking To Heal Little Tummies By Jenna Roberts and Natalie Hagood	A children's cookbook that follows the Specific Carbohydrate Diet. It was created by two mothers whose children are affected by autism. The cookbook contains easy-to-follow, kid-friendly recipes, as well as cooking tips and helpful information. It is a useful resource for providing variety and ease with your SCD cooking. Happy cooking!
Digestive Wellness/Digestive Wellness for Children By Liz Lipski www.digestivewellnessforchildren.com	Liz Lipski gives a broader understanding about how important good digestion is to overall health.
Eat Well Feel Well By Kendall Conrad www.eatwellfeelwellthebook.com	More than 150 Specific Carbohydrate Diet compliant recipes.
Food Allergy Field Guide—2006 www.savorypalate.com/ fafg. aspx	Light-hearted, practical handbook for families with children who have food-sensitivities to wheat, gluten, dairy, eggs, soy, corn, and peanuts. 100 kid-tested recipes.

A. Shopping, Food Sources, Books, APPS and Websites

The Gerson Therapy www.gerson.org	A nutritional program for cancer and other illnesses. This book reveals the healing effects of organic vegetables and fruit. Not only can juicing reverse the effects of degenerative illnesses, it can save lives.
The Gluten-Free Almond Flour Cookbook By Elana Amsterdam www.elanaspantry.com	Excellent website and excellent cookbooks using almond flour. I replace the agave syrup in her recipes with raw honey, organic maple syrup, or Stevia.
Gluten-Free 101—2006 www.savorypalate.com/gf101.aspx	Great for beginners; easy basic dishes without wheat.
Gluten-free Friends www.savorypalate.com/gff.aspx	An activity book for kids. A delightfully illustrated activity book for kids ages 4–11 that explains the gluten-free diet in simple, easy-to-understand terms.
The Kid-Friendly ADHD and Autism Cookbook By Dana Laake and Pamela Compart www.danalaake.com www.autismndi.com	The ultimate guide to the gluten-free, casein-free diet.
Nourishing Traditions Sally Fallon www.westonaprice.org	Sally Fallon puts the studies of Weston A. Price into a reader-friendly collection. The book contains fantastic recipes for fermented foods, helping to reintroduce lost variety and quantity of intestinal flora (probiotic).
Special Diets for Special People: Autism By Lisa Lewis, Ph.D. www.FHautism.com	Gluten-free and casein-free, food allergies. Recipes and diet plans to improve eating and digestion of children and adults.
Special Diets for Special Kids One **Special Diets for Special Kids Two** By Lisa Lewis, Ph.D. www.FHautism.com	Great-tasting recipes and tips for implementing special diets to aid in the treatment of autism and related development disorders.
1000 Gluten-Free Recipes www.savorypalate.com/1000GFR.aspx	The world's largest gluten-free cookbook.
Wheat Free Recipes www.savorypalate.com	A comprehensive cookbook, plus Carol's up-to-the-minute downloadable booklet on gluten-free baking.

JUICING AND RAW FOODS	
Juicing for Life By Cherie Calbom, MS, and Maureen Keane, MS, CUPN. www.juicinginfo.com www.keanenutrition.com	A guide to the health benefits of fresh fruit and vegetable juicing.
Total Juicing By Elaine LaLanne with Richard Benyo www.jacklalanne.com	More than 125 healthful and delicious ways to use fresh fruit and vegetable juices and pulp.
The Live Food Factor By Susan Schenck, Lac, MTOM www.livefoodfactor.com	The comprehensive guide to the ultimate diet for body, mind, spirit, and planet.
Living Foods for Optimum Health By Brian R. Clement www.rawfoodinfo.com	A complete guide to the healing power of raw foods.
The RAVE Diet and Lifestyle By Mike Anderson www.theravediet.com	The natural foods diet with meals that heal.
Ani's Raw Food Kitchen By Ani Phyo www.**ani**phyo.com/category/recipes	Easy delectable living foods recipes.

FOOD SOURCES

Need a better way of buying and finding healthful food? The neighborhood grocery store is often not the answer. These specialty food sources will help you find the ingredients you need.

FOOD BUYING CO-OPS AND CONSORTIUMS	
Bountiful Baskets Food Co-op Bountifulbaskets.org	BBFC is a group of people who work together for mutual benefit. This is a grassroots, all volunteer, no contracts, no catch co-operative. Since there are no employees at Bountiful Baskets, we as a group pay rock bottom prices on your food. This also means the co-op would not happen without volunteers.
Green People A food co-op, health food store, and natural food store search engine. Listings by state—www.greenpeople. org/healthfood.htm	Food co-ops, health food stores, natural food stores: 1630 listings alphabetically by state, city, Canadian province, and other countries. To view recently added listings, go to http://www.greenpeople.org/search2nd. cfm?type=Food_Coops
Your Health Source Provided by Traci Wroblski www.yourhealthsource.org Email: Monica@YourHealthSource.Org Voicemail/Fax: 888-280-0494	Co-op: foods and health product co-ops, home delivery, recipes, health fairs, special community e-groups. Dallas Fort Worth Metroplex locations and other states.

FOOD INGREDIENTS BY COMPANY AND WEBSITE

Food Ingredients by Company and Website			
Ingredients	**Company**	**Website**	**Phone**
Almond Butter	Justin's	www.justinsnutbutter.com	303-449-9559
Almond Flour	Lucy's Kitchen Shop	www.lucyskitchenshop.com	888-484-2126
Asafoetida Powder	Bob's Red Mill	www.bobsredmill.com	800-349-2173
	Herb Cupboard	www.herbcupboard.com	916-690-1761
Beans, Canned	Westbrae	www.Westbrae.com	800-434-4246
	Eden Organics	www.edenfoods.com	888-424-EDEN
Breads (Gluten-Free)	Ener-G	www.ener-g.com	800-331-5222
	Udi's	www.udisfood.com	303-657-6366
	Schar	www.schar.com	
	Rudi's	www.rudisglutenfree.com	877-293-0876
	Food For Life	www.foodforlife.com	800-797-5090
	Canyon Bakehouse	www.canyonbakehouse.com	
	French Meadow Bakery	www.frenchmeadow.com	
Broths	Pacific Foods	www.Pacificfoods.com	503-692-9666
	Imagine Foods	www.imaginefoods.com	800-434-4246
Beef Stock	Kitchen Basics	www.kitchenbasics.net	440-838-1344
Brown Rice Syrup	Lundberg Farms	www.lundberg.com	530-538-3500
California Almond Butter	Kettle Foods	www.Kettlefoods.com	888-4-kettle
Candy & Gum	Natural Candy Store	www.naturalcandystore.com	800-875-2409
	Spry Gum	www.xlear.com	
Capers	Krinos Foods	www.krinos.com	
Cashew Butter	Kettle Foods	www.Kettlefoods.com	888-4-kettle
Cheese (Dairy-Free)	Rice Vegan	www.galaxyfoods.com	
	Daiya Shreds	www.daiyafoods.com	
Coconut Milk	Thai Kitchen	www.thaikitchen.com	800-967-thai

Food Ingredients by Company and Website			
Cookies & Bars	Enjoy Life	www.enjoylifefoods.com	847-260-0300
	Orgran	www.orgran.com	+61 3 9776 9044
	Kinnikinnik	www.consumer.kinnikin-nik.com	877-503-4466
	Nana's Cookies	www.nanascookiecom-pany.com	720-945-1155
	LaraBars	www.larabar.com	707-462-6605
	AllerEnergy Bars	www.allerenergy.com	800-363-3438
	Schar Shortbread	www.schar.com	757-233-9495
	Pamela's	www.pamelasproducts.com	212-777-2227
	Glutino	www.glutino.com	866-646-7257
	Lucy's Cookies	www.drlucys.com	800-440-6476
	Tu-Lu's Bakery	www.tu-lusbakery.com	
	Gopal's Energy Bars	www.gopalshealthfoods.com	
	Kind Bar	www.kindsnacks.com	
	Boomi Bars	www.boomibar.com	
Crackers (Gluten-free)	Mary's Gone	www.marysgonecrack-ers.com	888-258-1250
	Schar Table Crackers	www.schar.com	800-363-3438
	Glutino	www.glutino.com	
	Back To Nature	www.backtonature-foods.com	
	Food Alive	www.foodsalive.com	+61 3 9776 9044
	Orgran	www.orgran.com	
Extracts	Simply Organic	www.simplyorganicupcom	800-437-3301
	Frontier	www.frontiercoop.com	800-669-3275
	Olive Nation	www.olivenation.com	
	Madagascar Pure	www.nielsenmassey.com	800-525-PURE
Dill	Generation Farms		903-326-4263
Extra -Virgin Olive Oil	Krinos Foods	www.krinos.com	

Flours & Mixes (GF)	Bob's Red Mill	www.bobsredmill.com	
	Gluten-free Pantry	www.glutino.com	
	Chebe	www.chebe.com	
	Pamea's Products	www.pamelasproducts.com	
	Orgran	www.orgran.com	
Fresh Express Spinach	Fresh Express Fresh Foods	www.freshexpress.com	800-242-5472
Garbanzo Beans	Eden Organic	www.edenfoods.com	800-441-3336
Hazelnut Butter	Kettle Foods	www.Kettlefoods.com	888-4-kettle

Food Ingredients by Company and Website			
Juices	Lakewood Organics	www.lakewoodjuices.com	800-434-4246 858-455-6998 888-569-6993 800-794-9986 +41 (0)71 466 48 48
	Sprout's Organics	www.sprouts.com	
	Mountain Sun Pure	www.mountainsun.com	
	Ceres Juices	www.ceresjuices.com	
	R.W. Knudsen	www.rwknudsenfamily.com	
	Evolution Fresh Juices	www.evolutionfresh.com	
	Biotta	www.biotta.com	
	Newman's Own	www.newmansown.com	
	Walnut Acres	www.walnutacres.com	
	Sunsweet	www.sunsweet.com	
Kalamata Olives	Krinos Foods	www.krinos.com	
Kombu	Eden Organic	www.edenfoods.com	800-441-3336
Lunch Meats	Applegate Farms	www.applegatefarms.com	866-587-5858
	All Natural Boars Head	www.boarshead.com	
Maple Syrup, Organic	Maple Valley	www.maplevalleysyrup.com	800-760-1449
Matcha Powder	Eden Foods	www.edenfoods.com	888-424-EDEN
Milks (Nondairy)	Pacific Foods	www.pacificfoods.com	503-692-9666 800-987-2329 866-388-7853 888-690-3958 800-550-6731
	Almond Breeze	www.almondbreeze.com	
	SoDelicious	www.turtlemountain.com	
	Tempt	www.livingharvest.com	
	Good Karma	www.goodkarmafoods.com	
Nuts and Seeds	Nuts Online	www.nutsonlinecom	
Oils, Cooking or Salad	Spectrum Organics	www.spectrumorganics.com	800-434-4246
Oregano	Krinos Foods	www.krinos.com	
Organic Foods—All Kinds	Diamond Organics	www.diamondorganics.com	888-674-2642

Organic Kuzu	Ohsawa		800-475-food (3663)
Organic Peanut Butter	Kettle Foods	www.Kettlefoods.com	888-4-kettle
Original Gelatin Unflavored	Knox Company	www.knoxgel.com	800-566-9435

Food Ingredients by Company and Website			
Pastas (Gluten-Free)	Ancient Quinoa Harvest	www.quinoa.bigstep.com	310-217-8125
	DeBoles	www.deboles.com	866-595-8917
	Tinkyada	www.tinkyada.com	416-609-0016
	Schar	www.schar.com	
	SamMills Corn Pasta	www.sammills.eu	
Rice Pasta Pastariso	Rice Innovations, Inc.	www.riceinnovations.com	
Pasta Sauces	Muir Glen	www.muirglen.com	
Pepperoncini Peppers	Krinos Foods	www.krinos.com	
Pine Nuts	Krinos Foods	www.krinos.com	
Popcorn (Organic)	Now Foods	www.nowfoods.com	888-669-3663
	K & W Non-GMO	www.kwpopcorn.com	660-359-2030
	Purcell Mountain	www.purcellmountain-farms.com	208-267-0627
Potato Chips	Boulder	www.bouldercanyon-foods.com	866-595-8917
	Terra Chips	www.terrachips.com	
	Kettle	www.kettlebrand.com	866-595-8917
	Garden Of Eatin'	www.gardenofeatin.com	
Red Wine Vinegar	Krinos Foods	www.krinos.com	
Rice Dream Milk	Imagine Foods	www.imaginefoods.com	800-434-4246
Rice Mixes	The Lundberg Farms	www.lundberg.com	530-538-3500
Roasted Vegetable Stock	Kitchen Basics	www.kitchenbasics.net	440-838-1344
Seafood—Wild Caught	Vital Choice	www.vitalchoice.com	800-608-4825
Sesame Butter	Kettle Foods	www.Kettlefoods.com	888-4-kettle
Spices	Eden Foods	www.edenfoods.com	888-424-EDEN (3336)
	Simply Organic	www.simplyorganicupcom	800-437-3301
	Frontier Spices	www.Frontiercoop.com	800-669-3275
Sunflower Butter	Kettle Foods	www.Kettlefoods.com	888-4-kettle
Tortillas (Rice)	Food For Life	www.foodforlife.com	

Food For Thought

By Company, Website, with Product Description

Authentic Foods Bean flour, bean flour mixes, and other baking supplies. http://pages.prodigy.com/autfoods	**Jowar Foods, Inc.** Mixes for breads, pastries, cookies www.jowar.com/
Bickford Flavors Flavorings, extracts. www.bickfordflavors.com	**King Arthur Flour** Naturally pure flour, mixes, xanthan gum. www.kingarthurflour.com
Bob's Red Mill Natural Foods, Inc. Wheat and gluten-free flours. **www.bobsredmill.com**	**Kingsmill Foods, Inc.** Breads, Cookies. www.kingsmillfoods.com
'Cause You're Special Company Mixes and baking supplies. www.causeyourespecial.com	**Kinnikinnick Foods, Inc.** Ice cream cones, crispy rice, cereal, baked goods. www.Kinnikinnick.com/
De-Ro-Ma Food Intolerance Center Pretzels, mixes, baked goods. www.cosmo2000.ca/deroma	**Kozy Shack** Gluten-free puddings. www.Kozyshack.com
Dietary Specialties, Inc. Flours, mixes, pasta, crackers, cookies, and condiments. www.dieteaspoonecupcom	**Miss Roben's Dietary Foods** Mixes, pasta, baking supplies. www.Missroben.com
Ener-G-Foods, Inc. Flours, baking supplies, baked goods. www.ener-g.com	**Nancy's Natural Foods** Variety of gluten-free products. 266 NW First Avenue, Canby, OR 97013, 877-862-4457
Latin American-Caribbean Specialty Foods and Spices Cassava meal, also called manioc flour. 408-375-5850	**Whole Foods Market** Information about a multitude of natural foods and specialty products, including gluten-free products. chemical sensitivities, mold allergies, for persons on rotation diets. www.wholefoodsmarket.com
Food For Life Breads. 909-279-5090	**Special Foods** Products are for persons with food allergies and/or intolerances. www.Specialfoods.com

Gluten-Free Delights www.Glutenfreedelights.com	
The Gluten-Free Pantry Mixes, pasta, baking supplies. www.glutenfree.com	
Glutino (DEROMA) Carries Schar and Nutricia products. www.glutino.com	

BY COMPANY, WEBSITE, WITH PRODUCT DESCRIPTION	
Other Sources	
Gluten-Free Friendly Inns Enjoying a new-found vitality with the gluten-free exclusionary diet, but feel like traveling is just, well, too complicated? This website is a resource for those who would like to travel like everyone else and remain gluten-free. www.innseekers.com/GFinns.htm	**Mr. Spice Healthy Foods** Gluten-free, salt-free, fat-free sauces and marinades. www.Mrspice.com
Francis Simon Bakery Baked goods. 3106 Commerce St. Dallas, TX 75226 214-741-4242	**Pamela's Products Inc.** Cookies, mixes, biscotti found at Whole Foods, Sprouts, Wegman's, Kroger, Winn Dixie, Safeway stores. www.pamelasproducts.com
The Sunflower Shoppe 5100 State Hwy 121 North Colleyville, TX 817-399-9100 Gluten-free foods, organic dairy and meat. Whole food supplements.	**Squirrel's Nest Candy Shop** All natural candy store provides natural alternatives. www.squirrels-nest.com
The Sunflower Shoppe 5817 Curzon Ave Fort Worth, TX 817-738-9051	**Interactive Menu Planner** National Heart Lung and Blood Institute. http://hp2010.nhlbihin.net/menu-planner/menu.cgi
	Body Mass Index Calculator National Heart Lung and Blood Institute. http://www.nhlbisupport.com/bmi/

Networking and Connecting	
Developmental Delay Resources www.Devdelay.org devdelay@mindspring.com 800.407.0944	Integrating conventional and holistic approaches. Connects families, professionals, and organizations.
Karina's Kitchen http://glutenfreegoddess.blogspot.com	Each week Karina shares her latest gluten-free recipes, focusing on fresh, seasonal ingredients. Living gluten-free has inspired her to get creative in the kitchen.

Autism and Allergy Resources, Websites, and Books

Find additional information and resources on autism spectrum disorder, websites and books with data on general information, medical developments, and legal and educational rights.

Defeat Autism Now (DAN) www.autism.com/dan/index.htm	Defeat Autism Now is part of the *Autism Research Institute* (ARI). According to the ARI website, "Defeat Autism Now! Is dedicated to educating parents and clinicians regarding biomedically based research, appropriate testing, and safe and effective interventions for autism."
Autism Research Institute www.autism.com	From the ARI website: "The Autism Research Institute (ARI) is the hub of a worldwide network of parents and professionals concerned with autism.... ARI also disseminates research findings to parents and others worldwide seeking help. The ARI data bank, the world's largest, contains over 40,000 detailed case histories of autistic children from over 60 countries."
About.com: Autism http://autism.about.com/lr/autism	Top 10 Websites for Autism.
Autism Network for Dietary Intervention (ANDI) www.autismndi.com/	Providing help and support for families using a gluten-free and casein-free diet in the treatment of autism and related developmental disabilities.
Autism Speaks www.autismspeaks.org	Autism Speaks is dedicated to increasing awareness of autism spectrum disorders, to funding research into the causes, prevention, and treatments for autism.
Autism Spot www.autismspot.com	Autism Spot is dedicated to providing parents, educators, professionals, and those living with autism with unbiased, comprehensive information. Includes little tricks and strategies for helping manage your autistic child in everyday life.

Autism-Therapy www.suite101.com/ autism-therapy	Suite 101's autism treatment subsection focuses on a wide variety of treatment options. From standard protocols and drug therapies like Risperdal to biomedical alternatives, this section offers many different therapies.
Connections: Special Needs Kids Directory www.specialneedskidsdirectory.com/	The directory provides free information to caregivers who have children with special needs in the Dallas/Fort Worth area, with over 550 resources in the area. Their website is dedicated to assisting parents to find, discover, and explore the resources that exist to better their child's quality of life.
Connections Project http://issuu.com/ connectionsproject	From the website: "Connections is a philanthropic for-profit organization underwritten/offset by Maverick Marketing Corporation. It is the goal of this project to create a grass roots movement of providers who provide and support free information to the population they serve with the goal of caregiver empowerment and increasing the speed of service/intervention to individuals with special needs. We connect resource providers and empower caregivers to: FIND quality resources, DISCOVER hope, and EXPLORE the possibilities. We celebrate resources!"
Developmental Delay Resources www.devdelay.org/	Integrating conventional and holistic approaches. Connects families, professionals, and organizations.
Generation Rescue www.generationrescue.org/	Jenny McCarthy's autism organization, Generation Rescue is an international movement of scientists and physicians researching the causes and treatments for autism, ADHD and chronic illness, while parent-volunteers mentor thousands of families in recovering their children.
QSAC-Quality Services for the Autism Community http://qsacupblogspot.com/2009/03/learning-web-sites-for-children-with.html	Learning websites for children with autism.
Talk About Curing Autism Foundation http://www.talkaboutcuringautism.org/medical/dan-protocol.htm	TACA provides information, resources, and support to families affected by autism. For families who have just received the autism diagnosis, TACA aims to speed up the cycle time from the autism diagnosis to effective treatments.

BOOKS ABOUT AUTISM, SPECIAL EDUCATION, AND ALLERGIES

Do you know of an autism book or other resource you would like to see posted on our website?

E-mail us at drkotsanis@kotsanisinstitute.com and Kendra@greatertots.org

GENERAL INFORMATION ON AUTISM

The Autism Answer Book: More Than 300 of the Top Questions Parents Ask

by William Stillman

Autism Spectrum Disorders: The Complete Guide to Understanding Autism, Asperger's Syndrome, Pervasive Developmental Disorder, and Other ASDs

by Chantal Sicile-Kira

Children with Autism: A Parent's Guide

by Michael D. Powers, Temple Grandin

Breaking the Vicious Cycle: Intestinal Health Through Diet

by Elaine Gottschall

Children with Starving Brains: A Medical Treatment Guide for Autism Spectrum Disorder

by Jaquelyn McCandless

Evidence of Harm: Mercury in Vaccines and the Autism Epidemic: A Medical Controversy

by David Kirby

Healthy Child Healthy World: Creating a Cleaner, Greener, Safer Home

by Christopher Gavigan

Mother Warriors: A Nation of Parents Healing Autism Against All Odds

by Jenny McCarthy

Nourishing Hope for Autism

By Julie Matthews

Healing and Preventing Autism: A Complete Guide

by Jenny McCarthy and Dr. Jerry Kartzinel

ADULTS WITH AUTISM

Thinking in Pictures: My Life with Autism

by Temple Grandin

SPECIAL EDUCATION AND LEGAL RIGHTS

Autism: Asserting Your Child's Right to Special Education

by David Sherman

School Success for Kids with Asperger's Syndrome

by Stephan Silverman, Rich Weinfeld

How to Compromise with Your School District without Compromising Your Child: A Practical Guide for Parents of Children with Developmental Disorders and Learning Disabilities

by Gary Mayerson

The Impossible Child!

By Doris J. Rapp, MD

This 160-page book is designed for caring but perplexed educators and parents who want to help children who have been erroneously labeled as dumb, lazy, nasty, rude, overactive, irritable, slow, or impossible. This book will enable you to recognize which children have allergies or food or chemical sensitivities that interfere with their ability to learn and behave normally. Practical, sensible ways to help children with these problems are discussed. With this information you may be able to alter the course of some child's life in a more positive direction—today! This book is also available in Spanish.

BOOKS ABOUT ALLERGIES BY DR. RAPP

Dr. Rapp has written many books to help children and adults. She has been a valued colleague of Dr. K and Beverly Kotsanis for many years. She is a globally recognized pediatrician and authority on allergies and environmental pollution. The first two books listed are the most helpful for those with allergies.

Is This Your Child?

This *New York Times* best seller has many examples of different types of children's allergies. This easy to understand 635-page book illustrates the way to tell which children or adults have environmental illness by the way the child or adult looks, feels, acts, and behaves. The writing, the pulse, or the ability to breathe also provides important clues. It tells how to pinpoint specifically the reason why certain children or adults are unable to learn in certain rooms, outside the school, or at certain times after specific exposures at school, home or work. It clearly explains ways to verify your suspicions using fast, easy, relatively inexpensive, and more expensive methods. If no one is listening, it tells you what to do and where to go for help! This book applies equally well to adults and to homes and workplaces, as well as schools.

Is This Your Child's World?

This book is written mainly about school-related allergies, but it is equally applicable to homes and workplaces. It has an endless number of practical tips to quickly help you to find and eliminate allergies. Dr. Rapp has tried to put herself in your position. What would most mothers, teachers and older children love and need to know about allergies? It has more practical information of the type you need than you can imagine. The tips are endless. You will read it and keep saying to yourself, Why did someone not tell me about this before? Why did I not think of that? The answers you need are often there and sometimes they are only a few hours away.

Environmentally Sick Schools

If you or a loved one is suffering from unexplained symptoms that could be due to allergies, any of Dr. Rapp's DVDs can provide clues to help you. You can also utilize these materials to show those around you that allergies could be causing the problem. Seeing is believing!

Our Toxic World: A Wake Up Call

This 510-page book is about chemicals and how they are hurting our children, our wildlife, our planet, and us. Find out how to protect yourself and your loved ones. We have polluted our air, water, soil, food, homes, schools, and workplace. WE MUST STOP IT! We now have epidemics of ADHD, cancer, fatigue, headaches, obesity, early puberty, sterility, brain defects, and muscle and visual problems, to name only a few. We must stop and figure out why. Eliminate the cause and there's nothing to treat. Chemicals are major causes of today's health challenges. Find out why you must make your own nest safe, now!

32 Tips That Could Save Your Life

We simply cannot continue to allow excessive toxic pollution of our air, food, water, homes, schools, and workplaces. Let's make some changes and give our newborns and everyone else a fighting chance. We have increasing numbers of illnesses that never existed before, including ADHD, ADD, arthritis, autism, bipolar illness, cancer, diabetes, thyroid disease, obesity, infertility, Alzheimer's, neuromuscular diseases, etc. At times, all of these medical problems can be solely caused by exposures in our environment. This book was written specifically to help you personally make your own little nests safer and more secure for yourself and your loved ones.

Integrative Cancer Therapy Resources

Book Title	Description
A Kinder, Gentler Cancer Treatment: Insulin Potentiation Targeted LowDoseTM Therapy By The Best Answer for Cancer FoundationSM www.kotsanisinstitute.com www.bestanswerforcancer.org	This is a powerful book exploring Insulin Potentiation Targeted LowDose Therapy and how a holistic cancer-targeted therapy kills the disease, not the patient. Contributing authors include licensed physicians Steven G. Ayre, Hendrieka Fitzpatrick, David C. Korn, Constantine A. Kotsanis, Thomas Lodi, Richard Linchitz, and Frank Shallenberger. Former patient contributing authors include Annie Brandt, Michael Short, and Charles Gray.
Beating Cancer Gently Compiled by Bill Henderson www.beating-cancer-gently.com	A wealth of information and resources on compassionate cancer care—complimentary, alternate, and adjuvant.
Treating Cancer with Insulin Potentiation Therapy By Ross A. Hauser, MD, Marion A. Hauser, MS, RD	Learn how insulin can help target chemotherapy and be used as part of a comprehensive natural medicine approach to reverse cancer and cancer physiology.
Medicine of Hope, Insulin Cellular Therapy By Jean-Claude Paquette, MD, ©1995. Translated from French by Aimée Ricci. www.IPTQ.org	The full text online in English and Spanish. This book provides an early history of IPT, explains how it works, and shares numerous patient case studies and outcomes.
Cancer as a Turning Point: A Handbook for Cancer Patients, Their Families, and Health Professionals By Lawrence LeShan, PhD www.cancerasaturningpoint.org *You Can Fight For Your Life: Emotional Factors in the Treatment of Cancer* *How to Meditate: A Guide to Self-Discovery*	This book helps those dealing with cancer to find a "turning point" or spiritual understanding that can be used to promote healing and to find the unrealized dream within that can provide inspiration.

ARTICLES AND PUBLISHED STUDIES

Location: www.iptforcancer.com

IPT: A New Concept in the Management of Chronic Degenerative Disease, S. G. Ayre, D. Perez Garcia y Bellon, and D. Perez Garcia, Jr.

IPT and Cachexia: A Dual-Purpose Approach to Cancer Management, Ayre and Tisdale.

New Approaches to the Delivery of Drugs to the Brain, S. G. Ayre.

Blood-Brain Barrier, Ayre, Skaletski and Mosnaim.

Neoadjuvant Low-Dose Chemotherapy with Insulin in Breast Carcinomas, S. G. Ayre, D. Perez Garcia y Bellon, and D. Perez Garcia, Jr.

Insulin, Chemotherapy, and the Mechanisms of Malignancy: The Design and the Demise of Cancer, S. G. Ayre, D. Perez Garcia y Bellon, and D. Perez Garcia, Jr.

The Insulin Potentiation Therapy (IPT) in the Treatment of Chronic and Oncological Diseases, Journal MED.

RESOURCE LIST: U.S. GOVERNMENT INFORMATION ON NUTRITION

The following government resources provide reliable, science-based information on nutrition and physical activity, as well as an array of tools to facilitate Americans' adoption of healthy choices.

Dietary Guidelines for Americans	http://www.dietaryguidelines.gov
MyPyramid.gov	http://www.mypyramid.gov
Physical Activity Guidelines for Americans	http://www.health.gov/paguidelines
Nutrition.gov	http://www.nutrition.gov
healthfinder.gov	http://www.healthfinder.gov
Health.gov	http://health.gov
U.S. Department of Agriculture (USDA)	
Center for Nutrition Policy and Promotion	http://www.cnpp.usda.gov
Food and Nutrition Service	http://www.fns.usda.gov
Food and Nutrition Information Center	http://fnicupnal.usda.gov
National Institute of Food and Agriculture	http://www.nifa.usda.gov
U.S. Department of Health and Human Services (HHS)	
Office of Disease Prevention and Health Promotion	http://odphp.osophs.dhhs.gov
Food and Drug Administration	http://www.fda.gov
Centers for Disease Control and Prevention	http://www.cdc.gov
National Institutes of Health	http://www.nih.gov
Let's Move!	http://www.letsmove.gov
Healthy People	http://www.healthypeople.gov
U.S. National Physical Activity Plan	http://www.physicalactivityplan.org

Note: The U.S. National Physical Activity Plan is not a product of the Federal Government.

B. Glossary of Specialized Ingredients

Agar Flakes Agar is a vegetarian gelatin substitute produced from seaweed and is widely used in Asia. It is sold in the form of blocks, powder, or flakes and is available in Asian markets and health food stores. Agar can be substituted for gelatin, but it has stronger setting properties so less is needed.

To use agar flakes in recipes, traditional directions call for 1 tablespoon of agar flakes to every cup of water or juice. Like normal gelatin, the agar is dissolved in the liquid in a small saucepan over medium-high heat, brought to a boil, and then simmered until thickened, about 5 to 7 minutes. It is then chilled in the refrigerator until set.

Almond Flour; Blanched Almond Flour Raw blanched whole almonds that have been ground into a fine powder. Can be used in cakes, cookies, sweet breads, and other desserts. It may be stored in the freezer to extend shelf life. We recommend an almond flour made by Bob's Red Mill; buy direct at www.bobsredmill.com, or try a good health food store for other brands of almond flour.

Almond Milk A milk substitute made from almonds, it is good for every aspect of cooking and baking. Creamy, a little sweet, and high in Vitamin E and other essential nutrients, almond milk is found with other non-refrigerated boxed beverages. While dairy-free, most are not soy-free as they contain soy lecithin.

Annie's Naturals Ketchup A brand of organic ketchup available either in health food stores or online at places such as amazon.com or shoprite.com.

Applegate Farms Black Forest Ham Find a local retailer at www.applegatefarms.com, or order online.

Applegate Farms Sunday Bacon Also available from Applegate Farms.

Arborio rice (Risotto) The classic risotto rice, it is probably the best all-around rice for cooking. Medium to long grain, it can absorb a lot of cooking liquid yet still retain a good bite when fully cooked.

Azuki or Adzuki Bean A small, dried, russet-colored bean with a sweet flavor. They can be purchased whole, powdered, or as a bean paste at Asian markets and are popular in Japanese cooking.

Food For Thought

Bacon Crustini Crumbles Crustini is an Italian appetizer consisting of small slices of grilled toast with various toppings, such as bacon in this instance. Bacon crustini crumbles is simply bacon crustini crumbled like bacon bits.

BHA and BHT Also known as butylated hydroxyanisole and butylated hydroxytoluene. Two of the more commonly used preservatives.

Biotta Elderberry Juice An elderberry juice made from organically grown berries from Biotta juices, it is a great antioxidant and immune system booster. It comes in a glass bottle and is a bit pricey. Find a local retailer at www.biottajuices.com, or just order online.

Biotta Exotic Juice Blend Find all of Biotta's juice blends at www.biottajuices.com.

Bob's Red Mill All-Purpose Flour A gluten-free flour by Bob's Red Mill, available direct at www.bobsredmill.com or use their website's store finder to find a local retailer.

Bob's Red Mill GF Oats Gluten-free oats available from Bob's Red Mill. Available in quick, rolled, or steel cut. Available at www.bobsredmill.com, or use their website's store finder to find a local retailer.

Bragg's Sprinkles seasoning A certified organic seasoning mix of all-natural herbs and spices, put out by Paul C. Bragg. Order at www.bragg.com.

Brown Rice Flour Stone-ground brown rice to make for a perfect gluten-free flour. Available from a number of brands and health food stores, including Bob's Red Mill.

Brown Rice Syrup A vegan and gluten-free liquid sugar substitute that can be used as a sweetener in baking and cooking with less calories and no refined sugar. It has a consistency similar to honey and tastes very sweet, but it has a flavor that is very different from other sweeteners, such as honey and agave nectar.

Casein A family of proteins found in mammalian milk; it makes up 80 percent of the proteins in cow milk and 65 percent of the proteins in human milk.

Chia Seeds The seed of a Central American plant in the mint family; it is rich in omega-3 fatty acids and provides protein, fats, and fiber. May be used whole or ground into flour. Available from a number of sources and health food stores, including Bob's Red Mill.

Chickpea Flour Chickpeas are also known as garbanzo beans. The flour is made from dried beans that are then ground into a fine powder. It can be used as a soup thickener and as a wheat substitute in baking breads. It is a pale yellow, powdery, with an earthy flavor best for savory dishes. It is gluten-free.

Coconut Flour Made from the meat of the coconut after the oils and milk have been extracted, it is hypoallergenic, gluten-free, contains no trans fat, and tastes sweet and slightly nutty. You can use it with other flours by substituting 10 to 30 percent of the flour with coconut flour.

Daiya Cheddar Shreds A dairy-free vegan product that has the melt, taste, and stretch of Cheddar cheese. It is made entirely from plant-based ingredients and is available from Daiya. Go to www.daiyafoods.com to find a retail store, deli, or restaurant that carries their products.

DeBoles Lasagna ready-bake noodles Made from rice by DeBoles, it is wheat and gluten-free. Go to www.deboles.com to find a local retailer.

B. Glossary of Specialized Ingredients

Dulse Seaweed Blend "Dulse" is a type of seaweed that is an energy food, rich in salt and iodine, good for the thyroid and adrenals, and will balance sugar levels and mood swings. Your local health food or specialty store should have some.

Earth Balance Soy Free (butter) A 100 percent vegan nondairy margarine spread with absolutely no whey, lactose, or casein, it has no hydrogenated oils and is cholesterol-free. It also tastes rich and buttery.

Egg-Replacer Powder A blend of starch, vegetable gum, and leaveners, including arrowroot, baking powder, and guar or xanthan gum. It can be used to replace eggs in most vegan recipes. One egg-replacer powder we recommend is produced by Ener-G.

Enjoy Life Chocolate Chips A high-quality chocolate made by Enjoy Life that is free of gluten, dairy, nut, soy, egg, and casein. Find out more about Enjoy Life's products at www.enjoylifefoods.com.

Enjoy Life Perky's Crunchy Flax Cereal A crispy rice-puff cereal with ground flax, naturally sweetened with fruit juice and honey.

Flax Seed Meal A good source of fiber, omega-3 fatty acids, and protein, it is made from ground flax seeds. You can buy it by the bag, on-line or at a health food or specialty store.

Fulvic Mineral Complex A supplement that has a combination of fulvic and humic acid. The most effective formulas also contain Norwegian Kelp. For more information on the benefits of fulvic and humic acids, go to www.HumifulvateRx.com.

Organic Raw Cane Sugar Pure powdered fructose, looks like regular sugar but sweeter, the granules being slightly smaller than table sugar. It can be purchased at many grocery stores and most health food stores. It can be used as a substitute for sugar in any food and baked good. Fructose is naturally occurring in fruits and some vegetables, and most of the powders now sold are made from corn. You can find specific brands that are made from only fruit sources, but most will be made from corn.

GAPS Diet A diet based on the work of Dr. Natasha Campbell-McBride, who started with the SCD Diet (Specific Carbohydrate Diet) and went further by describing the gut-brain connection in the book *Gut and Psychology Syndrome*. The term GAPS was then coined by her patients from that title.

GF Baking Powder Gluten-free baking powders are supplied by a number of brands and are fairly widely available. They are made from a variety of grains, beans, nuts, and seeds, so if you have a nut allergy, check the label to see exactly what it is made of.

Gluten A protein composite found in foods processed from wheat, barley, or rye. It is what makes dough elastic and provides a chewy texture to the final product.

GFCF Gluten-free and casein-free, referring to the components of the food in this type of diet.

Gluten-Free Vanilla Extract Organic vanilla, non-GMO, and gluten-free, made with organic alcohol and organic vanilla beans.

Glutino Sesame Pretzels Gluten-free, cholesterol-free, milk and casein-free sesame-coated pretzels produced by Glutino.

GMO Genetically Modified Organism. Any plant or animal that has been genetically modified.

Grapeseed Oil A pale delicate oil with a neutral and clean taste, extracted from grape pips. It is good for frying, making mayonnaise, and general kitchen use.

Green Tea Powder A powdered form of green tea, which itself is produced from leaves that are steamed and dried but not fermented. Such leaves make a greenish-yellow tea and slightly bitter flavor.

Guar (gwar) Gum Also called guaran, it is a thickener made from the ground seeds of guar beans.

Hazelnut Butter Hazelnuts are also known as cob nuts or filberts, and are rich in protein, unsaturated fats, and B vitamins. They are sweet and work well with chocolate. Creamed into butter, they are available in a wide number of brands, including "Justin's Chocolate Hazelnut Butter," which can be found at www.justinsnutbutter.com.

Hemp Protein Powder A more efficient protein powder than whey-based, it contains all eight essential amino acids, organic whole food, non-GMO. Nutiva Organic is the one we recommend; if you're having trouble finding it, go to www.nutiva.com.

Hemp Seeds, Organic Shelled organic hemp seeds, sold by the bag by Nutiva and Bob's Red Mill.

HFC High-Fructose Corn Syrup

Kombu Comes in strips 3 inches long and 1 inch wide wrapped in a clear cellophane package, it is a type of seaweed. The packaging helps it cook faster. You can find it in health food stores or Asian markets.

Lemongrass A tall grass native to warm tropical regions, it is a widely used herb in oriental cuisines for everything from teas, soups, and curries, to various meats. Fairly widely available.

Matcha Powder A finely milled green tea popular in Japan. Matcha is more finely ground and of higher quality than normal tea powder or green tea powder, and it comes in a variety of different blends.

Mimic Creme Healthy Top A nondairy, non-soy gluten-free whipping cream by MimicCreme, with no hydrogenated oils or trans fats and no polysorbate 60. It is made from organic virgin coconut oil, almonds, cashews, sweet almond oil, and natural cane sugar. Chill, then whip.

Monosodium glutamate (MSG) A sodium salt of glutamic acid, a nonessential amino acid. Used in a lot of East Asian cuisine, it was originally obtained by the use of seaweed extract until the chemical was isolated in 1907.

Muir Glen Tomato Sauces Muir Glen has a number of great sauces, including an excellent GFCF Pasta Sauce, Garden Vegetable Pasta Sauce, tomato sauce, and Veggie Pasta Sauce. You'll find them in any good grocery store.

Nature's Path Corn Flakes Sweetened with fruit juice, gluten-free, made with pure cornmeal.

B. Glossary of Specialized Ingredients

Nature's Path Rice Puffs Rice puffs made from brown rice. Note that they are produced in a plant that contains wheat.

Nitrite Free Pancetta. Pancetta is an unsmoked bacon, which is normally filled with nitrites. There are several manufacturers of nitrite-free meats, which should be carried in places like Whole Foods.

Nitrite Free Pepperoni. Pepperoni is normally filled with nitrites, unless you search out some nitrite-free varieties. It should be available anywhere that sells vegan.

Non-HFC Any food that does not contain high-fructose corn syrup.

Non-GMO Any food not made using genetically modified plant or animal sources.

Non-GMO Corn Tortillas. Tortillas made using corn that has not been genetically modified.

Nondairy Milk Powder A nondairy powder, it is typically made mainly of glucose syrup and vegetable oil. It is generally made from potatoes or rice and is not recommended for the specific carbohydrate diet.

Orange Zest The grated rind of an orange. Just take a cheese grater to the outside of an orange before peeling it.

Perky's Flax Cereal Made by Perky, it is a nut and gluten-free flax cereal sweetened with fruit juice and honey.

Potato Flour A gluten-free flour made from cooked, dried, and ground potatoes. Used as a thickener, and also in some baked goods because it produces a moist crumb.

Psyllium Husk, Mealed Psyllium is a soluble fiber used in laxative products. There are more than 200 species in the plant genus Plantago, from which several varieties of psyllium come. Most of the world's production of psyllium comes from India, though it grows in other parts of Asia as well as warmer parts of Europe. Search your health food or specialty store.

Quinoa A grain grown in Bolivia and Peru, it dates back to the time of the Incas. Small round grains that look similar to millet but are a pale brown in color. Mild taste, firm texture, slightly chewy. When cooked, the grains sweeten and become translucent with a white ring. Look for it in either your local health food store or farmer's market store.

Quinoa Pasta. Pasta made from quinoa.

Rice Milk A grain milk processed from rice, usually brown rice and unsweetened. Available in vanilla, chocolate, and almond flavors, as well as unflavored. An increasing number of regular supermarkets are now carrying it.

Rice Vegan Cheese A dairy-free cheese alternative made from rice. Melts just like cheese, comes in slices or blocks, and is available as substitutes for American, mozzarella, Cheddar, and cream cheeses.

Salba, Ground Salba is an ancient Aztec grain that is the most nutritionally complete grain in the world, is the richest plant-based source of omega-3 fatty acids, and has the highest protein content of any seed or grain, and plenty of fiber, antioxidants, calcium, magnesium, and iron. It's also non-GMO, vegan, gluten-free, and Kosher. You may have to hunt around in health food and specialty stores to find it though.

Schar Baguette A gluten-free baguette made from rice flower instead of wheat. Manufactured by Schar, one package contains two baguettes.

SCD Diet A diet created by Dr. Sidney V. Hass that limits the use of complex carbohydrates and eliminates refined sugar, grains, and starch from the diet.

SoDelicious Coconut Milk Kefir Made from coconut milk, fermented with kefir cultures and ten strains of bacteria; similar in taste and texture to drinkable yogurt. Manufactured by SoDelicious.

SoDelicious Coconut Yogurt Also from SoDelicious, it is a yogurt made from coconut milk instead of cow's milk.

Sorghum Molasses. A molasses made from sweet sorghum, which is a type of grass raised for grain. This type of molasses is more properly called "sweet sorghum syrup."

Soy Lecithin An additive derived from the oil of soybeans. Since most allergic reactions are to the actual protein, some people with soy allergies can tolerate soy lecithin. It should also be noted that since much of soy is also genetically modified, if you can eat soy products then you should look for those that are non-GMO or Identity Preserved (IP), in which the suppliers guarantee that their products are GMO-free.

Sprinkelz Chocolatey Vegan Sprinkles Sprinkelz manufactures a nondairy ice cream sprinkle, made from organic evaporated cane juice, organic cocoa powder, organic corn malt, syrup, water, and colored by fruit and vegetable extracts.

Stevia in the Raw Stevia, a sugar substitute, is an herb that grows natively in Paraguay and Brazil, with incredibly sweet leaves that have been used to flavor beverages for more than four hundred years. Stevia in the Raw is a product that minimizes the licorice-like aftertaste some Stevia products have. This is manufactured by the makers of Sugar in the Raw, so it should be found in many of the same places.

SweetLeaf Stevia A liquid Stevia sweetener by SweetLeaf; chemical-free, zero-calorie, zero-carb, zero-glycemic index. Comes in root beer, vanilla crème, and chocolate flavors.

Tahini Sauce A thick paste made from ground sesame seeds, used in many Middle Eastern and Greek dishes as a sauce and flavoring. Hain and Sunbutter are two brands.

Tamari Soy Sauce A type of Japanese soy sauce made without wheat and thus okay for anyone with wheat allergies. Use like dark soy sauce.

Tapioca Flour A starchy extract of the root of the cassava plant that is used as a thickener much like cornstarch, it is available in granules, flakes, pellets (called pearl tapioca), starch, and flour. The most widely used forms are tapioca flour (also called cassava flour) and pearl tapioca.

Terra Sweet and Beets Produced by Terra Chips, they are chips made with sweet potatoes, beets, and one or more of canola, Sunflower, or safflower oil.

Textured Vegetable Protein (TVP) Made from reduced-fat soybeans to replace or extend ground meat.

Unsweetened MimicCreme Nondairy, non-soy nut cream, gluten-free, vegan coffee creamer.

B. Glossary of Specialized Ingredients

Vanilla Bean Paste Usable in place of extract, it is made from whole vanilla bean pods, sugar, water, and a natural gum thickener. It is about as thick as a thin syrup, and you can see the seeds. You can find it at specialty stores such as Williams-Sonoma or Trader Joe's.

Grapeseed Vegenaise, Mayonnaise Substitute Made with grapeseed oil and organic; it's even good for the cholesterol.

Vegan Parmesan Topping A nondairy substitute for grated Parmesan cheese. Galaxy Nutritional Foods has a version that is soy-based, while other recipes for this involve yeast flakes and blanched almonds, so be sure to check what ingredients are in the vegan Parmesan that you buy in case you have any problems with soy or almonds.

Vegan Parmesan Sprinkles Same as the vegan Parmesan topping, just in a slightly different physical form; be careful to check ingredients because some versions use raw walnuts for those that have problems with nuts.

Xanthan Gum A thickening agent produced through fermentation of corn sugar by the bacteria Xanthomonas campestris. Since xanthan gum is corn-based, however, those with corn sensitivities should opt for products that use guar gum.

C. References

FOOD ALLERGIES, AUTISM, AND HEALTH:

For food allergies: View specifics on www.foodallergy.org

List of foods that may contain corn: www.adrenalfatigue.org

The Hope Center for Autism, Fort Worth: www.hopecenter4autism.org

National Institutes of Health: http://vsearch.nlm.nih.gov

www.autismspot.com

www.top8free.com

www.Organic.org

USDA Website for information on "Certified Organic"; www.usda.gov

www.disabled-world.com

RECIPE SOURCES:

The Sneaky Chef

www.pecanbread.com

Karina's Kitchen: glutenfreegoddessblogspot.com

Sunflower Shoppe

Living Without, recipe book

FOOD STORAGE:

USDA Food Safety Unit—Kitchen Companion on Food Safety

Food Marketing Institute

PESTICIDES:

www.whatsonmyfood.com contains information on the chemicals found on our food.

The Pesticide Action Network (PAN) Pesticide Database: A one-stop location for toxicity and regulatory information for pesticides. The database and website are updated and enhanced by Pesticide Action Network North America (PANNA): http://www.pesticideinfo.org/

C. References

NATURE'S FOOD PYRAMID—HOW THE BODY GETS ITS ENERGY:

Robin C. Hyman, DC, LCP, FRC, "Eat What You Are!" The publication that introduces the basic food pyramid model, research, and content from which Constantine A. Kotsanis, MD, created "Nature's Food Pyramid," introduced in Chapter 2. Special recognition goes to Dr. Hyman for his generosity in giving his permission to introduce the concepts he published in "Eat What You Are!"

WATER SECTION REFERENCES:

Rogan W. J., Brady M. T., the Committee on Environmental Health, and the Committee on Infectious Diseases. June 2009. Technical Report. Drinking water from private wells and risks to children. *Pediatrics,* 123:6 (DOI: 10.1542/peds2009-0751).

The National Institute of Environmental Health Sciences (NIEHS), which worked with the AAP on its recommendations involving children's safety, goes further in its own warnings. If you think your well has suffered structural damage, you are at risk of drinking tainted water and should have the water tested in case contamination occurred, says the NIEHS.

Essential information: Call the EPA's Safe Drinking Water Hotline (800-426-4791) to see whether your municipality provides free or inexpensive testing or to find a certified testing lab in your area. In addition, read their review of various types of water filters (ratings available to subscribers) and learn how to decipher your water report.

Drinking Water from Private Wells: A Risk to Children

A word of caution from the Committee on Environmental Health and Committee on Infectious Diseases.

Drinking water for approximately one sixth of U.S. households is obtained from private wells. These wells can become contaminated by pollutant chemicals or pathogenic organisms and cause illness. Although the U.S. Environmental Protection Agency and all states offer guidance for construction, maintenance, and testing of private wells, there is little regulation. With few exceptions, well owners are responsible for their own wells. Children may also drink well water at childcare or when traveling. Illness resulting from children's ingestion of contaminated water can be severe. (*Pediatrics* 123:1599–1605)

http://www.lifeionizers.com/water-facts/alkaline-water.html

Source: www.healthychild.org/live-healthy

At-home systems: http://www.berkeyfilters.com

FOOD LABELING:

Laurentine Ten Bosch, producer: Food Matters, www.drmercola.info, www.altmedangel.com, www.naturalnews.com, and www.bestofmotherearth.com.

Food For Thought

Appetite Journal, www.elsevier.com/locate/appet. Article: "Glutamate: Its Applications in Food and Contributions to Health."

www.truthinlabeling.org

Food Allergy and Anaphylaxis Network (FAAN): www.foodallergy.org.

Center for Science in the Public Interest, Summary of All Food Additives: www.cspinet.org/reports.

Food and Drug Administration, food website: http://www.fda.gov/food/default.htmusda

Federal Drug and Code of Federal Regulations

USDA National Nutrient Database for Standard Reference: http://www.nal.usda.gov/fnic/foodcomp/search/

ABA—APPLIED BEHAVIOR ANALYSIS:

http://www.autismspeaks.org/what-autism/treatment/applied-behavior-analysis-aba

The Association for Behavior Analysis International: www.abainternational.org/

For more general information about behavior analysis and ABA, see:

www.apbahome.net (The Association of Professional Behavior Analysts)

www.BACB.com (Behavior Analyst Certification Board)

www.apa.org/crsppp/archivbehav.html (American Psychological Association Archival Description of Behavioral Psychology)

www.behavior.org (Cambridge Center for Behavioral Studies)

Apps:

Search the iTunes App Store for the app called WHAT'S ON MY FOOD?

D. How to Contact Us

A Final Word

We are continually improving, learning, and especially sharing what we learn. **Kotsanis Institute** and **Greater Tots Organization** offer many programs and resources that may be of great assistance to you and your family and friends.

Go to www.foodforthoughtbook.com and click on our **Free Pantry Shopping List.** You may download it and use it to customize your own list.

We encourage you to visit our websites. Like us on Facebook and Twitter. Sign up for our event calendar notices. We look forward to hearing from you!

Websites:	www.FoodforThoughtbook.com
	www.kotsanisinstitute.com
	www.greatertots.org
Email Addresses:	Foodforthought@kotsanisinstitute.com
	Drkotsanis@kotsanisinstitute.com
	kendra@greatertots.org
Meet Up:	Sign up for scheduled events at www. FoodforThoughtbook.com
Facebook:	See websites
Twitter:	See websites

Kotsanis Institute

Constantine A. Kotsanis, MD, MD(H), CCN

Beverly D. Kotsanis, BS

2260 Pool Road

Grapevine, Texas 76051

Phone: 817-481-6342

Greater Tots Organization

Kendra Finestead, M.O.M.

139 Olive Street

Keller, Texas 76248-2238

817-726-7850

About the Authors

Constantine "Gus" Kotsanis, Medical Director, Kotsanis Institute

About the Authors

Constantine A. Kotsanis, MD, MD(H), CCN is board certified in otolaryngology (ear, nose, and throat) by the American Board of Otolaryngology, Head and Neck Surgery, and a fellow in the American Academy of Otolaryngic Allergy. He has been a practicing physician for twenty-five years. He is also licensed by the Arizona State Board of Homeopathic Medicine and is a Certified Clinical Nutritionist (CCN). He serves as associate professor at University of Texas Southwestern School of Medicine, and he was one of the founding members of Defeat Autism Now! (DAN!) in 1995. His mission is to change the way health is delivered to the world one person at a time.

Dr. K practices in Dallas-Fort Worth, Texas, treating autism, learning, and behavior disorders and lecturing internationally on this and other topics. Years ago, Dr. Kotsanis realized that all chronic conditions share common ground. He has incorporated nutritional treatments into his practice that address neuro-endocrine-immune system pathways for patients from all over the world. Dr. Kotsanis is trained in homeopathy, acupuncture, neural therapy, and other forms of energy medicine. His treatments incorporate nutrition, homeopathy, oxidative, and botanical medicine in addition to other methods.

Many of his treatments are nutrition-based and include the cleansing and healing of the digestive tract for the proper nutrients to be absorbed and used by the body. Once this is accomplished, he addresses the neuro-endocrine-immune pathway by correcting other functional and metabolic imbalances such as enzyme and hormone systems. He incorporates detoxification protocols for heavy metal toxicities and has pioneered new therapies for the treatment of autism and learning disorders.

Dr. Kotsanis was born in Greece and lived on a farm there until he was thirteen, when he left and settled in Chicago. He attended Northern Illinois University, Athens Medical School in Greece, and Loyola University of Chicago. His favorite recreational activities are traveling, attending medical meetings, discovering new healthy recipes, and playing chess. He is an avid study of social, medical, and political history. He lives in Colleyville, Texas, with his wife Beverly, his children Andrew, 25, Katerina, 18, and Jacob, 8, their Rottweiler Doberman Hound dog.

"Better health through the integration of functional and complementary medicine."

Beverly D. Kotsanis, CEO, Kotsanis Institute

Beverly D. Kotsanis, BS, has been the CEO and director of operations for the Kotsanis Institute since 1983 when she and her husband Constantine "Gus" Kotsanis, MD, MD(H), CCN, opened their practice in Grapevine, Texas.

She holds a Bachelor of Science degree in psychology from Loyola University of Chicago and has attended postgraduate studies in business at Rosary College, River Forest, Illinois, and at Southern Methodist University in Dallas, Texas.

Beverly is passionate about learning new ways to help patients and families through conventional and complementary healing approaches, and she is a warehouse of clinical knowledge.

A gourmet and practical chef, one of her favorite activities is trying out new recipes. Beverly is always seeking leading edge knowledge about nutrition, cooking, and diets for patients and families. For years, patients have requested copies of recipes she collected. It is because of her tenacity and commitment to "getting the word out" that this special book is now in print!

Kendra Jean Finestead, Founder Greater Tots Organization

Kendra Jean Finestead, M.O.M., is a Mom On a Mission to redefine the "happy meal."

Having a daughter on the spectrum who experienced significant improvement with a specialized diet and biomedical treatment plan inspired Kendra to inform, instruct, and encourage other parents in their "special" kitchens. And so, Greater Tots Organization was founded, a 501c3 organization created for the special dieters in Kendra's community and beyond. Greater Tots provides a platform for families to connect and to gather information and inspiration. Mastering a daily cooking regimen for a toddler who requires a gluten-free, casein-free, egg-free, sugar-free, yeast-free diet (Candida diet) has earned Kendra her stripes as the creative GFCF expert she is today. Special diets are not easy, but they can be conquered and they can make miracles happen. Never underestimate the power of a mom (dad, or guardian) on a mission, and always eat happy food!

4794801R00249

Printed in Great Britain
by Amazon.co.uk, Ltd.,
Marston Gate.